GOD'S
TERRORISTS

GOD'S TERRORISTS

The Wahhabi Cult and the Hidden Roots of Modern Jihad

Charles Allen

LITTLE, BROWN

LITTLE, BROWN

First published in Great Britain in February 2006 by Little, Brown

Copyright © Charles Allen 2006

The moral right of the author has been asserted.

Unless otherwise stated, maps drawn by John Gilkes.

A CIP catalogue record for this book is available from the British Library.

ISBN 0 316 72997 3

Typeset in Caslon by M Rules
Printed and bound in Great Britain by Clays Ltd, St Ives plc

Little, Brown
An imprint of
Time Warner Book Group UK
Brettenham House
Lancaster Place
London WC2E 7EN

www.twbg.co.uk

'There is no God but Allah, and Mohammed is the prophet of Allah.' Such is the cry which electrifies 250 millions of the inhabitants of this globe. Such is the cry which thrills them so that they are ready to go forward and fight for their religion, and consider it a short road to Paradise to kill Christians and Hindus and unbelievers. It is that cry which at the present time is echoing and re-echoing through the hills and mountain fastnesses of the North-West Frontier of India. It is that cry which the *mullahs* of Afghanistan are now carrying to mountain hamlets and to towns in Afghanistan in order to raise the people of that country to come forward and fight. That is a cry which has the power of joining together the members of Islam throughout the world, and preparing them for a conflict with all who are not ready to accept their religion . . . And it is especially these Mohammedans on the North-West Frontier of India who have this intense religious zeal – call it what we will, fanaticism or bigotry – but which, nevertheless, is a power within them overruling every passion.

Dr Theodore Pennell,
Missionary Doctor at Bannu, *Among the Wild Tribes of the Afghan Frontier*, 1909

Contents

Maps

Preface

Since 9/11 a lot has been said and written about global jihad, the international movement which seeks to bring about Islamic revival by forcing the Islamic and non-Islamic worlds into violent confrontation. Understandably, the focus has been on modern events and on how and why rather than whence. This book is not about the present. It is a history of the ideology underpinning modern jihad and, in particular, a first full account of one important strand in that founding ideology: Wahhabism. This initially took shape in Arabia at the end of the eighteenth century, and was then brought to the Indian sub-continent early in the nineteenth century. It took on the Sikhs, the British and mainstream Muslim society. Time and time again it was suppressed, only to reform and revive, eventually to find new life in Pakistan and Afghanistan in the late twentieth century. This history offers no solutions but it does illustrate patterns of behaviour, successes and failures from which lessons might be drawn.

The following pages contain a great many personal names that may sound alien to those unfamiliar with Muslim tradition, where it is customary to use Arabic names hallowed by religious connotations, the most obvious example being 'Muhammad' and its diminutive 'Ahmad', both meaning 'praised'. To get over the inevitable duplication of personal names Islamic custom makes good use of honorific titles (e.g., *Sheikh* – man of learning) and terms that define status (e.g., *Shaheed* – martyr), occupation (e.g., *Maulana* – learned priest), place names (e.g., Delhvi – of Delhi), and paternity (e.g., *ibn*, *bin* – son of). Assumed names are often used as, indeed, are *noms de guerre*. Patience is called for, of the sort familiar to non-Russian readers of Count Tolstoy's novels. As an aid, the first time the name of a Muslim figure of importance appears (or reappears after a long gap) the most commonly used short version of his name is in small capitals, and used thereafter: for example, Amir-ul-Momineen Shah SYED AHMAD Barelvi Shaheed (Commander of the Faithful King Syed Ahmad of Bareli Martyr). To guide the reader through this minefield of names, a list of the main Muslim personalities featured is provided. There are also two charts at the back of this book. The first illustrates the ties between the two families who first secured Wahhabism in Arabia: the second sets out what I have dubbed the 'Wahhabi' family tree in India, showing the key promoters of the several strands of Wahhabi revivalist theology in the nineteenth century. A glossary is provided.

The English spelling of Arabic, Persian, Pashtu and Hindustani names and words is always problematic, not least because the Victorians transliterated these words very differently from modern usage. For example, the Arabic word for a descendant of the Prophet is usually set down in English as 'Saiyyed' but is also written 'Sayyed', 'Sayyid', 'Syed', 'Syad' or 'Said'. Here, to help delineate different individuals and groups of people, 'Saiyyed' is used for the central meaning; 'Sayyed' to describe the two clans occupying the Khagan valley in northern Hazara and Sittana in the Indus Valley; 'Sayyid' in relation to Sayyid Nazir Husain Muhaddith of Delhi, suspected leader of the Delhi Wahhabis in 1857 and after; 'Syad' for the moderniser Sir Syad Ahmad Khan of Alighar; and 'Syed' for the Indian revivalist-cum-revolutionary Syed Ahmad. In much the same way, 'Shah' denotes kingship but is also an honorific title granted to Saiyyeds; here it is used chiefly to identify Shah Waliullah, founder of the Madrassah-i-Rahimiya school in Delhi, his son Shah Abdul Aziz and grandson Shah Muhammad Ishaq.

With many sources still closed to me, this history can best be described as a work in progress. Corrections and further information on this subject are invited and can be posted on my website at www.godsterrorists.co.uk.

Charles Allen, 2006

Acknowledgements

Some informants have asked not to be named. My particular thanks to them and also to Bashir Ahmad Khan, Omar Khan Afridi, Major Tariq Mahmood, Rahimulla Yusufzai, Gulzar Khan, Hugh Leach, Ron Rosner, Sue Farrington, Theon and Rosemary Wilkinson; Norman Cameron, Secretary of the Royal Society for Asian Affairs; Dr Peter Boyden, Assistant Director, and staff of the National Army Museum; Nicholas Barnard, Curator of the South Asian Department, and Tim Stanley, Asian Department, at the Victoria and Albert Museum; Alison Ohta, Curator, and Kathy Lazenbatt, Assistant Librarian, at the Royal Asiatic Society; Muhammad Isa Waley, Curator of Persian and Turkish Collections at the British Library; Matthew Buck at the Royal Artillery Museum; Helen George, Prints and Drawings, and the Director and staff of the Oriental and India Office Collection at the British Library; the Director and staff at the University of Cambridge Library; the Director and staff at the Cambridge Centre for South Asian Studies. I am particularly grateful to David Loyn for reading my manuscript and correcting a number of factual errors. While I have sought advice and listened, I should make it clear that the reading which follows is my own. Some passages have previously appeared in *World Policy Journal*, Volume XXII, Number 2 (Summer 2005) and are republished here by kind permission of Karl Miller, Editor, *World Policy Journal*.

A special *shukria*, also, to the many kind persons who have helped to make my visits to Pakistan and Afghanistan memorable for the best of reasons. Their Pakistan and their Afghanistan are not well represented in this book, but it is they and others like them who embody the virtues of Islam.

Lastly, my continuing thanks to that inner band without whom no author can hope to get by: my editor Liz Robinson, for her unsparing determination to keep me on the path of literacy; at Time Warner, my commissioning editor Tim Whiting, for having faith in me, and also Linda Silverman and Iain Hunt; my agent at Sheil Land, Vivien Green, for continuing moral support; and my life partner, Liz, for always being there. *Bismallah*.

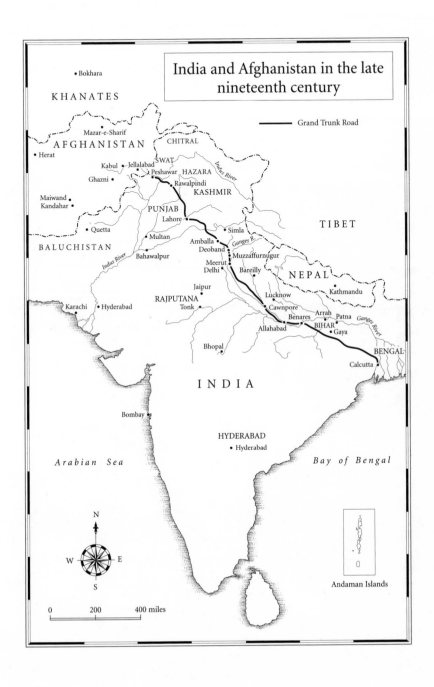

India and Afghanistan in the late nineteenth century

Introduction: 'Am I not a Pakhtun?'

When the Pathan is a child his mother tells him, 'The coward dies but his shrieks live long after,' and so he learns not to shriek. He is shown dozens of things dearer than life so that he will not mind either dying or killing. He is forbidden colourful clothes or exotic music, for they weaken the arm and soften the eye. He is taught to look at the hawk and forget the nightingale. He is asked to kill his beloved to save the soul of her children. It is a perpetual surrender – an eternal giving up of man to man and to their wise follies.

Ghani Khan, *The Pathans*, 1947

A few years ago, while researching an episode of British imperial history, I made a brief journey to Kabul by way of the Khyber Pass, that notorious defile which opens on to the plains of India. Ever since men first learned to march under one banner this fatal chink in the mountain ranges guarding the Indian sub-continent's north-western approaches has been a zone of conflict. Down through this rocky pass wave after wave of invaders have picked their way, intent on securing for themselves the three traditional prizes of the plunderer: *zan, zar, zamin* – women, gold and land. Among those invaders are the present incumbents of Afghanistan's eastern and Pakistan's western borders, a group of some two dozen tribes, large and small. While each clings fiercely to its own territory and tribal identity, they refer to themselves collectively as the *Pakhtuna* or *Pashtuna*, better known to the West as the Pathans. All claim descent from one or other of the three sons of their putative ancestor, Qais bin Rashid, who went from Gor in Afghanistan to Arabia and was there converted to Islam by the Prophet Muhammad himself. Although Sunni Muslims, they follow their own code of ethics, known as *Pakhtunwali*, which by tradition takes precedence even over the Islamic code of law known as *sharia*. There is a common Pathan proverb which states, 'Obey the mullah's teachings but do not go by what he does.'

Almost everyone I met on this journey was a Pathan, as was my guide and mentor Rahimullah Yusufzai, a gentle, scholarly journalist based in Peshawar, the ancient frontier town which an early British administrator long ago termed the 'Piccadilly of Central Asia'. When I came knocking on his door Rahimullah was already well known among journalists and foreign correspondents – and is even better known today. Because he broadcast for the BBC World Service in Pashtu, the Pathan language, his voice was familiar on both sides of the border – so much so that the mere sound of it was enough to bring a group of panicky guards to their senses after they had begun poking Kalashnikovs through our car windows at a check-post: 'Ah, Rahimullah Yusufzai,' they cried, shouldering their weapons and beaming at us. 'Come inside and have a cup of tea!'

Rahimullah Yusufzai had been covering the fighting in Afghanistan since before the withdrawal of Soviet troops in 1989 and the civil war that raged thereafter as the *mujahedeen* ('those who engage in struggle for the Faith', but most often interpreted as 'holy warriors') who had liberated their country from the infidel

Russians turned on each other and transformed an already war-torn region into Mad Max country, where warlord fought warlord and both terrorised the civil population.

Rahimullah's contacts were legendary, so it was only to be expected that when a new phenomenon appeared on the Afghan scene in the autumn of 1994 he was the first journalist to note it and the first to appreciate its significance. This new phenomenon came in the form of earnest, unsmiling young men with untrimmed black beards who wore black turbans and black waist-coats, and who almost invariably carried either Kalashnikov automatic rifles or grenade launchers. They called themselves *Taliban* or 'seekers of knowledge' and they expressed allegiance not to a general or a tribal leader but to a one-eyed cleric by the name of Mullah Muhammad Omar.

Rahimullah Yusufzai and BBC correspondent David Loyn were on hand to cover the swift advance of these new insurgents north-wards from Kandahar. They followed them as they fought their way through the gorges carved in the mountains by the Kabul River and observed how they combined military incompetence with extraordinary valour, charging the enemy without a thought to tactics or personal safety, secure in the belief that their death in *jihad* (the struggle against forces opposed to Islam) would win them the status of *shahid* (the martyr who goes straight to Paradise). It was this religious madness that vanquished their opponents, causing large numbers to switch sides. Of their leader, Mullah Omar, little was known other than that he had lost an eye fighting the Russians, and that before and after taking up arms against the infidels he had spent years studying the faith in a number of *madrassahs*, or religious schools, across the border in Pakistan. Some said that he had returned to the struggle after the Prophet Muhammad appeared to him in a dream and ordered him to bring peace to Afghanistan; others that he had grown so disgusted by the corruption of the warlords – in particular, the very public marriage of one such warlord to his young catamite –

that he had become a willing puppet of Pakistan's secret intelligence agency, the ISI. Whatever the case, in April 1996 Mullah Omar appeared on a rooftop before a large crowd of mullahs in Kandahar, draped in the city's most precious relic: the Mantle of the Prophet Muhammad. This was in deliberate imitation of the ceremony by which the second Caliph, Omar ibn al-Khattab, had established his right to rule over all Muslims before going on to enter Jerusalem riding on a white camel in the year 637. The parallel was further reinforced when Mullah Omar was proclaimed *Amir ul-Momineen* (Commander of the Faithful), a title first used by the Caliphs in the days of Islam's golden age. In September 1996 Kabul fell to the Taliban, the Amir ul-Momineen entered the city in a minivan, the deposed former President was castrated and hanged from a lamp-post, and Afghanistan was declared an Islamic state under the divinely ordained laws of Islam (*sharia*).

Our journey to Kabul took us through country shattered by civil war and the depredations of the warlords. Every foot of the road had been fought over and the roadsides were littered with both buried mines and the graves of Taliban martyrs. Prominent among the latter was a whitewashed stone surrounded by green flags on poles and marked with a notice inscribed in Arabic which Rahimullah translated for me: 'Hajji Mullah Burjan, military commander of the Taliban Islamic Movement, was martyred at this spot leading an attack against the miscreant and illegal Rabani forces at the Silk Gorge, while trying to bring sharia to Afghanistan.' A year earlier Mullah Burjan had stood on this same spot being interviewed by Rahimullah and the BBC's David Loyn before leading a suicidal attack against enemy tanks blocking the road.

Wherever we went it was clear that the Taliban were the heroes of the day: they had brought peace to the land and restored the rule of law – and indeed there was a great deal to admire in them. The groups of black-clad militiamen who manned the check posts and who guarded Jellalabad's one functioning hotel were disciplined and courteous, if strict in their demands. Those who were willing to talk to us came across as hardened campaigners, but with a naivety and a lack of curiosity about the outside world which reminded me of Red Guards I had met at the time of China's Cultural Revolution in 1966–7. Where they differed markedly from the Red Guards was in their behaviour off duty, when, as often as not, they pulled out pocket mirrors, tweezers, eyeliner and various unguents and began preening themselves.

Rahimullah's explanation was that many of the Taliban were youngsters orphaned by war, who had been brought up and educated in the hundreds of religious schools set up in Pakistan with funds from Saudi Arabia. For many thousands of young Pathan boys the madrassah had been their home and its male teachers – men like Mullah Omar – their surrogate parents. Here the bonds and shared purpose had been forged which had given these 'searchers after truth' their extraordinary aura of invincibility, for the madrassah was not so much a school as a seminary, with a curriculum made up entirely of religious instruction and the study of the Quran. Here they had spent their adolescence rocking to and fro as they learned to recite by heart an Arabic text whose meaning they did not understand but which they knew conferred on them absolute authority in all matters governing social behaviour.

Only once on our brief foray into Afghanistan did Taliban militiamen show us hostility, when we drove south from Jellalabad to the site of a famous Buddhist monastery from the centuries before the advent of Islam. Here we found unusually large numbers of armed guards, and were soon told to go back the way we had come. Only later did it become clear why: in 1996 Mullah Omar's Taliban Government had given sanctuary to a Yemen-born Saudi national who had earlier helped channel vast sums of Saudi Arabian petro-dollars into the war against the Soviets. His name was Osama bin Laden and he had recently been joined by an Egyptian doctor named Ayman al-Zawahri.

Kabul in 1997 was a city still racked by war, strewn with mines and unexploded ordnance, with entire suburbs roofless and deserted, inhabited only by pariah dogs. We very soon returned to Peshawar, where the contrast could not have been greater, for it was almost literally bursting with humanity: a city that had numbered no more than 250,000 souls when I first came through here in the early 1970s now held ten times that number. Then, it had consisted of two quite clearly demarcated areas: the old city, squeezed within walls laid down centuries earlier; and the civil station, set down outside the city walls in expansive British Raj pattern in the mid-nineteenth century. Now there was suburban sprawl on every side, but especially north of the Grand Trunk Road linking Peshawar to Nowshera and Islamabad. The ploughed fields of twenty-five years before lay under a shanty-town of corrugated iron roofs and mud walls extending far across the Vale of Peshawar. This was the Afghan Colony, home to more than two million refugees.

From Peshawar my travels took me northwards to Hoti Mardan, which stands almost at the centre of the Vale, bounded on one side by the mountain ranges of Swat and Buner and on the other by the Kabul and Indus rivers. Hoti Mardan is now the Pakistan Army's Punjab Regimental Centre, but for well over a century it was the headquarters of that most famous of British India's frontier regiments, the Queen's Own Corps of Guides Cavalry and Infantry, formed by twenty-six-year-old Lieutenant Harry Lumsden in 1847 from volunteers drawn from the surrounding tribes. The first of these irregular soldiers were Yusufzai or 'sons of Joseph', a Pathan tribe originally from Kandahar in southern Afghanistan which had conquered the Peshawar valley and the mountains to the north at about the time that King Henry VII was establishing his Tudor dynasty in England and Wales. The Yusufzai today are one of the largest of the Pathan tribes and their territories extend northwards from the Kabul River for a hundred miles into the mountain fastnesses of Swat and Buner. They are honoured among the Pathans as the purest of their number in terms of their blood-line.

The Yusufzai were of special interest to me as the first of the Pathan peoples to come into contact with the British when the East India Company pushed northwards across the Punjab in the 1840s. Because the British came to the Vale of Peshawar as conquerors of the Sikhs, who had long oppressed the Pathans, the Yusufzai greeted them as liberators when they took over from the Sikhs as governors of Peshawar city and began administering the surrounding countryside. The young British officers who came to speak to their tribal chiefs and clan leaders, the *khans* and *maliks*, were polite and friendly. Indeed, so upright and honest were they in their dealings that they were credited with a facial deformity that made it impossible for them to lie. These early political officers were also keen to know more of the ways of the Yusufzai and, moreover, they were recognised by the Pathans as *Ahl al-Kitab*, People of the Book, who shared with them the revelations of the early prophets – unlike the Sikhs, who were heathen *kaffirs* and proven enemies of Islam.

The first agent of the British East India Company to arrive in these parts was the political envoy Mountstuart Elphinstone, leading an embassy to the Amir of Kabul in 1809. He found a lot to admire in the character of the Yusufzai and the other Pathan tribes: 'They are fond of liberty, faithful to their friends, kind to their dependents, hospitable, brave, hardy, frugal, laborious and prudent.' But Elphinstone came to Peshawar as a guest and potential ally, whereas the Britons who followed in his footsteps were agents of what is now termed imperial expansionism but was at the time called the Forward Policy, the extension of British India's frontier beyond the Indus so as to leave no political vacuum for any other imperial power – such as France or Russia – to occupy. To Harry Lumsden and his fellow politicals the Pathans were potential subjects, and their strengths and weaknesses were seen in that light. Working alongside Lumsden at Hoti Mardan for many years was Dr Henry Bellew, attached to the Corps of Guides as their surgeon. Bellew was an outstanding linguist and got to know the Yusufzai well, later compiling an ethnographic study still regarded as a classic of its kind. Like Elphinstone before him, the doctor was impressed by the Pathans' rugged individualism. 'Each tribe under its own chief is an independent commonwealth,' he wrote, 'and collectively each is the other's rival if not enemy . . . Every man is pretty much his own master. Their khans and maliks only exercise authority on and exact revenues from the mixed population . . . They eternally boast of their descent, their prowess in arms, and their independence, and cap all by "Am I not a Pakhtun?"'

What Bellew and other British officials also discovered was that Pathan pride went hand in hand with Pathan violence. 'It would seem that the spirit of murder is latent in the heart of nearly every man in the valley,' observed Judge Elsmie when he came to write his *Notes on some of the Characteristics of Crime and Criminals in the Peshawar Division of the Punjab, 1872 to 1877.* 'Murder in all its phases: unblushing assassination in broad daylight, before a crowd of witnesses; the carefully planned secret murder of the sleeping victim at dead of night, murder by robbers, murder by rioters, murder by poisoners, murder by boys, and even by women, sword in hand . . . Crime of the worst conceivable kind is a matter of almost daily occurrence amongst a Pathan people.'

The Yusufzai settled in the Vale of Peshawar and elsewhere in the plains could be coerced into paying taxes and accepting British authority, provided it was not too heavy-handed. However, their fellow-tribesmen in the mountains took a very different view. Like all the larger Pathan tribes, the mountain Yusufzai in Swat and Buner were divided into numerous sub-tribes and clans that were constantly at each other's throats, but the moment the British so much as threatened to encroach these same sub-tribes and clans at once put aside their feuds to unite under one banner. They had united to resist the best efforts of the Great Mughal, Akbar, and they did the same with the British. There are places in those mountain strongholds overlooking the Vale of Peshawar whose names came to resonate loud and long in the British public consciousness because of pitched battles fought and hard won, among them 'Ambeyla' and 'Malakand'.

Dr Bellew saw the mountain Yusufzai at their best and worst, and, after many years of bitter, first-hand experience, concluded that their worst was pretty awful:

> The circumstances under which they live have endowed them with the most opposite qualities – an odd mixture of virtues and vices. Thus they are hardy, brave and proud; at the same time they are faithless, cunning and treacherous. Frugal in their own habits, they are hospitable to the stranger, and charitable to the beggar. The refugee they will protect and defend with their lives, but the innocent wayfarer they will plunder and slay for the pleasure of the act. Patriotic in a high degree, and full of pride of race, yet they will not scruple to betray for gold their most sacred interests or their nearest relations . . . Under no authority at home, they are constantly at feud with each other, and hostility with their neighbours. Murder and robbery are with them mere pastimes; revenge and plunder the occupation of their lives . . . Secure in the recesses of their mountains, they have from time immemorial defied the authority of all the governments that have preceded us on the frontier.

The British soon concluded that not just the Yusufzai of Swat and Buner but all the Pathans in the mountains were best left alone. Recognising them to be well-nigh ungovernable, the British Government of the Punjab devised a system that reflected the realities of the situation. British rule was deemed to extend to the foot of the mountains and this was termed the 'Settled Areas'; all the tribespeople who had their villages in this area were expected to pay their taxes and follow the Indian Penal Code, with some minor modifications. Beyond this belt of settled land was a second strip that extended deep into the mountains to the north and west; this became known as the 'Tribal Areas'. Not until 1893 was a set frontier established between Afghanistan and British India, when the Durand Line was drawn up by a senior British official in consultation with the Amir of Kabul; today it forms the agreed frontier between Afghanistan and Pakistan. This British legacy cuts right through Pathan territory and is arguably the most porous border in the world – and the most difficult to police. It always has been, and still is, a no-go area for outsiders.

After wandering over the battlefields of Ambeyla (not to be confused with the town of Amballa, of which more later) and Malakand I moved on westwards to the hill country of Hazara. I had said my goodbyes to Rahimullah Yusufzai and was now travelling in a vehicle provided by another authority on frontier matters and tribal history, Bashir Ahmad Khan, former political officer and diplomat, whose Yusufzai Swati ancestors had long ago crossed the Indus to claim the delightful Mansehra Valley in upper Hazara. As well as briefing me before I set out, the ever-generous Bashir Khan had also provided me with a detailed set of notes on what I was to look out for.

To get to Hazara I had to skirt the mountains of Buner, which as they approach the Indus Valley push southwards into the Vale of Peshawar to form a large spur shaped like a closed fist. This is the Mahabun Mountain: more accurately, a massif some thirty miles wide and fifteen deep made up of a jumble of mountain peaks linked by jagged ridges and riven by steep-sided valleys (see Map 2, 'The Peshawur Valley'). Before the Muslim conquests it was venerated by Buddhists as Udiyana, the Paradise Garden, and by Hindus as the Great Forest (*Mahaban*), a favourite retreat of sages and hermits. Among Muslims, too, it had come to be regarded as a place of particular sanctity, so that many *pirs* (holy men) had been drawn to settle there. 'It forms an important

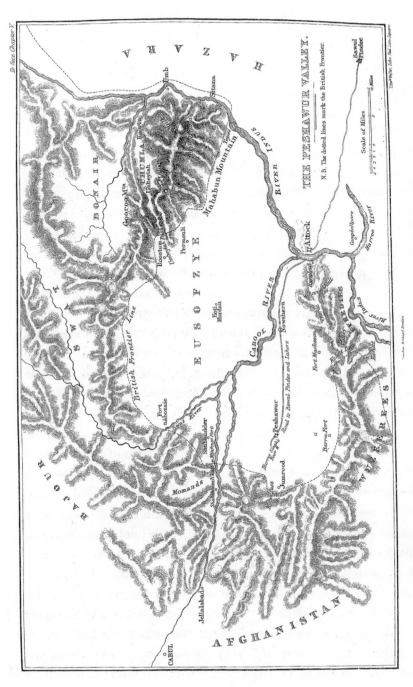

'The Peshawur Valley': John Adye's map of 1863 showing the Yusufzai country and Mahabun Mountain

and striking feature on that part of the frontier,' wrote John Adye, one of the first British officers to penetrate this mountain fastness in 1863:

> Its sides for the most part are steep, bare, and rugged, the higher summits being fringed with forests of fir, and in the winter capped with snow. There are, however, occasional plateaux of cultivation and numerous small villages belonging to the tribes, and in some parts dense forest runs down almost to the plains. The roads are few and bad – in fact, mere mule-tracks between the villages. The mountain on its eastern side is very abrupt, and is divided by the Indus from our province of Hazara; while all along, at the foot of its southern slopes, lie the plains of Eusofzye.

No fewer than six Pathan tribes and sub-tribes inhabit the Mahabun Mountain: the Yusufzai Chamlawals in the north-west; the Yusufzai Khudu Khels in the west; the Gaduns in the south; the Waziri Utmanzai in the south-east; the Yusufzai Isazai in the north-east; and, lastly, the Yusufzai Amazai sandwiched between the Chamlawals and Isazai.

The south-eastern corner of the Mahabun Mountain, occupied by the Utmanzai, is the point where the Indus finally cuts through the mountains to debouch on to the plains. In the late 1960s the Government of Pakistan built the Tarbela Dam here, whose waters now extend northwards up the gorge for some miles. The road crosses the Indus just below the dam. At this point, according to Bashir Khan's notes, I was to be aware that on the left side of the gorge looking up it – that is to say, on the eastern slopes of the Mahabun Mountain, and now all but submerged under the waters of the Tarbela Lake – was Sittana, which Bashir Khan described simply as 'the site of the camp of the Hindustani Fanatics'.

The term 'Hindustani Fanatics' meant absolutely nothing to me then. But it should have rung bells, because I was already aware from my researches that, before raising the Corps of Guides, Harry Lumsden had at the age of twenty-four led a force of three thousand Sikh infantry into northern Hazara, then nominally under Sikh control. He had faced stiff opposition from the local tribesmen, the Sayyeds of the Khagan Valley, whose resistance had been greatly strengthened by the presence of a small group of Hindustanis – not Hindus, as the word might suggest, but Muslims from Hindustan, the lands east of the Indus River. These Hindustanis, he noted in his report, had led the Sayyeds into battle and they had fought the fiercest. Several were taken prisoner and sent down under guard to Lahore, capital of the Punjab, where Harry Lumsden's chief, Henry Lawrence, made them welcome and praised them for their courage. Nearly all were found to be plainsmen from Patna, a large town on the Ganges between Benares and Calcutta, and they were led by two brothers named Ali, also from Patna: 'They begged for mercy and were permitted, under promise of future good conduct, to go to their homes in India.'

And there were other clues I had missed – one of them set down in a fascinating document written by that delightful eccentric James Abbott, the first British administrator of Hazara, giving pen-portraits of all the tribal chiefs in the area with details of their dispositions and foibles. Abbott had attached a number of notes and postscripts, and one of these read, in part: 'Khagan is important partly on account of its contact with independent states – but more, owing to the disposition of the *Hindustanee fanatics*, followers of Achmed Shah, to make it their place of arms ... I understand that there are still some of the Hindustanees fostered there by Syud Zamin Shah, & that intercourse is maintained between the Syuds & the fanatics at Sittana.'

Tucked away among Abbott's numerous letters to Henry Lawrence in Lahore were further references to this same 'remarkable nest of Immigrants from Hindustan' that I had earlier failed to note. Abbott had become convinced that some sort of secret supply chain had been set up, by which money, materials and men were being smuggled across the plains of India to Sittana. His men had intercepted messengers carrying letters concealed inside bamboo canes and with gold coins hidden under their waistcoats. Young Muslim men from Tonk, Rohilkhand and elsewhere in India were crossing the Indus River at Attock 'disguised as beggars and students' and then making their way north to the Mahabun Mountain, where they discarded their disguises and took up arms. At Sittana itself, large *godowns* (warehouses) were being built for the storage of grain, transported there by *kafila* (camel caravans). Over a period of four years, between 1849 and 1853, Abbott had become increasingly concerned by the growing threat these 'enthusiasts' posed to his neighbouring district of Hazara, and had asked for armed check-posts to be set up along the Indus. He had been told that there were no grounds for alarm, for 'all the enemies of the British Government have recently been defeated'.

Finally, there was the overlooked detail in the seditious letters intercepted by the authorities at Peshawar at the time of the outbreak of the Sepoy Mutiny of 1857, the so-called Indian Mutiny. As described in the Punjab *Gazetteer of the Peshawar Division*, these letters had been sent by 'Muhammadan bigots in Patna and Thanesar to soldiers of the 64th Native Infantry, revelling in the atrocities that had been committed in Hindustan on the men, women and children of the "Nazareenes" [Christians] and sending them messages from their own mothers that they should emulate these deeds, and if they fell in the attempt they would at least go to heaven, and their deaths in such a case would be pleasant news at home. These letters alluded to a long series of correspondences that had been going on, through the 64th Native Infantry, with the fanatics in Swat and Sitana.'

The fruit of my travels and researches was *Soldier Sahibs: The Men Who Made the North-West Frontier*, published in 2000. It told the story of a pioneering band of political officers, known collectively as 'Henry Lawrence's Young Men', young military officers who served under Lawrence on what was then the north-west frontier of the Punjab but which became the North-West Frontier Province of British India. Besides Harry Lumsden and James Abbott, these frontiersmen included Herbert Edwardes, John Nicholson, Reynell Taylor and Neville Chamberlain, all of whom carved out extraordinary reputations for themselves in their dealings with the frontier tribes – and who between themselves and the Pathans helped to create the lasting mystique of 'the Frontier'. From then on India's North-West Frontier became increasingly romanticised, as much by the political officers on the spot as by anyone else. I particularly recall the words of perhaps the last of these British frontiersmen, Sir Olaf Caroe, Governor of the North-West Frontier Province from 1946 to 1947, who described his feelings to me in the following terms:

> The stage on which the Pathan lived out his life was at the same time magnificent and harsh – and the Pathan was like his background. Such a contrast was sometimes hard to bear, but perhaps it was this that put us in love with it. There was among the Pathans something that called to the Englishman or the Scotsman – partly that the people looked you straight in the eye, that there was no equivocation and that you couldn't browbeat them even if you wanted to. When we crossed the bridge at Attock we felt we'd come home.

Exactly the same attitude came into being in Britain's dealings with the desert tribes of Arabia. Early adventurers such as Doughty, Burton and Palgrave and later politicals such as St John Philby and T. E. Lawrence unwittingly conspired to create a romance of a stark landscape sparsely populated by manly *Badawin*, better known today as Bedouin, whose harsh moral code mirrored that of the Pathans in almost every respect. It may be going too far to say that the tendency to view these two regions and their two peoples through rose-tinted preconceptions had fatal consequences, but it most certainly blurred the realities.

The first British officer to attach this aura of romance to the Pathans was Herbert Edwardes, in *A Year on the Punjab Frontier*, published in 1851. Yet Edwardes recognised that many of the qualities he admired in the Pathans were double-edged: their individualism and manliness was accompanied by intense egoism and vengefulness; strong clan identity meant intense inter-clan enmity; codes of friendship and hospitality were matched by deceit and betrayal. But perhaps the most striking paradox was that the Pathans' much-vaunted independent nature was accompanied by an extraordinary degree of religious dependence. Edwardes was a devout Christian evangelical, brought up to regard his own values as the benchmark of modern civilisation, as demonstrated by the conspicuous success of the British Empire. He had no time for what he saw as the Pathans' religious credulity, which in his opinion made them prey to exploitation by the many categories of persons known collectively as *ulema*, or 'those learned in the ways of Islam', the Muslim clergy. 'The Moolah and the Kazee, the Peer and the Syud descended on the smiling vale,' wrote Herbert Edwardes of the Waziri tribes south of Peshawar,

> armed with a panoply of spectacles and owl-like looks,
> miraculous rosaries, infallible amulets, and tables of
> descent from the Prophet Muhommud. Each newcomer,
> like St Peter, held the keys of heaven; and the whole, like
> Irish beggars, were equally prepared to bless or curse to all
> eternity him who gave or him who withheld . . . To be
> cursed in Arabic, or anything that sounded like it; to be
> told that the blessed Prophet had put a black mark against
> his soul, for not giving his best field to one of the Prophet's

own posterity; to have the saliva of a disappointed saint left in anger on his doorpost; or behold a Hajee, who had gone three times to Mecca, deliberately sit down and enchant his camels with the itch, and his sheep with the rot: these were things which made the dagger drop out of the hand of the awe-stricken savage, his knees knock together, his liver turn to water, and his parched tongue to be scarce able to articulate a full and complete concession of the blasphemous demand.

The Corps of Guides surgeon Dr Henry Bellew also noted this same propensity for religious subservience among the Yusufzai. 'They are', he declared, 'entirely controlled by their priests, and are at all times ready for a *jahad* [jihad], be the infidels black or white ... An inordinate reverence for saints and the religious classes generally is universal, and their absurdly impossible and contradictory dicta are received and acted upon with eager credulity.' Half a century later Winston Churchill, then a junior officer with the 4th Hussars, came to exactly the same conclusion. 'Their superstition', he wrote of the Pathans, 'exposes them to the rapacity and tyranny of a numerous priesthood – *Mullahs, Sahibzadas, Akhundzadas, Fakirs* – and a host of wandering *Talib-ul-ulms*, who correspond with the theological students in Turkey, and live free at the expense of the people.'

When Dr Bellew came to set down his *General Report on the Yusufzais* in 1864, he singled out two groups of clergy as having particular influence over the Pathans. The first were the Saiyyeds, of Arab extraction and believed to be the direct descendants of Caliph Ali, the son-in-law of the Prophet: 'Their origin being from so holy a source, they are, of course, esteemed as uncommonly holy persons. Their bold, obtrusive, and continual publication of their sacred character and descent draws from the ignorant a reverential and awful respect, and at the same time gives them great influence over the mass of the population they dwell among. They use this to their own advantage and manage to get from the Afghans [i.e., Pathans] considerable tracts of land in gift as a perpetual and hereditary possession.'

Bellew's second group provided the most active portion of the clergy. Every mosque had its *imam*, who led the congregation in prayers, supported in the larger mosques by a number of religious teachers, known variously as *mullahs*, *maulvis* or *maulanas*: 'They call the *azan* [summons to prayer], and perform the prayers and other duties of the Imam in his absence. They are mostly occupied in teaching the *Talib-ul-ulm* the Kuran [Quran], the forms of prayer, and the doctrines of Islam, and the village children how to repeat their "belief" and say their prayers.' Dr Bellew's 'Talib-ul-ulm' were more correctly *taliban-ul-ulm*, literally 'seekers of knowledge', or religious students. He categorised them as 'a mixed class of vagrants and idlers, who, under the pretence of devoting themselves to religion, wander from country to country; and, on the whole, lead an agreeable and easy life. Wherever they go they find shelter in the mosques, and can always get a sufficiency of food for the mere asking. As a rule, they are very ignorant and remarkably bigoted.'

Edwardes, Bellew and the British officers who came after them loathed these saiyyeds, imams, mullahs, maulvis, maulanas and taliban in equal measure. They saw the ulema, because of their influence over their flocks, as a threat to British authority and their influence on the tribespeople as wholly negative. That loathing was returned in equal if not greater measure by the sayyeds, mullahs, maulvis, maulanas and taliban, who considered the British not merely a threat to *their* authority but also a threat to their religion. In 1847 a would-be assassin caught and disarmed by Herbert Edwardes' guards was found to have been acting on the instructions of a mullah. In 1853 John Nicholson shot a man advancing on him with a sword, an assailant whom he later described as 'religiously mad'. This man, too, had been put up to it by what Nicholson described as a 'religious instructor'. As the gravestones in the Christian cemeteries of Peshawar, Kohat, Bannu and elsewhere on the Frontier testify, scores of acts of violence against individual Britons were perpetrated over the next century.

My youngest daughter has a beautiful gold-threaded scarf that once belonged to an English doctor named Flora Butcher. Miss Butcher wanted to be a doctor at a time in Britain when women were not allowed to enter the profession, so she went to Belgium to study. After qualifying, she had hoped to practise in India but was refused permission to do so by the British authorities. Undaunted, she proceeded up the Khyber Pass, to set up a medical mission in tribal territory, where she and a small band of devoted Indians ministered with great success to the local tribespeople. Towards the end of 1927 her friends became concerned by the non-appearance of the pack ponies that kept her supplied, enquiries were made, and it was discovered that Miss Butcher and most of her staff had been murdered. She was only one of a number of doctors targeted and assassinated on the Frontier at that time by what the British termed 'fanatics'.

In *Soldier Sahibs* I interpreted these killings by tribesmen as part and parcel of the Pathans' traditional propensity for violence and their antipathy to outside interference. I was quite wrong. What I had missed was something infinitely more serious: a series of insurgencies and assassinations increasingly directed by a movement whose adherents saw themselves as engaging in a great religious struggle in defence of Islam but who were (as they still are) profoundly at odds with that same religion; a movement dedicated not simply to protecting Islam, as its adherents protested (and still protest), but to the destruction of all interpretations of religion other than its own; a movement that worked time and time again to bring the people of the Frontier out in armed revolt, and which in 1857 played an unacknowledged part in the struggle to overthrow British rule in India; a movement brought to the verge of extinction many times over but whose ideology was always kept alive – and which today is not only back in business but whose appeal and authority is greater than it has ever been.

The founder of this movement saw himself as a reformer and described those who followed his teachings as *Al-Muwahhidun*, or the Unitarians. But to their many enemies they became known, after their movement's founder, as *Al-Wahhabi* – the Wahhabi. One of the many curious features of their subsequent history is that the Wahhabis were very well known to people of my great-grandparents' generation. Indeed, one of my great-grandfathers was standing beside Lord Mayo, the then Viceroy of India, when he was knifed by what was almost certainly a Wahhabi-directed assassin in 1871. To the British authorities in India in the nineteenth century these Wahhabis were best known as the Hindustani Fanatics, and their fighting base in the mountains was always spoken of as the 'Fanatic Camp'. A generation later, in my grandparents' time, the same movement reappeared in Arabia, revitalised and now calling itself *Al-Ikhwan* – the Brotherhood. Meanwhile, on the Indian sub-continent Wahhabism had mutated into a more respectable form, now rebranding its religious ideology *Salafi*, or 'following the forefathers'. Then in our own times these two streams, re-energised by new political ideologies associated with nationalism, separatism and pan-Islamism, converged and cross-infected on the Afghanistan–Pakistan fault line. Out of this coming-together emerged two very different bodies, one tight-knit and localised, the other loose-knit and with global aspirations: the Taliban and Al-Qaeda.

Wahhabism is declared by its defenders to be no more than Islam in its purest, original form, and without links to either the Taliban or Al-Qaeda. A number of serious academics and political observers have taken the same view, representing Wahhabism as little more than a puritanical reformist teaching within Islam which still has political clout in Saudi Arabia but little relevance to modern-day events elsewhere, particularly when it comes to the driving ideologies of men like the Yemeni Osama bin Laden, the Egyptian Ayman al-Zawahri, the Afghan Mullah Omar and the Jordanian Abu Musab al-Zarqawi, and others who use terror in the name of Islam as a political weapon.

The founder of Wahhabism saw himself as a reformer and revivalist reacting against corruptions inside Islam. He declared holy war on those corruptions and took that war to his fellow Muslims. But his Wahhabism very quickly developed its own militant politico-religious ideology built around an authority figure who was both a temporal and spiritual leader. It became, in essence, a cult.

Wahhabism of itself never enjoyed mass support. Its ideology always was and remains rooted in violent intolerance, which has few charms for most people. It would have gone the way of all extremist cults but for the fact that it appeared as a champion of faith at a time when the world community of Islam, the *umma*, began to question why it was that the triumph of Islam was not proceeding as ordained.

Islam's first great crisis of faith occurred at the time of the eruption of the Mongols in the late twelfth century, but a second and more serious crisis began with the rise of Western capitalism. At the time of Sultan Suleiman the Magnificent the Ottoman Empire appeared invincible: a world of shared faith under one central authority, the *khalifa*, and one rule of law, sharia, governing all aspects of Muslim behaviour. This was the civilisation of *dar ul-Islam*, the 'domain of Islam', inhabited by those who had submitted to the will of God, surrounded on all sides by *dar ul-harb*, the 'domain of enmity', inhabited by unbelievers who would all finally convert to Islam and become subject to sharia. But with the failure of the siege of Vienna in 1663 the Ottomans began a long, slow retreat before the advance of Christian Europe. That advance was much more than brute imperialism: it was all-enveloping, neatly summed up in the triumphalist words of the British missionary doctor Dr Theodore Pennell when he wrote in

1909 that 'The Old Islam, the old Hinduism, are already doomed, not by the efforts of the missionaries, but by the contact of the West, by the growth of commerce, by the spread of education, by the thirst for wealth and luxury which the West has implanted in the East.'

The questions 'How can this be?' and 'What can we do?' came to be asked with increasing concern by ordinary Muslims. By tradition it was the local ruler, the amir and the nawab, who defended Islam in the name of the Caliphate, but these secular leaders were giving way to Christian governors. In their absence it was the ulema who increasingly came forward with the answers that people wanted to hear. One response was Islamic revivalism, which continues today under the generic term of 'pan-Islamism', a movement for reshaping the world along Islamic lines, to which many disparate individuals and groups turned (and continue to turn) for comfort and salvation. This remains a perfectly legitimate ideal, no different from Christians wishing to see all non-Christians saved – until it is subsumed by the employment of compulsion, violence and terror as instruments to achieve that ideal. What made this terrorising not merely acceptable but a religious duty was the ideology articulated in Wahhabism.

Now it is the West's turn to ask the questions. Since 9/11 immense efforts have been made to understand the phenomenon of Islamist extremism. An entire industry of think-tanks and defence centres has sprung up to satisfy the demand for explanations. Most of this attention has been focused on recent events, with correspondingly little notice being taken of origins. Wahhabism is only part of the answer, but it is an important part, and one aspect of Wahhabism in particular has been all but ignored. Here I have tried to make good that gap in our understanding.

1

Death of a Commissioner

He was the beau ideal of a soldier – cool to conceive, brave to dare, and strong to do . . . The defiles of the Khyber and the peaks of the Black Mountain alike bear witness to his exploits . . . The loss of Col. Mackeson's life would have dimmed a victory: to lose him thus, by the hand of a foul assassin, is a misfortune of the heaviest gloom for the Government, which counted him among its bravest and its best.

> Part of a tribute from Lord Dalhousie inscribed on the memorial to Colonel Frederick Mackeson, Commissioner of Peshawar, died 14 September 1853

On the afternoon of 10 September 1853 Colonel Frederick Mackeson was working on the veranda of his bungalow in the Civil Lines at Peshawar. As Commissioner of Peshawar, Mackeson was the most senior British official on the North-West Frontier of the Punjab, overseeing the work of a dozen or so assistant commissioners and magistrates. He was also the most experienced political officer in the region; he had made it his business to know the Pathans and their ways, and was liked and respected, both by his junior officers and the tribal chiefs, among whom he was known affectionately as *Kishin Kaka* or 'Uncle Mackeson'. One of his first acts on his appointment two years earlier had been to build a new *kutcherry* or office, together with a residential bungalow. These new quarters were on open ground between Peshawar city, where the native inhabitants lived, and the cantonment housing the British political and military officers and their troops. This was in keeping with the political philosophy that Mackeson and his fellow politicals had imbibed from their chief, Henry Lawrence, which was that they should always make themselves accessible.

Having completed his official duties in the kutcherry, Mackeson had walked across the road to his bungalow to work on his papers. It was his habit to see petitioners only in the morning, so when a tribesman advanced towards him holding out a roll of paper, Mackeson told him to come back the next day. He was unknown to Mackeson's staff but had earlier been seen praying outside the office. As recounted to a young officer named Sydney Cotton, newly arrived on the frontier, the stranger then fell down at the feet of the Commissioner and, clasping his hands, implored him to read his petition: 'Colonel Mackeson then took the paper and commenced to read, and being intent on its contents, the native suddenly sprung upon the Colonel, and plunged a dagger into his breast.' The Commissioner died four days later.

The assailant was seized and interrogated. He had come from a village outside British territory, in Swat, declared himself to be a talib, and claimed to have acted to stop the British invading his land. Further questioning revealed him to be a 'religious fanatic' who saw himself as a mujahedeen set on a course of martyrdom. He was duly tried and hanged. He died, according to Cotton, 'glorying in his deed of blood'. To prevent his grave becoming a martyr's shrine his remains were burned and the ashes thrown in the river.

As for the unfortunate Mackeson, fears that his body might be further violated led to his being interred not in the Christian cemetery, which lay outside the perimeter on the cantonment, but in a garden known as the Company Bagh. A black marble obelisk was erected over the grave, inscribed with a fulsome tribute penned by the Governor-General of India himself, Lord Dalhousie.

Because of the name Mackeson had made for himself among the frontier tribes, his friends found his murder incomprehensible. There were rumours, angrily dismissed, that the Commissioner had violated Pathan taboos by making advances to one of their women. There was also talk of a *fatwa* or religious edict having been proclaimed, and of a reward being offered for his head. The reality was that the murder was both an act of revenge and the first successful blow against the British Government in India by a secret organisation intent on revolution.

This organisation was, in fact, already known to the authorities. Back in 1848 Lieutenant Harry Lumsden had reported the presence of Hindustani outsiders among the Sayyed tribesmen of Hazara. He had captured their two leaders – two brothers named Ali – who after questioning had been returned under custody to their homes in Patna. Then in August 1852 the Assistant Magistrate of Patna, Charles Carnac, had sent details to the Governor-General of a plot involving a sect of Muslims in his city who were 'mixed up with a band of Moslem fanatics in the distant hills of Sittana and Swat'. A bundle of letters had been intercepted which revealed that a 'treasonable correspondence' was taking place between these fanatics in the mountains and members of a prominent Muslim family living in the Sadiqpore district of Patna. The latter were apparently despatching *kafilas* or caravans of men, arms and funds to the frontier along a secret trail that went from Patna to Peshawar by way of Meerut, Amballa and Rawalpindi, for the express purpose of waging war against the Government of India.

Acting on this information, Mr Carnac had raided the Sadiqpore mansion-cum-caravanserai in Patna, only to find that the occupants had been forewarned and had destroyed all their letters. However, the head of the family, one Maulvi Ahmadullah, had subsequently assembled several hundred armed men in his premises and had declared that 'he was prepared to resist any further prosecution of the Magistrate's enquiries and, if attacked, would raise the standard of revolt'.

After taking advice from his home minister and members of his council, Lord Dalhousie had then set out a formal Minute in Council in which he expressed himself satisfied that there was no cause for concern. For years these fanatics had been doing their best to 'induce the Mussulmans [Muslims] in India to join in a holy war' and nothing had come of it: 'The letters now detected seem to me to show that their efforts have met with very little success. They ask for money, they ask for arms and recruits, and the terms in which they write seem to me conclusive of the fact that they have obtained very little of the one and very few of the other.' The Governor-General had himself seen 'a sort of ballad', picked up in the back streets of Calcutta, which enjoined 'all true Mussulmans to join the standard of the faith and rise against the infidel'. But that sort of thing was only to be expected. His Lordship could see 'no reason to suppose that there is any more movement or intrigue at present going on than must at all times be expected among the Mussulmans in India'.

This first Minute had then been followed by a second, written by Dalhousie in October 1852 in response to further discoveries of treasonable activities, now involving attempts to subvert sepoys of the Bengal Native Infantry on service in the Punjab. Again, the evidence pointed to a group of Muslim mullahs in Patna being deeply involved in treasonable conspiracy against the state. But Government, according to Dalhousie, was on top of the situation, and the law as it existed was fully capable of dealing with it. Instructions were subsequently sent to all the provinces under British rule reminding the local authorities how they were to deal with such cases. Where it could be proved that treason was being plotted, the ringleaders of plots were to be shown no leniency – but magistrates were to avoid taking any action that might be seen as oppressive by the native population. As for the fanatics up in the Mahabun Mountain at Sittana, they were best left untouched: 'Since they are insignificant, they may be let alone as long as they are quiet. At any rate, this is not a propitious time for such a movement. We have already irons enough in the fire on the north-west frontier without heating another unnecessarily.'

Barely eight weeks after the Governor-General recorded this second Minute, Commissioner Mackeson had himself led a small punitive force across the Indus River from British territory in Hazara. This was in response to an appeal from a local tribal chief, the Khan of Amb: some Hindustani foreigners had occupied one of his forts on the banks of the Indus and he needed help to expel them. These Hindustanis were the same Moslem fanatics of Sittana of whom the Magistrate of Patna had complained eighteen months earlier. Among the officers who accompanied Mackeson on this raid was a young lieutenant of the 41st Bengal Native Infantry, George Rowcroft, for whom it was his first taste of frontier warfare. 'Sittana', he wrote in a private memoir, 'was a place built and inhabited by Mahomedan Hindustanis and Bengalis; refugees and outlaws, men who had left the British territories either as criminals fleeing from justice, or as fanatics renouncing the "Feringee" [the British] and all his works. They were a thorn in the side of the civil and political authorities on the Frontier, and made frequent raids across the Indus into British territory, often succeeding in carrying off, for ransom, some of our subjects; generally a Hindu trader.' Having kidnapped a victim they would send a ransom demand to his relatives and, if this wasn't answered, follow up with a second message accompanied by the victim's ear: 'A further neglect to pay up resulted in the head of the victim being sent, and a sarcastic message that they were now relieved of the expense of feeding him.'

Ordered by Mackeson to give up the Khan of Amb's fort, its Hindustani occupants responded with a defiant letter declaring that they would die first. Accordingly, on 6 January 1853 two regiments of Sikh infantry were ferried across the Indus and advanced on the fort from below, while at the same time a party of matchlock-men supplied by the Khan of Amb took up a position on the heights above. The sight of columns of troops advancing in good order was enough to send the occupants scurrying up the mountainside. 'In spite of the boasts of the Hindustanis,' wrote Colonel Mackeson in his official despatch, 'they were all, to the number of from 200 to 300, in full flight from the fort of Kotla.' In the meantime, the Khan of Amb's matchlock-men had seized the Hindustanis' main base at Sittana, higher up in the mountains. But here, too, the Hindustanis dispersed into the surrounding crags and ravines, leaving behind a small rearguard party to hold off the attackers. According to George Rowcroft's account, by the time the Sikhs arrived the fighting was over: 'The latter, on arriving at Sittana – a partially fortified village surrounded by a dense belt of dried thorns – found that the able bodied portion of the occupants had fled, and the few (some dozen or fifteen of sick and wounded) left behind, had been promptly disposed of by the gallant Tunawallis.'

The camp at Sittana was levelled, the belt of thorns fired, and the expedition withdrew, taking with it a number of wounded prisoners. In Peshawar the Guides' Assistant Surgeon, Dr Robert Lyell, treated these wounded men and was impressed by their fortitude and their refusal to talk. Only after one of his nursing assistants had gained their confidence did they begin to give information about themselves and their organisation, whereupon it became clear that this was no rabble of outlaws but a disciplined army, well organised and with a clear agenda. It had an established chain of command, and was currently led by the younger of two brothers named Ali following the recent death of the elder brother. Although they lived frugally on stewed pulses and unleavened bread, they were armed with carbines and were kept well supplied by their supporters in the plains. The prisoners boasted that many pious Muslims contributed to their cause, including the rulers of a number of leading Muslim princely states in India.

Mackeson could have put an end to the Hindustani Fanatics at Sittana in January 1853. But the Commissioner had just received the Governor-General's Minute, telling him to leave things as they were. So he did not order a pursuit, later justifying his inaction on the grounds that he had done all that was required of him: 'He considered their flight, without offering resistance, would generally increase the contempt in which they were held by the surrounding tribes, and would be more useful to us than any persecution of them could be.'

Mackeson's failure to follow up his raid probably cost him his life. Had he done so, the history of the North-West Frontier might well have been very different. But Frederick Mackeson, like Lord Dalhousie before him and many others who came after, underestimated the Hindustani Fanatics. Intelligence existed to show the movement's true nature, but this information was disregarded. It was not the first time the Hindustani Fanatics were let off the hook, and it was certainly not the last.

What the British came to know as the Fanatic Camp at Sittana had been established almost a quarter of a century earlier on the eastern slopes of Mahabun Mountain overlooking the Indus Valley. It was on land granted in perpetuity as a religious gift by the local Yusufzai back in the sixteenth century to a renowned saint named Pir Baba, who was a Saiyyed descended from the Prophet. After the Sikhs annexed neighbouring Hazara and the Vale of Peshawar, Sittana became a refuge and a rallying point for resisters – or, as a British intelligence officer put it, 'the refuge for

outlaws and offenders from Yusufzai and Hazara, and the ren-
dezvous of all the discontented Khans and their followers'. Then
in the winter months of 1827–8 a very different kind of resister
appeared on the Frontier: SYED AHMAD of Rae Bareli, founder
and first of the Hindustani Fanatics.

Syed Ahmad was born Syed Ghullam Muhammad in 1786 in
the town of Rae Bareli, on the Gangetic plains between Lucknow
and Allahabad in the kingdom of Oude. As his first name implies,
his family claimed descent from the Prophet, which marked him
out as someone to be respected by virtue of his inherent sanctity
and to be accorded the honorific title of *shah* (king). According to
his several biographers, he grew up into a model of perfection: tall,
strong and fair, with close-knit eyebrows and a long and bushy
beard. He was said to have had a great appetite for physical sports,
including wrestling, swimming, archery and shooting. This gave
him an imposing physique that set him apart from most clerics,
yet he was apparently taciturn and gentle in demeanour, with a
quiet voice that could be heard by all who wished to hear him. As
one biography put it, 'All the perfections . . . were implanted from
his birth in this holy man, as evidenced from the delight which he
took in the exercise of piety and practice of virtue from his child-
hood.' Like the Prophet, he fell from time to time into deep
ecstatic trances, indicating that he was in direct communication
with God.

After his father's death in 1800 the fourteen-year-old moved to
Delhi to become a talib of the leading scholar of the age, SHAH
ABDUL AZIZ, principal of a small but greatly respected religious
school known as Madrassah-i-Rahimiya, tucked away in the back
streets of the old city. According to the author of *Sirat-ul-
Mustaqim*, the best known of the biographies, 'When he was
admitted into the society of the venerated Sheikh Abdul Aziz,
who received him as a disciple of the Nakshbandia school, by the
propitious effects and influence of the enlightened spirit of his
instructor, the concealed excellencies of his nature developed

themselves in a natural succession of wonders.' Among these
wonders were three dreams: in the first the Prophet fed the boy
with three dates; in the second the Prophet's daughter Fatima
bathed him, washed him and dressed him in garments 'of exceed-
ing richness'; in the third God placed him on his right hand,
showed him his treasures and said to him 'This I have given to
you, and I shall give you yet more.' Clearly Syed Ahmad was des-
tined for great things – although it should always be borne in
mind that the hagiographers who wrote about him did so as leading practitioners of the cult of Syed Ahmad that developed after
his untimely demise.

Syed Ahmad was extremely fortunate in having Shah Abdul Aziz
for his teacher, for he was the eldest son and religious successor
of the renowned Sufi scholar and reformer SHAH WALIULLAH
of Delhi, who has been described by a leading modern historian
as 'the bridge between medieval and modern Islam in India'. Half
a century earlier Shah Waliullah had set out to make Islam more
accessible by translating the *Quran*, the word of God divinely
revealed to his Prophet Muhammad, from Arabic into Persian.
He had also called for moral reform and a return to the pristine
Islam of the days of the Prophet as set down in the Quran and the
Hadith, a corpus of accounts of the deeds and sayings of the
Prophet as remembered by his companions. As part of this process
of reform Shah Waliullah had broken with religious convention by
setting himself up as a *mujtahid*, one who makes his own interpretations of established religious law by virtue of informed
reasoning.

In the public mind, however, Shah Waliullah had been best
known for his unavailing efforts to restore Muslim rule to
Hindustan, culminating in a famous appeal to the Afghan ruler
Ahmad Shah Abdali to invade India, destroy the Hindu Marathas
in battle and bring back the golden years of the Mughal Emperor
Aurangzeb. In the event, Ahmad Shah had been forced to retreat
to Afghanistan and the Marathas had once again become the

dominant power in northern India. But the dream of an Islamic revival and of Hindustan under sharia had been kept alive by Shah Waliullah's four sons, with the Madrassah-i-Rahimiya acknowledged as the most influential seminary in all Hindustan.

Islam east of the Indus River had developed along different lines from that followed in the faith's heartlands. It had reached almost every corner of the sub-continent, but was a minority religion everywhere other than in East Bengal (now Bangladesh) and in perhaps half a dozen regional centres such as Delhi, Lucknow and Hyderabad. Contrary to what some Hindu nationalist historians would have us believe, most conversions to Islam had been voluntary, inspired as much by the challenge to the Hindu caste system represented by Islamic egalitarianism as by the examples of Sufi saints, who in many areas preceded the Muslim invasions. Islam represented a rare opportunity for social betterment, so it followed that most of these converts came from the bottom of the pile, as exemplified by the weavers and artisans of East Bengal. Most of them became willing if ignorant followers of the Hanafi school of law, the oldest, most inclusive and least hierarchical of the four schools of jurisprudence of the Sunnis, the Islamic mainstream which followed the precedents established by the Prophet and his immediate successors and acknowledged the authority of the line of caliphs who came after them.

The many waves of Turko-Afghan invaders who settled in northern India were also Sunnis, again mostly Hanafis, whereas the Persians who came with the Mughals were predominantly Shia, the largest minority sect in Islam, which regarded Imam Ali and his line as the legitimate descendants of the Prophet and thus the only true source of religious authority – a view considered heretical by orthodox Sunnis. However, centuries of contact with Hinduism also led to a measure of synthesis between it and both Sunni and Shia interpretations of Islam – an intermingling of views and practices that reformers such as Shah Waliullah and his sons found highly objectionable.

Elements of racism also came into play. Even though Islam stood for the equality of all men before God, the Muslim community in India developed a hierarchy that in many respects mirrored the Hindu caste system, a pecking order in which Hindustani Muslims descended from Hindu converts were at the bottom and those of Arab descent at the top, closely followed by Mughal, Persian and Afghan settlers. At the very pinnacle, naturally enough, were the Saiyyeds, whose descent from the Prophet accorded them respect bordering on veneration, enabling them to exercise what was generally a moderating influence on society by acting as mediators in disputes and as religious patrons. A significant number among this Muslim aristocracy resented their loss of power and equated it with the watering-down of Islam's core values since the days of Emperor Aurangzeb. Many also embraced Sufi mysticism. The reformer Shah Waliullah was himself a follower of the Naqshbandi Sufi school, based on a movement originating in Bokhara in the fourteenth century which eschewed music and dance in favour of silent contemplation, and sought to recapture the simple intensity of early Islam through personal devotion. However, there are Sufis and Sufis. Prior to Shah Waliullah, the best-known Naqshbandi Sufi in India was Sheikh AHMAD SIRHINDI, who had been so appalled by the religious tolerance promoted by Emperor Akbar that when Jehangir succeeded him he began a political campaign to restore what he regarded as true Muslim values. These were centred on the overarching importance of *tawhid*, the oneness of God or absolute monotheism, as the basis of true religion, and on the need to combat all innovations and deviations from tawhid, as represented not only by Shia beliefs but also by many of the popular customs that had been adopted by Sunnis over the centuries. Ahmad Sirhindi's application of Naqshbandi Sufism expressed itself in violent intolerance of Sunni backsliders and in the persecution of Shias and Hindus. Despite being proscribed in later years, the Sirhindi movement continued to inspire Sunni fundamentalists –

among them Shah Waliullah, his four sons and those who studied under them at Delhi's Madrassah-i-Rahimiya.

Thus the adolescent Syed Ahmad became a student of probably the most radical and reactionary school in India at a time when the *umma*, the world community of Islam, felt itself threatened to a degree not experienced since the days of the Great Khans. The Ottoman sultanate, after centuries as the pre-eminent power in Eastern Europe and Western Asia, was suffering one reverse after another at the hands of the Austrians, Russians and French, while at the same time its authority was being undermined from within by a series of revolts by regional viceroys. In India it was the same story. As Mughal power at the centre waned, local Muslim governors were breaking away to set up their own regional principalities. These, in their turn, were being taken over one after another by the British East India Company, beginning in Bengal and the Carnatic and then pushing into the interior: in 1799 Tipu Sultan was defeated and killed at Seringapatam; in 1803 the Mughal emperor Badshah Shah Alam, great-great-grandson of Emperor Aurangzeb, suffered the last in a series of humiliations at the hands of foreign invaders when he signed over what little authority remained to him to become a pensioner of the British in Delhi.

Unable to match the growing military and economic power of Europe, Islam responded through religious revival in a variety of forms. Disgusted at his emperor's craven response to the takeover of his city by the British, Syed Ahmad's teacher Shah Abdul Aziz issued a fatwa that Delhi had been enslaved. 'In this city the *Imam ul-Muslimin* [religious leader of the Muslims; thus, the Mughal Emperor] wields no authority,' he declared. 'The real power rests with the British officers. There is no check on them, and the promulgation of the commands of *kufr* [heathenism] means that in administration and justice, in matters of law and order, in the domain of trade, finance and collection of revenues – everywhere the *kuffar* [heathen infidels] are in power.' He therefore declared Hindustan to be a domain of enmity (*dar ul-harb*), and that henceforward it was incumbent on all Muslims to strive to restore India to that blessed state which had prevailed in earlier times.

This fatwa was little more than a symbolic act of defiance, but there can be no doubt that young Syed Ahmad left the Madrassah-i-Rahimiya thoroughly radicalised and with the conviction that un-Islamic forces were threatening his faith. As an expression of this radicalisation he abandoned the name 'Muhammad' as blasphemous, and became Syed Ahmad.

Biographies of Syed Ahmad such as that already quoted from state that after eight years of study in Delhi he married and moved back to his home town of Rae Bareli as a mullah. But there are other versions, including a biography written by a nephew, which give widely differing accounts and dates – suggesting that the writers were following very different agendas. They demonstrate that Syed Ahmad gathered under the umbrella of his leadership a number of factions that were only willing to sink their religious differences while he remained alive. One has to pick one's path through these competing histories with caution, but it seems highly probable that Syed Ahmad abandoned his studies in Delhi in his late teens to join his elder brother, an irregular horseman in the forces of a Pathan freebooter named AMIR KHAN.

Even the most hagiographical accounts accept that Syed Ahmad did indeed spend time with Amir Khan, although the claim is that he did so as *pesh-imam* or chaplain to the troops, during which time he exercised moral influence over Amir Khan's band of Pathan soldiery, besides performing several miracles. What is glossed over is that Amir Khan was no jihadi fighting for Islamic values but a deeply unpleasant mercenary, a Yusufzai originally from the mountains of Buner who fought for whoever paid the most or offered the best prospect of booty. At this period Amir Khan commanded the cavalry of the half-mad Maratha warlord

Jaswant Rao Holkar; in effect, he was helping a Hindu to plunder central India. In British eyes Amir Khan and his Pathans were nothing less than *pindaris* or marauders, notorious for their acts of cruelty and rapine. Colonel James Tod, who witnessed Amir Khan's depredations at first hand, describes him in his *Annals of Rajasthan* as 'one of the most notorious villains India has ever produced'. Nevertheless, as a means of bringing order to central India the British authorities in Bengal entered into negotiations with Amir Khan, and in 1817 recognised him as the ruler of a new principality named Tonk.

This alliance with the British was seen as a betrayal by Syed Ahmad, who quit Amir Khan's service to return to the Madrassah-i-Rahimiya in Delhi, where he became one several radical teachers, all disciples of Shah Abdul Aziz in the school of Shah Waliullah. Very soon, however, Syed Ahmad was marking out his own territory, making a name for himself through the intensity of his preaching and the forcefulness of his personality. Leaving his now elderly master, he took up residence in Delhi's Akbar-abadi mosque beside the city's famous Red Fort, to which crowds flocked to hear him preach and deliver religious judgements. Among the many who came to hear him was a man seven years his senior named SHAH MUHAMMAD ISMAIL, a nephew of Shah Abdul Aziz. After hearing Syed Ahmad preach one evening, Shah Muhammad Ismail was invited to join him in his room, where the two of them spent the night in a state of silent rapture contemplating God. Shah Muhammad Ismail then took the oath of religious allegiance known as *baiat* to become Syed Ahmad's first disciple. He was soon joined by SHAH ABDUL HAI, a son-in-law of Shah Abdul Aziz, as Syed Ahmad's second disciple. It is said that these two were Syed Ahmad's 'lovers', although the word should probably be seen in the Sufi context of intense ecstatic devotion to one's spiritual master. In the case of Shah Muhammad Ismail, this devotion extended to ghosting at least some of Syed Ahmad's published writings and to writing the first biography. Indeed, there is a good case for concluding that the disciple had a major hand in smoothing out and filling in his master's thinking: that Syed Ahmad was a man of action who spoke from the heart rather than the head, leaving his disciples to sort out the theological details.

From 1818 onwards Syed Ahmad's name and his message of Islamic reform and revival began to be heard in Sunni mosques and meeting-places right across northern India, greatly assisted by the efforts of his more learned disciples. As he toured through the plains country north and west of the Jumna River, hundreds pledged themselves to his work by taking the oath of baiat. Yet it seems that Syed Ahmad was still at this time seeking to come to terms with Sufism, since he is on record as having himself taken oaths of allegiance not only to the order of Naqshbandi Sufism followed by his mentors but also to three other Sufi schools. The outcome of this search seems to have been a rejection of many aspects of Sufism as idolatrous, and a hardening of attitude.

At some point on Syed Ahmad's preaching tour he arrived at the great city of Lucknow, then in chaotic decline but still the most important seat of Muslim learning on the sub-continent outside Delhi. Here his sermons were heard by a talib from Patna named WILAYAT ALI, then aged about eighteen or nineteen, who was won over to his cause and duly took the oath of allegiance. That, at least, is the received account of the conversion to Syed Ahmad's cause of the man who was to follow him as the most influential leader of his movement – but there is an alternative version, of which more latter.

In about 1819 Syed Ahmad's first disciple Shah Muhammad Ismail set down his master's theology in a work entitled *Sirat-ul-Mustaqim* (the Straight Path). It laid great stress on the doctrine of the oneness of God (*tawhid*), and on the importance of struggling against all heretical practices associated with innovation (*bidat*). 'The law of the Prophet is founded on two things,' it declares:

First, the not attributing to any creature the attribute of
God [tawhid]; and second, not inventing forms and
practices which were not invented in the days of the
Prophet, and his successors of Caliphs [bidat]. The first
consists in disbelieving that angels, spirits, spiritual guides,
disciples, teachers, students, prophets or saints, remove
one's difficulties; in abstaining from having recourse to any
of the above creations for the attainment of any wish or
desire; in denying that any of them has the power of
granting favour or removing evils; in considering them as
helpless and ignorant as one's self in respect to the power
of God . . . True and undefiled religion consists in strongly
adhering to all the devotions and practices in the affairs of
life which were observed at the time of the Prophet. In
avoiding all such innovations as marriage ceremonies,
mourning ceremonies, adorning of tombs, erection of large
edifices over graves, lavish expenditure on the
anniversaries of the dead, street processions and the like,
and in endeavouring as far as may be practicable to put a
stop to these practices.

This was exactly the theology to be expected of a student of
the school of Shah Waliullah. Indeed, the only real difference
between Syed Ahmad and his predecessors at this stage lay in his
boldness in taking his message beyond the confines of the
mosque and the madrassah and into the streets. He and his disciples were the first Muslim proselytisers to exploit the new
medium of printing, taking their lead from the Christian missionaries in Bengal. These printed texts were mostly set down in
Urdu, the language of the masses, rather than in Persian or Arabic.
    Featured prominently in these new publications was the call
for jihad. A printed appeal issued in Syed Ahmad's name in 1821
speaks of jihad as 'a work of great profit; just as rain does good to
mankind, beasts and plants, so all persons are partakers in the

advantages of a War against the Infidel'. It asks the faithful to compare the state of affairs in Hindustan as it now is with what it was in the days of Shah Jehan and Aurangzeb, and calls on them to struggle against all un-Islamic forces that have beset the land. However, this call does not go so far as to declare jihad, for according to the rules of Islamic jurisprudence, as Syed Ahmad understood them, such an act was a formal declaration that could only be made by an *imam* (religious leader) – which he evidently did not consider himself to be – acting with the support of an *amir* or secular leader. In India only the Emperor of Delhi had the necessary authority to declare jihad, by virtue of his dual role as religious head of the Muslim community in India and *khalifa* or viceroy of the Ottoman caliphate. A further complication was that jihad could only be launched from a country where Islamic sharia prevailed: a *dar ul-Islam* (domain of Faith) – and, in Syed Ahmad's eyes, Hindustan was no longer a domain of Faith but a domain of enmity. If a jihad was to be launched at all it would have to be from outside Hindustan, just as long ago the Prophet had launched his first jihad on the domain of enmity of Mecca from the domain of Faith of Medina.

Syed Ahmad's call for spiritual revival and jihad went all but unnoticed by the British authorities. As the Indian civil servant and historian Sir William Hunter was afterwards to put it, 'He traversed one Province with a retinue of devoted disciples, converted the populace by thousands to his doctrine, and established a regular system of ecclesiastical taxation, civil government, and apostolic succession. Meanwhile, our officers collected the revenue, administered justice, and paraded our troops, altogether unsuspicious of the great religious movement which was surging around them.'

Early in 1821 Syed Ahmad announced that he was to make the *hajj*, the pilgrimage to Mecca which constitutes one of the five pillars of Islam. He invited his followers to join him, and some four hundred assembled in his home town of Rae Bareli before accompanying their master on a grand progress down the Ganges by boat, with stops at all the major cities.

Nowhere was Syed Ahmad received with more enthusiasm than at the ancient city of Patna, on the Ganges approximately half-way between Delhi and Calcutta. This was the home of his new disciple Wilayat Ali, and it is probable that he and his brother INAYAT ALI – three years younger, so then aged eighteen to Wilayat Ali's twenty-one years – marshalled their family and friends to organise this welcome. Patna's large Muslim community turned out en masse to receive Syed Ahmad like a major prophet, the most important Muslims in the city taking off their shoes and running beside his palanquin as it was carried through the streets. So warm was his reception that the preacher stayed on for some weeks as a guest of the wealthiest men in Patna, among them the heads of three houses that were to combine together to become the bastions of Wahhabism in India: FATAH ALI, descended from a long line of religious leaders and saints, and father of the two men who became notorious in later years as the 'Ali brothers'; Fatah Ali's close friend and contemporary ELAHI BUX, doctor, bibliophile and philanthropist, four of whose sons became Syed Ahmad's lieutenants; and Syed MUHAMMAD HUSSAIN of Sadiqpore, brother-in-law of Elahi Bux, whose daughters married the sons of Elahi Bux and whose house and *serai* in Sadiqpore Lane in Patna became the movement's headquarters and central seminary (see Appendix 2, the 'Wahhabi' family tree in India).

For three generations the male members of these three houses combined to run the movement initiated by Syed Ahmad, initially as his counsellors and lieutenants and subsequently as devotees of his cult. They have been portrayed as saints and martyrs in the cause of Indian freedom, but it would be more accurate to compare them to the Mafia families of Sicily and America. Both organisations conspired to impose their exclusive views of society through violence and by working to eliminate the opposition –

which in this instance meant not only the governing *Nazrani* (Christians) but also Hindus, Sikhs, Shias, and even most schools of Sunni Islam. Both organisations worked in secret, swore oaths of loyalty to their leaders, followed their own exclusive code of morality, and believed themselves to be God-fearing, the only striking difference being that one party put its faith in the family godfather, the other in its spiritual leader.

From Patna, Syed Ahmad continued his triumphal progress downriver to Calcutta, where so many of the faithful flocked to his banners that he was unable to initiate them individually by his hand and they had to make do with touching the folds of his unrolled turban. So great was the stir created by his arrival in the city that some professedly 'loyal' Muslims presented a petition to the police declaring Syed Ahmad to be planning an uprising against the British. Enough donations had now been received to allow Syed Ahmad's organisation to book passages to Arabia for some eight hundred and fifty pilgrims. In the spring of 1821 (or possibly the following year) they set sail in ten vessels for the Red Sea port of Jedda.

Syed Ahmad was away from India for at least one and possibly two years. He returned with a vision of militant Islam that was to divide the Muslim community.

2

The Puritan of the Desert

This Puritan of the desert, who was no doubt a reformer, believing in the early teachings of Mahomet, determined to bring back El Islam to its ancient simplicity. With a great following, after denouncing the superstitions and corruptions of those who professed his religion, he commenced by destroying the tombs of saints, even those of Mahomet and Husein, inculcating at the same time a higher state of morals.

William Wing Loring,
A *Confederate Soldier in Egypt*, 1884

The man who gave his name to this new vision of Islam was an Arab, Muhammad ibn Abd AL-WAHHAB, born in 1702 or 1703 in the town of Uyainah in the desert country of Nejd, a rocky plateau in the hinterland of the Arabian peninsula. However, the true roots of Wahhabism go back a lot further – to the late thirteenth century, and a time when Islam faced its first great challenge in the form of the eruption of the Mongols into the heartlands of the faith. In 1258 the Mongols overthrew the historic caliphate of

Arabia in the mid-nineteenth century

Black Sea

Caspian Sea

TURKISH OTTOMAN EMPIRE

Tigris River

Euphrates River

• Tehran
• Qum

Mediterranean Sea

• Damascus

SYRIA

Baghdad •
Karbala •

• Isfahan

• Jerusalem

PERSIA

Cairo •
• Suez

Basra

JABAL
SHAMMAR

Kuwait •

Bushire •

Persian Gulf

HIJAZ

• Hail

Uyainah •

NEJD

Bahrain •

Nile River

Dariya • • Riyadh

EGYPT

• Medina

WAHHABI

Muscat •

ARABIA

OMAN

Jedda •
• Mecca

Red Sea

HADRAMAUT

SUDAN

• Khartoum

Arabian Sea

YEMEN

Aden •

0   200   400 miles

Baghdad and went on to make the lands of the Middle East tributary to the Great Khans. One of the many caught up in this conquest was a Sunni jurist named Sheikh IBN TAYMIYYA, born in what is now Syria in 1263. His father was a refugee from the destruction of Damascus in 1259, and he grew up believing the Mongols to be enemies of Islam.

Out of the ruins of the caliphate a brilliant, inclusive Islamic civilisation flowered under the Mongols, centred on Persia, rooted in Sufism, and predominantly Shia. But to Ibn Taymiyya and others who followed the Hanbali code of jurisprudence – the last, strictest and least popular of the four main schools of law in the Sunni tradition – this civilisation was anathema and an offence to God. In the centuries following the first dramatic expansion of Islam under the aegis of the Prophet and his first caliphs, these four schools had developed to interpret and pronounce on all matters of sharia, the divinely ordained laws of Islam governing human behaviour. By about AD 900 a consensus had been arrived at in the Sunni community that every outstanding issue concerning right belief had been resolved by learned and righteous men from one or other of the four schools of jurisprudence; this came to be known as *taqlid* (community consensus). It followed that there was no further scope for *ijtihad* (independent reasoning), the traditional phrase being that 'the gates of ijtihad were now closed'.

In the wake of the Mongol invasion Ibn Taymiyya set out to 'break the shackles of taqlid'. He declared himself qualified to be a *mujtahid*, one who makes his own interpretations by virtue of informed reasoning, and began to redefine the laws of Islam. He first came to prominence with his literalist interpretations of the Quran and his strictures against innovation (*bidat*). He attacked the great Sufi mystic of the age, Ibn al-Arabi, and condemned as polytheistic and heretical many folk practices that had entered the Sunni mainstream. As if this direct challenge to religious custom were not enough, Ibn Taymiyya went on to challenge the central authority of the caliphate, arguing that a true caliphate had ceased to exist after the death of the last of the four caliphs who followed the Prophet as religious and political leaders of the early Islamic world. The true Muslim state, he argued, was one where the *amir* (temporal leader) governed only in partnership with the *imam* (religious leader), who had the authority not only to interpret sharia but also to guide the amir's administration with the support of other members of the Muslim clergy (*ulema*): the mullahs, magistrates (*qadis*), and judges (*hakims* and *muftis*). In keeping with this view of the ulema as the senior partner in government, Ibn Taymiyya made it clear that only with the authority of the imam could the amir go to war – and only the imam could proclaim jihad.

It is in the context of this last subject, jihad, that Ibn Taymiyya is best remembered – and both admired and execrated. And not without reason, since his reinterpretation of jihad lies at the heart of modern Islamist revivalism.

In the first centuries of Islamic expansion, jihad had been recognised as an obligation on the part of all Muslims to strive for the faith until the entire world had converted or submitted to Islamic authority. That uncompromising view had inevitably set Islam on a collision course with Byzantine Christendom. But as Islam was transformed from an Arab faith into a cosmopolitan, multi-ethnic world religion in which learning and diversity of interpretation was celebrated, so the literalist view of jihad gave way to a more pragmatic reading. Included in the Hadith is a famous pronouncement made by the Prophet Muhammad on his return from the battle of Bard, which marked the end of his military campaign against the polytheists: 'We are finished with the lesser jihad (*jihad kabeer*); now we are starting the greater jihad (*jihad akbar*).' This division of jihad now came to be interpreted in Islam as meaning that the outer and less important physical struggle for Islam was over and had given way to the more important inner, moral struggle. Even Ahmad bin Hanbal, the ninth-century jurist who gave his name to the most restrictive of the four Sunni schools of law, took this view. The dramatic spread of Sufi mysticism and the Sufi brotherhoods throughout the Islamic world community in the twelfth century helped to develop further this concept of jihad as a spiritual, inner struggle.

Ibn Taymiyya, however, declared the Prophet's division of jihad to be inauthentic, on the grounds that it contradicted the words of God as set down in the Quran. Taking two verses (chapter 2, verse 193; and chapter 8, verse 39) from the Quran as his authority, Ibn Taymiyya defined jihad in strictly literal terms: as unrelenting struggle against all who stood in the way of Islam's destiny.

This uncompromising interpretation has to be seen in the context of the threat to Islam posed by the Mongols and by the unorthodox, Shia beliefs they supported. Ibn Taymiyya declared the Mongol khans to be unbelievers, and called on all true Muslims to unite against them in battle as a matter of religious duty. In 1300 he actively participated in an important military victory over the Mongols outside Damascus, encouraging the troops on the battlefield by preaching jihad from the sidelines and even involving himself in their military training. But jihad, in his view, was much more than a matter of military defence: it was active belligerence against all who refused to heed the call of Islam or who disobeyed the strictures of Islam. It was, in his own words, 'the punishment of recalcitrant groups, such as those that can only be brought under the sway of the Imam by a decisive fight . . . For whoever has heard the summons of the Messenger of Allah, peace be upon him, and has not responded to it, must be fought.'

Ibn Taymiyya further declared jihad to be the finest act that man could perform: 'Jihad against the disbelievers is the most noble of actions and moreover it is the most important action for the sake of mankind . . . Jihad implies all kinds of worship, both in its inner and outer forms. More than any other act jihad implies love and devotion for God . . . Since its aim is that the religion is

Allah's entirely and Allah's word is uppermost, therefore according to all Muslims, those who stand in the way of this aim must be fought.'

Ibn Taymiyya classified the enemies of Islam into four distinct groups: infidels such as Christians, with whom it was permissible to make peace agreements and share meals, whose women Muslims might marry and whose lives might be spared after they had been made prisoners; those Muslims who had reverted to infidel habits, with whom no peace could be made and who must be fought if they refused to return to the fold; those who declared themselves Muslims but were not carrying out Islam's rituals properly, and were therefore to be killed without mercy; lastly, those who rejected Islam while still claiming to belong to it, and were thus deserving of no mercy under any circumstances.

It should always be remembered that Ibn Taymiyya's literalist, dogmatic, intolerant ideology was widely condemned in his own lifetime. He was frequently in trouble with the religious author-ities, imprisoned on several occasions and branded a heretic. His theology has never found a place in the Sunni mainstream. But it was never forgotten and it continued to attract adherents, of whom the most famous – until recent times – was the Arab named Muhammad ibn Abd al-Wahhab, born in Nejd soon after the beginning of the eighteenth century.

At that time Nejd was no more than a barren stretch of scrub-land surrounded on all sides by desert wastes, sparsely inhabited by tribes of Bedouin camel-herders and graziers engaged in end-less internecine struggles for the possession of grasslands and oases. Indeed, for many Arabs Nejd had only negative associ-ations. There was a popular saying that 'Nothing good ever came out of Nejd', and it was related in the Hadith that the Prophet had three times been called upon to ask God to bless Nejd and had three times refused, answering on the third occasion, 'Earthquakes and dissension are there, and there shall arise the horns of Satan.' In the years following the ministry of Al-Wahhab there were many who argued that this prophecy had been confirmed.

Al-Wahhab was of the impoverished tribe of Beni Temin, known only for the quality of their horseflesh. According to his many critics, he was a provincial bumpkin with little access to Islamic scholarship. This view was given some substance by his Wahhabi biographers, who wished to emphasise the learning he received from his father, a judge descended from a long line of respected jurists who followed the Hanbali school of law, holding that the interpretation of sharia had to be based exclusively on the Quran and the Hadith. But from the first Al-Wahhab was a devoted student of religion, and by the age of ten could recite the Quran from memory. As an adolescent talib he visited Medina and Basra, as well as flirting briefly with Sufism at Qum. A decade later he returned to Medina to sit at the feet of a number of renowned teachers drawn from all over the Muslim world. Whatever gloss his biographers later put on it, it was here that he acquired the extreme views associated with his name.

At Medina Al-Wahhab studied initially under a fellow Nejdi, Abd Allah ibn Ibrahim ibn Sayf, a known admirer of the theology of Ibn Taymiyya, who then introduced him to an Indian immigrant named MUHAMMAD HAYAT of Sind, a prominent teacher of Hadith. Although a follower of the Shafi school of jurisprudence and not a Hanbali, Muhammad Hayat was a Naqshbandi Sufi of the line of the sixteenth-century hardline revivalist Sheikh Ahmad Sirhindi – and he too was an admirer of the heretical Sheikh Ibn Taymiyya. Muhammad Hayat and his father are known to have taught a great many students in Medina. Besides Al-Wahhab from Nejd these talibs included a young man from Delhi: Shah Waliullah.

Few historians seem to have realised that Shah Waliullah of Delhi, born in 1703, and Al-Wahhab of Nejd were not only contemporaries but studied in Medina over the same period and with at least one teacher in common. Shah Waliullah went to Mecca on

hajj in 1730 at the age of twenty-seven or twenty-eight and subsequently spent fourteen months studying in Medina. Al-Wahhab
(born 1702/1703) is known to have returned to Medina to continue his studies in his late twenties. How long he spent there is
not recorded, but the odds are that his time overlapped with Shah
Waliullah's period of stay. Shah Waliullah's principal instructor of
Hadith in Medina was the venerable Kurd Shaikh Abu Tahir
Muhammad ibn Ibrahim al-Kurani al-Madani – who had earlier
taught Muhammad Hayat of Sind, Al-Wahhab's main teacher.
Thus the intriguing possibility presents itself that these two
young revolutionaries-to-be may have sat in the same classes and
even exchanged ideas. Muhammad Hayat and his father, both
followers of Ibn Taymiyya, encouraged their students to reject the
rigid imitation of precedent, to make their own interpretations of
religious law, and to view militant jihad as a religious duty. The
consequences of their studies in Medina were that both Al-
Wahhab and Shah Waliullah went home to become the two great
Sunni revivalists of their time, each to implement the radical
teachings learned in Medina in his own way.

It is no coincidence that in Saudi Arabia today Ibn Taymiyya
occupies a place of honour second only to that of Al-Wahhab. The
latter's debt to Ibn Taymiyya is huge. Inspired by Ibn Taymiyya's
example, and further encouraged by Muhammad Hayat, Al-
Wahhab returned to Nejd to expound a new faith, later
summarised by the Wahhabi apologist Sheikh HAFIZ WAHBA as
'restoring Islam to what it was in the time of the holy Prophet and
the great caliphs'. This was precisely what Shah Waliullah also set
out to do in Delhi – yet the one became honoured as a great
revivalist and the other hated as a schismatic.

In Delhi, Shah Waliullah operated in a highly informed religious community wherein his every pronouncement was challenged
and tempered through debate and argument. In provincial Nejd,
however, there were few scholars with the legal expertise and
debating skills to stand up to Al-Wahhab. In consequence, he was

able to construct and apply almost unchallenged a brand of holier-than-thou, confrontational and heartless Islam the like of which had not been seen since the days of Mahmud of Ghazni, the butcher who led twelve loot-and-destroy raids through northern India in the eleventh century, justifying his actions in the name of Islam. Al-Wahhab's fundamentalism went way beyond the return to Islamic first principles that Shah Waliullah called for. It was strictly literalist and uncompromising, applied with an aggressive intolerance not shared by his former fellow student.

The name Al-Wahhab gave to this new theology was *ad Dawa lil Tawhid*, usually translated as The Call to Unity. Those who espoused it termed themselves *al-Muwahhidun* or Unitarians. Very quickly, however, both the teaching and its followers became known, after its founder, as *Wahhabi* – a term that soon came to be used in most of the Islamic world as an insult, an epithet to describe a schismatic, and a byword for religious intolerance.

The tenets of Wahhabism were first set down in a treatise entitled *Kitab al-Tawhid* (The Book of Unity), originally little more than a series of notes but afterwards worked up by his successors into four thick volumes. It reduced Islam to absolute monotheism (*tawhid*), rejected all innovation (*bidat*) and declared there to be but one interpretation of the Quran and the Hadith – Al-Wahhab's, by virtue of his competence to exercise independent reasoning. The rise of Islam had been accomplished only by jihad against idolaters and polytheists. It followed that there was only one course of action open to those who regarded themselves as true Muslims. They had, first, to swear absolute loyalty to their religious leader; secondly, to follow his teaching in every respect; thirdly, to join him in armed jihad against all apostates, blasphemers and unbelievers; and fourthly, to hate those same apostates, blasphemers and unbelievers. In return, they were promised the protection of God and the love and companionship of their fellow believers, and were assured of an immediate ascent to heaven should they die as martyrs while striving for Islam. There was no other path to salvation. 'The only way', wrote Al-Wahhab, 'is by love to those who practise *tawhid* of Allah, by devotion to them, rendering them every kind of help, as well as by hate and hostility to infidels and polytheists.'

This new vision was badly received in Nejd. It placed Al-Wahhab at odds with other contemporary religious teachers, including his father and uncle. 'He claims', declared the latter, Sulayman, 'to follow the Holy Quran and *al-Sunna* [the example of the Prophet and his companions as accepted by Sunnis] and dares to deduce from their teachings, paying no heed to any opposition. Anyone who opposes him he calls a heretic, although he possesses none of the qualifications of the *mujtahedeen* [those who exercise independent reasoning].' In his home village of Uyainah he was denounced as a schismatic and ordered to leave. He went to join his father, who had moved to the settlement of Huraymila, but there too his teachings so angered his new neighbours that he was ordered to keep his views to himself, which he did until his father's death in about 1740. He then took over as judge and began to act and pronounce judgment in accordance with his new teachings. Increasingly outraged, the populace finally turned on him, and an attempt was made to kill him under cover of darkness. He fled Huraymila and sought refuge back in Uyainah.

There Al-Wahhab gained the ear of the new governor, whose aunt he married. With his new patron's backing he once more began to apply the doctrines of the Call to Unity, gaining particular notoriety through a number of violent acts that became the hallmark of his teaching. These included inciting and then leading a mob to tear down the tomb of a Companion of the Prophet, and sentencing to death a woman who refused to abandon a sexual liaison outside marriage – an action made all the more shocking by Al-Wahhab's active participation in the stoning to death that followed. This last act seems to have been the final straw for the local ulema. He was charged with heresy in seeking to set up a new school of Islamic interpretation, and with acting violently against those who did not support his views. The tribal chieftain intervened and Al-Wahhab was again ordered to move on – now to the little hamlet of Dariya, where his teachings had won him a number of converts.

This retreat to Dariya subsequently came to be represented among the Wahhabis as a re-enactment of the Prophet's famous migration from the *dar ul-harb* of Mecca to the *dar ul-Islam* of Medina, from which he began his spiritual conquest of Arabia. Here in Dariya Al-Wahhab won the support of the local chief, MUHAMMAD IBN SAUD, leader of a sub-branch of the powerful Aneiza tribe and already admired for his abilities as a warrior. Muhammad ibn Saud became not only a convert to Wahhabism but, by marrying his eldest son ABD AL-AZIZ IBN SAUD to Al-Wahhab's daughter, the founding father of the Saud–Wahhabi dynasty, the future rulers of Saudi Arabia (see chart in Appendix 1: the roots of the Al-Saud–Al-Wahhab family alliance).

In about 1744 a remarkable partnership was forged between Muhammad ibn Saud and Al-Wahhab. This was formalised in an oath-swearing ceremony between the two by which the former took upon himself the role and title of *emir*, or secular leader, and the latter became the imam, soon afterwards assuming the rather grander title of *Sheikh ul-Islam*. This alliance allowed the one to become a powerful local ruler and the other to transform the province of Nejd by stages into a dar *ul*-Islam, that much sought-after domain of Faith wherein true sharia prevailed. In the words of a convert to the cause, Harry St John Philby, writing a century and a half later,

> The true faith was purged of the dross of ecclesiastical pedantry, and the salient facts of a moribund creed were made to shine forth again as beacons to every wanderer in the wilderness of doubt. The unity and jealousy of God, the vital necessity of belief and the certainty of reward to

all believers – these were the cornerstones of the edifice, which prince and priest set to work to erect upon the shifting sands of nomad society; and the edifice that grew out of those foundations was an Arabian Empire.

The Bedouin tribes of Arabia were mainly pastoralists, seemingly united by shared customs but as inveterately hostile to each other as the Pathans, with whom they shared many qualities. 'The Arab', noted the Swiss scholar and traveller J. H. Burckhardt, after visiting Mecca and Medina in disguise in 1816, 'displays his manly character when he defends his guest at the peril of his own life, and submits to the reverses of fortune, to disappointment and distress with the most patient resignation ... the Bedouin learns at an early period of life, to abstain and to suffer, and to know from experience the healing power of pity and consolation.' Like the Pathans, the Bedouin valued their independence above all else: 'Their primary cause is that sentiment of liberty, which has driven and still keeps them in the Desert, and makes them look down with contempt upon the slaves that dwell around them ... The Bedouin exults in the advantages he enjoys; and it may be said, without any exaggeration, that the poorest Bedouin of an independent tribe smiles at the pomp of a Turkish Pasha.'

A prohibition on inter-tribal marriage helped to reinforce this sense of independence. Writing about the Wahhabis a few years before Burckhardt, Louis Alexandre Olivier de Corancez, the French Consul at Aleppo, noted that this ban 'circumscribes the number of members of each tribe within extremely narrow limits, preserving unity within them through blood ties. Each tribe may therefore be described as an extended family whose father is the sheikh chosen by the Arabs ... Since time immemorial, some of the tribes have been at war, and others in alliance with one another.'

By marrying his son into Al-Wahhab's tribe Muhammad ibn Saud broke with custom but initiated a process that led to the unification of a number of disparate tribes under one leader. 'Thus', added de Corancez in his *Histoire des Wahabis*, 'was born among the Arabs, in the very heart of their country, a new people which fashioned greatness out of its own wretchedness.'

The unification of Bedouin society under one green banner had been achieved once before, but only after a great deal of military coercion. Now once again those who had no wish to share one man's vision of God were made to do so. The religious ideology to which Al-Wahhab gave his name created a community united in its total submission to God in the person of his emir. Every man who joined Muhammad ibn Saud's inter-tribal commonwealth was required to take an oath of allegiance, on pain of losing his place in Paradise, to observe the law according to the Wahhabi tenets, and to pay religious tax at the rate of one Spanish dollar for every five camels and one for every forty sheep, those owning land or property paying by providing a certain number of armed camel-riders. To enforce compliance Imam Al-Wahhab instituted a cadre of religious policemen known as the *mutawihin*, guardians of public morals. Burckhardt describes them as 'Constables for the punctuality of prayers . . . with an enormous staff in their hand, [who] were ordered to shout, to scold and to drag people by the shoulders to force them to take part in public prayers, five times a day.' But the mutawihin were much more than enforcers of religious laws, for as well as ensuring conformity in almost every aspect of life from dressing modestly to closing shops at prayer-times, they also served as the movement's religious commissars, seeing to it that only the Call to Unity was preached in the Friday mosques and taught in the madrassahs.

In return for their allegiance Muhammad ibn Saud offered his followers the prospect of conquest. Raiding one's neighbours had been part and parcel of Bedouin life since before the days of the Prophet, but in 1746 Imam Al-Wahhab issued a formal proclamation of jihad against all those who refused to share his vision of Unity. Taking the early struggles of the Prophet against non-

believers as its model, the Emir's *ghazu* or war-parties began raiding deep into what were now proclaimed infidel territories,
attacking the weakest first while their Imam secured non-aggression pacts with their more powerful neighbours. 'By attacking the
weaker singly and compelling them to join his standard against
their neighbours,' observed Lieutenant Francis Warden, author of
the first British report on the Wahhabi phenomenon, *Historical
Sketch of the Wahabee tribe of Arabs 1795 to 1818*, 'the Wahabee [i.e.,
Muhammad ibn Saud] gradually increased his power to a height
which enabled him to overawe the greater States.'

Whatever spiritual gloss he cared to put on it in his writings,
under Al-Wahhab's tutelage the Bedouin of Nejd became not so
much holy warriors as fanatics without scruples. They preyed on
their neighbours, each man in the raiding party setting out to
plunder, destroy and kill bolstered by the conviction that he did
so as a jihadi. One-fifth of the proceeds from these raids went to
their emir, the rest being divided among the participating tribes.
As for the imam and his Wahhabi ulema, they received the normal
zakat or religious tax as required by the Quran of all true believers.
Thus there was something in it for everyone – provided they
were Wahhabi.

When in July 1929 the Wahhabi envoy Hafiz Wahba set out to
explain the Wahhabi philosophy to his British audience at the
Central Asian Society in London, he was at pains to draw parallels
with the Protestant reformers in Europe, likening Ibn Taymiyya
to his contemporary Martin Luther. The first European observers
of the Wahhabis also drew parallels with their own Church. 'The
religion of the Wahabys may be called the Protestantism or even
Puritanism of the Mohammedans', noted J. H. Burckhardt:

> The Wahaby acknowledges the Koran as a divine
> revelation; his principle is, 'The Koran, and nothing but
> the Koran' . . . He reproves the Muselmans of this age, for

their impious vanity in dress, their luxury in eating and smoking. He asks them whether Mohammed dressed in pelisses, whether he ever smoked the argyle or the pipe? All his followers dress in the most simple garments, having neither about their own persons, nor their horses, any gold or silver; they abstain from smoking, which, they say, stupefies and intoxicates. They reject music, singing, dancing, and games of every kind, and live with each other (at least in the presence of their chief) on terms of most perfect equality.

Although Al-Wahhab's main targets were the Sufis and the Shias, many of the most popular practices of Sunni Islam were also condemned as innovations or reversions to paganism. They included a host of expressions of religious devotion that had developed over the centuries, such as invoking the intercession of the Prophet, the saints or the angels; visiting or praying at the graves of holy men or erecting monuments over their graves; celebrating the Prophet's birthday or the feasts of dead saints; and making votive offerings. At the same time, many everyday habits were also declared sinful, among them smoking tobacco or hashish, dancing, playing music, fortune-telling, dressing in silks, telling beads or wearing talismans. The shaving of beards, the wearing of robes that failed to show the ankle, the use of rosaries to count the ninety-nine names of God and much else besides was declared un-Islamic.

But the parallels with Puritanism went only so far. According to the Wahhabi code, the moment a Muslim deviated from Al-Wahhab's interpretation of monotheism he became an unbeliever – and the moment he became an unbeliever his life and goods became forfeit. 'Any doubt or hesitation', states The Book of Unity, *Kitab al-Tawhid*, 'deprives a man of immunity of his property and his life.'

When asked to name the chief qualities of their faith, Muslims almost invariably describe it as a religion of peace, using the adjectives 'merciful' and 'compassionate' to describe God, as set out in the famous invocation that makes up the first chapter of the Quran. The Arabic of the Quran is a richly symbolic language, full of nuances, ambiguities, and words that when pronounced with different inflections can convey wider meanings. It is also a source text full of seeming contradictions that demand scholarly guidance to be fully understood. By its exclusive interpretation of the Quran and the Hadith, Al-Wahhab's theology threw overboard all the checks and balances that Islamic jurisprudence had developed over centuries of learning to shape a confusing and conflicting series of revelations delivered in hard times in a hard country in the seventh century into a model for civilised, theocratic living. And by its selective reading and its focus on those passages which gave licence to anathematise, persecute, and kill without mercy, Al-Wahhab's Islam effectively sidelined the Quran's central message of charity, tolerance, forgiveness and mercy.

At the heart of this selectivity was Al-Wahhab's interpretation of jihad. Following Ibn Taymiyya's lead, he dismissed as inauthentic the Prophet's declaration of an end to the lesser jihad and the beginning of the greater. This proclamation finds no place either in the Book of Unity or in Al-Wahhab's other key publication, *Kitab al-Jihad*, the Book of Struggle. Its author recognised the purpose of jihad to be the defence of Islam and the Islamic community – but for him, as for Ibn Taymiyya, that defence took only one form: violence against all who stood in Islam's way. Polytheists and pagans were to be given one opportunity to convert, and became fair game thereafter. If they refused to submit or resisted they were to be killed, and if they were made prisoner and still refused to submit they should still be killed, although certain categories such as women, children, the elderly and slaves (and mullahs) might be spared. As for those who called themselves Muslims but were deviants and apostates who failed to acknowledge their falsehoods, they were to be shown no mercy. On the other hand, those who heeded and followed Imam Al-Wahhab's teachings became sanctified warriors or, in his own words, 'the army of God'. It became their duty to make jihad at least once a year as ordered by their Imam. This jihad could only take place by his specific order, and on his terms.

It has been argued recently on the basis of a study of Al-Wahhab's writings preserved in Riyadh that the violence which characterised Wahhabism was the work of his successors and not promoted by the man himself. His writings do indeed show that Al-Wahhab always gave his neighbours an opportunity to convert before the Wahhabi ghazu were unleashed on them, and that when it suited him or when his neighbours were too powerful he made non-aggression pacts with them. Hitler applied much the same philosophy. What these writings also demonstrate is that the Wahhabi interpretation of jihad followed the selective trail first marked by Ibn Taymiyya. Nowhere in either the Book of Unity or the Book of Struggle is there to be found a single example of the many verses in the Quran that refer to non-violent means of defending Islam or propagating the faith, or which place specific restrictions on fighting (e.g., chapters and verses 2,109; 2,190; 2,194; 5,13; 6,106; 15, 94; 16,125; 22, 39-40; 29, 46; 42,15; 50,39; etc.). In the Book of Struggle Al-Wahhab turns for authority to just four verses from the Quran, precisely those verses most frequently cited by past militants such as Ibn Taymiyya and by present Islamist extremists whenever the call to jihad goes out. These include the much-quoted and much-abused 'Verse of the Sword' (chapter 9, verse 5), usually only quoted in part. The full verse reads: 'Then, when the sacred months are over, kill the idolaters wherever you find them, take them [as captives], besiege them, and lie in wait for them at every point of observation. If they repent afterwards, perform the prayer and pay the alms, then release them. God is truly All-Forgiving, Merciful.' In none of these four instances is reference made to the specific circumstances in which the Prophet originally dictated his statements. In the case of the Verse of the Sword, scholars of the Quran will point out that the whole chapter relates to the ending of a truce with non-believers that the Prophet Muhammad and his followers had entered into, and that the verse should not be read in isolation. But then, literal and selective reading lies at the heart of fundamentalism, whether Muslim, Christian, Jewish or Hindu.

In 1766 Muhammad ibn Saud was assassinated while at prayer and was succeeded as emir by his son Abd al-Aziz ibn Saud. The new emir built on and added to his father's military successes – with his father-in-law at his elbow as both spiritual and tactical godfather. Even those biographies which extol his saintly virtues make it plain that Imam Al-Wahhab saw his duties as extending into the battle-field. He introduced firearms where the Bedouin had previously relied on the spear and the scimitar and he personally taught recruits how to handle this new weaponry. He also issued every holy warrior a *firman* or written order addressed to the gate-keeper of heaven, requiring him to be admitted forthwith as a martyr should he die in battle. The cult of martyrdom in Islam is traditionally associated with the Shias, arising from Imam Hussein's seeking of martyrdom at Karbala. Now under the Wahhabis the prospect of dying in battle as a *shahid* or martyr became a powerful motivating factor, a consummation devoutly to be wished. Thus Emir Abd al-Aziz ibn Saud's jihadis found themselves in a win-win situation: if they triumphed in battle they gained material benefits; if they were vanquished they went directly to Paradise.

Like the Pathans in their mountains, the Bedouin had always turned their hostile environment to their advantage. 'Hunger, thirst and fatigue are the Wahabis' natural allies,' noted Louis de Corancez:

They have no discipline in combat, and are wary of engaging the enemy before he is weak enough to have lost the will to defend himself. Thus they pillage rather than wage war. They waver at the first sign of resistance, and are as speedy in fleeing from the enemy's range as in pursuing him from beyond it. They cling to this course of action tenaciously, fleeing the enemy when he faces them and following in his steps when he in turn takes flight. Thus they spy on him for days on end, awaiting the opportunity to surprise and slaughter him without great danger, convinced that the finest victory lies in destroying everything without incurring any loses themselves.

The young emir and his older imam together improved upon this hit-and-run mode of warfare by inculcating a new sense of discipline among their soldiers, teaching them to make better use of the skills they already possessed: 'Ibn Saud ordered that each dromedary should be mounted by two soldiers. He rationed not only the soldiers' food, but also that of the camels, so that each was able to carry rations for a twenty-day journey . . . The two riders carry nothing except two goatskins, the one filled with water, the other with barley flour. When they become hungry they mix the flour in a little water. This is their only sustenance for weeks . . . Henceforth many armies were able to scour the desert and take their defenceless enemies by surprise.' All these warriors were tribal levies, but three hundred of the best were selected to form a permanent force under the emir's personal command. They were given fast horses, weapons and armour as well as other special privileges, and they became the vanguard of the Wahhabi ghazu or war party.

As his spiritual mentor grew older Emir Abd al-Aziz ibn Saud assumed greater authority, enforcing his father-in-law's hard-line teaching with ever-increasing ruthlessness. According to Burckhardt, every non-Wahhabi tribe was first given the option to convert, and if its people refused they were condemned as *meshrekin* or heretics: 'The Wahaby (as Ibn Saud, the chief, is emphatically styled) propagates his religion with the sword. Whenever he purposes to attack a district of heretics, he cautions them three times, and invites them to adopt his religion; after the third summons, he proclaims that the time for pardon has elapsed, and he then allows his troops to pillage and kill at their pleasure. All who are taken with arms are unmercifully put to death. This savage custom has inspired the Wahabys with a ferocious fanaticism that makes them dreadful to their adversaries.' De Corancez confirms this ruthless approach to conversion:

> At the moment when they were least expected, the Wahabis would arrive to confront the tribe they wished to subject, and a messenger from Abd al-Aziz ibn Saud would appear bearing a Koran in one hand and a sword in the other. His message was stark and simple: 'Abd el Aziz to the Arabs of the tribe of ——, hail! Your duty is to believe in the book I send you. Do not be like the idolatrous Turks, who give God a human intermediary [a reference to the Wahhabi belief in a unitary God]. If you are true believers, you shall be saved; otherwise, I shall wage war upon you until death.'

Faced by such a stark choice, few tribes resisted. In 1773 the Emir's strongest opponent in Nejd was defeated and the Wahhabis won the town of Riyadh, which now became the military base for further conquests extending far beyond the Nejd plateau.

In that same year Al-Wahhab, by then aged seventy, resigned the office of imam. Whether this was a voluntary or involuntary surrender is unclear. But the title was then assumed not by his eldest son or by some other leading figure from the Wahhabi ulema, as might have been expected, but by the Emir, Abd al-Aziz ibn Saud. The word *imam* means 'one who leads' and is usually read in Sunni Islam as 'one who leads the prayers', but it is quite clear that

Abd al-Aziz ibn Saud used the title to present himself as spiritual head of the Wahhabi ulema. Nor is it possible to ignore the word's associations with the supreme religious authority and infallibility of the imams who guided the early Islamic community in the first decades after the death of Muhammad and are revered as the *al-Salaf al-Salih* or 'the Righteous Forefathers'. When Emir and Imam Abd al-Aziz ibn Saud took the title for himself he may have done so in much the same spirit as that in which King Henry VIII assumed the title of Defender of the Faith after breaking away from the authority of Rome – but it was at this juncture that Wahhabism began to take on the characteristics of a cult built around the infallibility of its emir-cum-imam.

For the next two decades Abd al-Aziz ibn Saud alone directed the Wahhabi expansion in the dual role of temporal leader and spiritual head of the Wahhabi ulema, his genius as a military commander and popular ruler enabling him to enlarge his Wahhabi chiefdom to an extent his father and father-in-law could scarcely have dreamed of. His first mentor and father-in-law Muhammad ibn Abd al-Wahhab died in 1792, leaving twenty widows and eighteen children, five of whom became renowned Wahhabi religious teachers in their turn. This dynasty became known as the *Aal as-Sheikh*, the Family of the Sheikhs, with its most senior male members assuming the title of *Mufti* or chief judge of the Wahhabi ulema, so helping to maintain the dynastic links between the Ibn Sauds and the Aal as-Sheikh which continues to this day.

By the start of the nineteenth century a common identity had begun to take shape among the disparate tribes of the Arabian peninsula, superseding all other local loyalties. It was an Arab identity but also a Wahhabi identity, both personified in Emir and Imam Abd al-Aziz ibn Saud. As Burckhardt put it:

All the Arabs, even his enemies, praise Saud for his
wisdom in counsel and his skill in deciding litigations; he
was very learned in the Muselman [Muslim] law; and the

rigour of his justice, although it disgusted many of his
chiefs, endeared him to the great mass of his Arabs . . . A
country once conquered by the Wahaby enjoys under him
the most perfect tranquillity. In Nejd and Hedjaz the roads
are secure, and the people free from any kind of
oppression. The Muselmans are forced to adopt his
system; but the Jews and Christians are not molested in
exercising the respective religions of their ancestors, on
condition of paying tribute.

By all accounts Abd al-Aziz ibn Saud was handsome in
demeanour and modest in disposition, his only extravagance a
passion for fine horses and his only weakness, in Arab eyes, a
morbid fear of assassination that caused him to direct his armies
into battle from a secure position to the rear. Yet it remains an
incontrovertible fact that under his aegis the Wahhabi ghazu
brought terror to large parts of Arabia as far south as Oman and the
Yemen, and to the lands to the north as far as Baghdad and
Damascus.

In 1802 a Wahhabi raiding band led by the Emir's eldest son
Saud ibn Saud attacked Karbala in modern-day Iraq, the most
sacred shrine of the Shias, containing the tomb of their chief saint,
Husayn, grandson of the Prophet and son of Imam Ali. 'They pil-
laged the whole of it and plundered the Tomb of Hossein,' wrote
Lieutenant Francis Warden, 'slaying in the course of the day, with
circumstances of peculiar cruelty, above five thousand of the
inhabitants. This event, which made a deep impression on the
minds of the Turks, Arabs and Persians, was attributed to the
guilty negligence of the Turkish Government, in failing to keep
the Tomb of Hossein in a proper state of defence.' Huge amounts
of booty were seized, the emir-cum-imam taking the usual one-
fifth for himself and sharing out the rest among his Wahhabi
soldiery, a single share to every foot-soldier and a double share to
every horseman.

In 1803 Abd al-Aziz ibn Saud requested and obtained the permission of the Sharif of Mecca, guardian of Islam's holiest shrine, to perform the Hajj to Mecca, whereupon his Wahhabis laid waste to Islam's holiest shrine. According to T. E. Ravenshaw, author of *A Memorandum on the Sect of Wahabees*, 'They killed many Sheikhs and other believers who refused to adopt Wahabeeism; they robbed the splendid tombs of the Mahomedan saints who were interred there; and their fanatical zeal did not even spare the famous Mosque, which they robbed of the immense treasures and costly furniture to which each Mahomedan Prince of Europe, Asia and Africa had contributed his share.'

In 1804 a Wahhabi army again crossed the great desert into the Hijaz and destroyed tombs in the ancient cemetery at Medina, despoiling the grave of the Prophet Muhammad. In the following year the Wahhabis entered Mecca for the second time and, having massacred those who refused to accept their creed, now claimed it for themselves.

The shock waves of the fall of Mecca to the Wahhabis were felt in the farthest corners of the Ottoman Empire. To most Muslims it was sacrilege of the grossest kind, made all the worse by the Wahhabis' violation of the tomb of the Prophet. By shutting down the pilgrimage route, the Wahhabis also closed off the path to salvation for all Muslims except those of their own sect. There were those who could place only one interpretation on these events: they marked the descent to earth of the false prophet Ad-Dajjal, as foretold by the Prophet Muhammad, and the beginning of the end of the world. Others were more sanguine, but concerned that they might lead to an Islamic revival. 'The Wahabis are now united under the banner of a single leader where their power was formerly scattered among a thousand small tribes,' wrote de Corancez in 1810:

This union has moulded vagrant hordes weakened by internecine wars into a people; and through this union the might of this people will soon spread beyond the desert itself . . . These Arabs lament their past glory, and impatiently await the time to regain it. Everything therefore points to the Wahabis becoming in our time – at least in the East – what the Arabs once were, and such a revolution can surely no longer be remote.

The British Government in India and the Turkish rulers of the Ottoman Empire now became involved, though from very different motives. Today one need only tap in 'Wahhabi+British' on the search engine of a PC to bring up any number of websites claiming a British hand behind the rise of Al-Wahhab and the Wahhabis as part of the Crusader war against Islam. Many take as their source the purported memoirs of a British spymaster named Mr Humphrey, who in the mid-eighteenth century supposedly infiltrated the Ottoman caliphate in the guise of a Muslim and thereafter guided Al-Wahhab's every move. One such site declares of the Wahhabis that 'their false love of religion traces back to a *dajjal* [devil] who went by the name of Muhammad bin Abdul-Wahhab, who was a man sponsored, educated, paid, and helped by the British to eradicate the Uthmani [Ottoman] empire, as well as the rest of the *Ummah* from within.' Mr Humphrey is in fact a fiction, part of a German-inspired effort to destabilise the Indian war effort in the Second World War. The author was most probably the anti-British ex-Grand Mufti of Jerusalem, Muhammad al-Husseini, also known as 'Hitler's Mufti'.

In the real world the British played no part in these affairs until two Wahhabi dhows attacked and boarded the sloop HMS *Sylph* in the Persian Gulf in November 1818, cutting the throats of all the non-Muslims on board. This threatened the East India Company's profitable sea trade with Persia and Iraq: the Governor of Bombay reacted by forming an alliance with the rulers of Oman and Muscat and despatching a squadron of armed frigates to sweep the shipping lanes. After a few Wahhabi dhows had been blown out of the water and a sea-port shelled the Wahhabis turned their attentions elsewhere, and the EICo's political agents stationed at Bushire in the Persian Gulf reverted to the role of interested observers.

For the rulers of the Ottoman Empire, however, the Wahhabis posed a far more direct challenge. Under Emir and Imam Abd al-Aziz ibn-Saud Wahhabism was now questioning the ancient suzerainty of the Caliphate over all Muslims.

'If there was one point of the Wahauby faith which was more prominently odious to the Ottoman government than another,' wrote the British diplomat Sir Harford Brydges, 'it was that which divested the grand signor of the sacred character of visible Imamm, or spiritual head of the followers of Islam.' Furthermore, the closing down of the Hajj by the Wahhabis had removed an important source of revenue for the Sultan of Turkey in the form of pilgrim tax, besides denting his claim to be the protector of the holy places of Islam.

After the failure of a succession of half-hearted military cam-paigns directed from Baghdad, Egypt's Muhammad Ali Pasha was given the responsibility of reclaiming the Hijaz for the Caliph and reopening the pilgrimage routes to all Muslims. Ali Pasha too began by underestimating the strength and mobility of his oppo-nents, entrusting his army to his eighteen-year-old son. In 1811 an eight-thousand-strong Egyptian force was defeated by a united force of Bedouin tribes led by a hard core of Wahhabi fighters from Nejd. A year later the Egyptians returned with a larger force and recaptured Medina, forcing the Wahhabis back to Mecca. The Egyptians then made the mistake of looting Jedda, alienating the local Arab chieftains and causing them to pledge allegiance to the Wahhabis once more.

In 1806 Emir and Imam Abd al-Aziz ibn Saud died at the hand of a vengeful Shia from Karbala while saying his prayers. His capable son Saud ibn Saud assumed his father's twin titles and continued to apply his aggressive policies until his own death from fever in 1814, when he was succeeded by his son Abdullah ibn Saud. But Abdullah lacked the fighting qualities of his paternal line, and in February 1815 the combined forces of the Wahhabis and their allies were crushed by the Egyptians in a decisive battle fought seven days' march west of Riyadh. Among those present on the battlefield was an Italian adventurer named Giovanni Finati, who had joined Mahomet Ali Pasha's army as an officer by claiming to be a convert to Islam and taking the name of Mahomet. At this engagement Fanati noted what increasingly became a characteristic feature of the Wahhabi phenomenon: that the majority of the Arabs fighting alongside them were at best lukewarm supporters of the Wahhabi creed but had joined because they saw the Egyptians and Ottomans as invaders of their land. Initially the battle went their way, but a well-executed withdrawal of their own centre by the more disciplined Egyptians drew their opponents down from their strong position and exposed them to the Egyptian cavalry. Many of their allies turned and ran, leaving the Wahhabis to fight on alone. 'Courage', noted Finati, 'was all that the Wahabees had to oppose us; but it did not forsake them to the last, the fight being protracted, even in that desperate condition . . . The slaughter made of the enemy was prodigious, the whole field remaining strewed over with their headless bodies.'

The Egyptian Pasha had offered six silver coins for every head brought to him, with the result that the ground before his headquarters was soon covered in pyramids of human heads. The lives of three hundred prisoners were deliberately spared, but only so that they could be impaled in batches before the gates of Mecca and Jedda and at the ten staging-posts in between.

In 1818 the Egyptians laid siege to the surviving Wahhabis under Emir-cum-Imam Abdullah ibn Saud at Dariyah. The defenders held out for several months before starvation forced them to surrender. Ibrahim Pasha rounded up all the Wahhabi ulema he could find, some five hundred in all, and herded them into the main mosque, where for three days he presided over a theological debate in which he sought to convince them of their errors. By the end of the fourth day his patience had worn out and he ordered his guards to fall on them and kill them, so that the mosque at Dariyah became, in the words of the traveller William Palgrave, 'the bloody tomb of Wahhabee theology'. Abdullah ibn Saud and five male members of the family were sent as prisoners first to Cairo and then on to Constantinople where, 'after having been paraded through the streets for three days, they were beheaded and their bodies were exposed to the outrages of the mob'. Other members of the family were sent to Medina and placed under house arrest. A year later the Wahhabi stronghold at Riyadh was taken and the fortress built there by the great Abd al-Aziz ibn Saud razed to the ground.

The destruction of the Wahhabi empire was greeted with satisfaction and relief by their Muslim contemporaries. The celebrated early nineteenth-century Hanafi scholar Muhammad Amin ibn Abidin had only harsh words for the founder of Wahhabism and his theology: 'He claimed to be a Hanbali, but his thinking was such that only he alone was a Muslim, and everyone else was a *mushriq* [polytheist]. Under this guise, he said that killing the Ahl as-Sunnah [those who follow Sunni tradition] was permissible, until Allah destroyed his [people] in the year 1233 AH [AD 1818] through the Muslim army.'

Lieutenant Burden and other members of the British mission at Bushire took a more practical line. With the destruction of the Wahhabi empire the main threat to stability in the Gulf had been removed. 'Thus', concluded Burden in the closing paragraph of his *Report*, 'rose and fell – it is to be hoped never to rise again – the extraordinary sect of the Wahabees.'

3

The False Dawn of the Imam-Mahdi

From 1820 some Moulvees of India declaring themselves to be disciples of Syud Ahmed of Bareilly, whom
they styled Ameerul Momeneen and Iman Homan
(chief and leader of the faithful), began to preach the
Wahabee creed in this country . . . They preached to the
common people that Hindustan is now a Darool Harab
(or country of the infidels): therefore it behoved all the
good Mehomedans to wage war against the infidels.

Moulvee Syud Emdad Ali Khan,
An Epitome of the History of the Wahabees, 1871

The desecration of the tomb of the Prophet in Medina in 1804
by Abd al-Aziz ibn Saud's jihadis and the subsequent occupation
of Mecca shocked the entire Muslim umma, Sunnis and Shias
alike. But there were those among the orthodox Sunnis who saw
the iconoclasm of the Wahhabis as acts of cleansing and restoration, among them a group of pilgrims from Sumatra present in
Mecca at the time of the first Wahhabi raid in 1803. On their
return home two years later their leader, a fakir named Miskin bin

Rahmatullah, set out to apply the Wahhabi programme to the uplands of central Java, where islanders of Hindu and Buddhist faith who had resisted early attempts at conversion were concentrated. According to a Muslim scholar of that period, 'They looted and robbed the wealth of the people and insulted the *orang kaya* [important peoples]. They killed the *ulama* and all the *orang yang cerdik* [Brahmin Pandits]. They captured married women, wedded them to their men, and made their women captives their concubines. Still they called their actions "actions made to perfect religion".' What became known as the Padri Movement briefly involved Stamford Raffles during that confusing period between 1811 and 1815 when the British and Dutch East India Companies were swapping islands like playing-cards. Thereafter it became both a revivalist and an anti-colonialist struggle in the interior, only finally suppressed in 1842.

Other pilgrims were equally inspired, including a number of individuals from India who subsequently returned to apply Al-Wahhab's theology in their homeland, each in his own style. Besides Syed Ahmad, three deserve more than a mention: GHULAM RASUL of Benares, and the two Bengalis Hajji SHARIATULLAH (the word *Hajji* being a term of respect given to one who has made the Hajj to Mecca) and TITU MIR.

Of the three, Ghulam Rasul is the least well-known. He is said to have spent many years studying Hadith in Arabia soon after the start of the nineteenth century, not in Mecca or Medina but in the Wahhabi heartland of Nejd. When Ghulam Rasul eventually returned to Benares he took the name of Hajji Abdul Haq and became known as the Nejdi Sheikh. He also brought with him a radical version of Islam that caused great offence in local religious circles. However, the real significance of Ghulam Rasul/Hajji Abdul Haq to this narrative is that one of his disciples in Benares was Wilayat Ali, the young man who as an adolescent became an ardent follower of Syed Ahmad after his visit to Lucknow in 1818. By this account, Wahhabism was already being taught in India well before the return of Syed Ahmad from his pilgrimage to Mecca.

The Bengali Shariatullah was almost certainly in Arabia at the same time as Ghulam Rasul. He was living in the Hijaz in 1805, when Mecca fell to the Wahhabis, and chose to stay on, only quitting Arabia after the destruction of the Wahhabi stronghold of Riyadh in 1818. On his return to Bengal he began to preach what is probably best described as a diluted form of Wahhabi theology, very similar to that being promoted at this same time by Shah Waliullah's son Shah Abdul Aziz of Delhi. He declared the country to be a domain of enmity because it was now ruled by the East India Company; and because he laid great stress on *faraiz*, the Muslim's duty to obey sharia, his movement became known as Faraizi. Despite his opposition to British rule, both Hajji Shariatullah and the son who followed him as leader of the Faraizis believed they had a duty to work with rather than against the British in bringing about dar ul-Islam, a view that had considerable support until it was challenged by his fellow Bengali Mir Nasir Ali, better known as Titu Mir.

Born in 1782, Titu Mir began life as a small cultivator with an appetite for violence. Forced off the land, he turned to crime and then drifted to Calcutta, where he spent some time as a professional wrestler before taking service with a powerful landowner as a *lathial*, a 'big-stick man' or enforcer. At some point he was found guilty of affray by a British magistrate and sent to prison. He was, in the words of a British judge, 'a man of a bad and desperate character'. After his release he went to work as a bodyguard for a minor member of the Mughal royal family in Delhi, and in that capacity accompanied him to Mecca on pilgrimage. There in 1821 or 1822 Titu Mir met a fellow Hindustani who already had a great following: the charismatic Syed Ahmad of Rae Bareli.

By the time Syed Ahmad and his followers landed at Jedda to begin the Hajj – the early summer of 1821 or 1822 – the holy

places of Mecca and Medina were back in the hands of the Sharifs
of the Hijaz under the protection of the Egyptians. However,
deep in the Arabian desert the surviving Wahhabis had regrouped.
TURKI IBN SAUD, an uncle of the executed emir Abdallah ibn
Saud and grandson of Muhammad ibn Saud, had escaped from
house arrest and was now beginning a fresh campaign to regain
the lands won by his half-brother – and to restore Al-Wahhab's
teachings. After failing to recapture the old stronghold of Riyadh,
Turki ibn Saud retreated into the desert and there began to
rebuild the tribal alliances first forged by his grandfather.

It was at this juncture, with the Wahhabis greatly weakened but
still threatening to take on the Ottoman Empire, that the ten
boatloads of Hindustani pilgrims arrived in Mecca. Having completed the Hajj, most of the party then returned to the coast and
sailed back to India. However, Syed Ahmad and his closest companions stayed on. He began to preach in the mosques, and word
of his preaching soon came to the attention of the religious authorities, very much on the alert for the slightest whiff of sedition
or heresy. What they heard was enough to merit Syed Ahmad's
expulsion, which suggests that he was preaching rather more
than the revivalism of Shahs Waliullah and Abdul Aziz. None of
the several biographies written by his followers goes into details
about Syed Ahmad's period in the Hijaz, and with good reason,
for by the time they came to be written 'Wahhabi' had become
a term of abuse and the movement was working hard to present
itself as something other than a sectarian force promoting a
creed imported from Arabia. What is remarkable about these
biographies is the degree to which they differ over how long
Syed Ahmad was away from India, and where he went. Shah
Muhammad Ismail, the first disciple, declares that after visiting
Mecca and Medina they travelled northwards together as far as
Constantinople before returning to Arabia, taking six years in all.
This allowed them to see the true dar ul-Islam of the Ottomans
and to compare it with the dire state of affairs in British India. Not

so much as a word is said about the Wahhabism that had so recently convulsed the Islamic world.

Whatever Shah Muhammad Ismail has to say on the matter, it seems most likely that Syed Ahmad returned to India early in 1824, after an absence of at least two years. He went ashore briefly in Bombay and was fêted as a saint by all sections of the Muslim community of the city. Again, there was talk of prophecies being fulfilled and of the approach of the end of days – and it seems to have been at this point that Mahdism first entered Syed Ahmad's newly enlarged religious vocabulary.

Both Sunnis and Shias shared the belief that at the end of days a messiah-figure known as the *mahdi*, or the 'expected one', would come to the rescue of Islam. He would return to Mecca at the head of all the forces of righteousness to take on the forces of evil in one final, apocalyptic battle, after which he and the lesser prophet Jesus would proceed to Jerusalem to kill the devil. Thereafter the world would submit to his rule until the sounding of the last trumpet, and Judgement Day. There were, however, significant differences between the Sunnis and Shias over the origins of the Mahdi, in that the latter held him to be the twelfth and last of the imams of early Islam. Unlike his predecessors, this twelfth imam had not died and gone to heaven but had disappeared from the sight of man to become the 'Hidden Imam'. He was said to be concealed in a cave in the mountains, waiting for the call from the righteous, when he would reappear as a *padshah* or 'great king' to lead the faithful to victory.

In Muslim India these distinctions and qualifications had become blurred over the centuries, like so much else in Islam. In the last decades of the Delhi Sultans in the mid-sixteenth century a Sunni mullah named Sayyid Muhammad of Jaunpur, near Benares, had proclaimed himself the Mahdi and had attracted a large following. His early death failed to discourage his adherents, who had proclaimed themselves the Mahdawis and set up a cult characterised by extreme asceticism, and violence towards other Muslims. 'They always carried swords and shields, and all kinds of weapons,' wrote the chronicler Nizamuddin Ahmad in his history *Tabaqat-i-Akbari*, 'and going into cities and bazaars, wherever they saw anything that was contrary to the law of the Prophet, at first they forbade these things, with gentleness and courtesy. If this did not succeed, they made people give up the forbidden practices, using force or violence.' The Mahdawi cult gained many converts among the Afghan leadership in India, so many in fact that it eventually provoked an orthodox backlash and was declared a heresy. Nevertheless, the belief in a messiah figure who would appear from the mountains to the west as the King of the West took hold among all sections of the Muslim community in India, becoming increasingly popular as Muslim power there waned.

A second and less successful eruption of Mahdism had occurred in Syed Ahmad's own lifetime, in western India in January 1810, when a Muslim named Abdul Rahman proclaimed himself the Imam-Mahdi, collected a band of followers of the Bohra sect of Sunnis and seized the fort of Mandvi in Eastern Surat. The insurgents had then marched on the nearest town, calling on all Hindus to embrace the faith or be killed. The British political agent at Surat had been sent a written demand calling on him to convert, and had responded by summoning troops from Bombay. Four companies of infantry and two troops of cavalry were landed on 19 January and a one-sided encounter followed in which the aspiring Imam-Mahdi and some two hundred insurgents were killed, after which the uprising fizzled out.

There was thus a well-established predisposition among all sections of the Muslim community in India to respond to the call of the true Imam-Mahdi in a time of religious crisis, and this now became an established part of Amir Syed Ahmad's Wahhabi platform in India: the belief that the end of days was drawing nigh and with it the imminent return of the Hidden Imam-Mahdi, the King of the West.

From Bombay Syed Ahmad and the other hajjis sailed on round the coast to Calcutta, where they finally disembarked.

The Hindustan to which Syed Ahmad returned was fast being reshaped on British terms. The last of the Pindari freebooters had been destroyed, the wings of the Maratha warlords clipped, and the Jat ruler of Bharatpore, holed up in his great mud fortress near Agra with eighty thousand men, was in the process of being brought to heel. Except for the Punjab, where the Sikhs still held sway, all Hindustan was now under direct or indirect East India Company control. So it was not surprising that Syed Ahmad and his twin messages of Islamic revival and armed struggle against the infidel were received with an enthusiasm bordering on hysteria. And nowhere was this enthusiasm more marked than at Patna, the seat of his most loyal supporters, headed by the three families of Fatah Ali, Elahi Bux, and Syed Muhammad Hussain.

Syed Ahmad's second stay in Patna marked a turning point in the progress of his movement. Word had spread through all sections of the Muslim community that the Hajji had returned to restore India, if not the world, to a domain of Faith under Islamic sharia. His first two disciples were now likened to the Prophet's two closest Companions, and Syed Ahmad himself was seen by his followers as travelling in the footsteps of the Prophet as His messenger. He was proclaimed amir of his movement, and each day hundreds came forward to be blessed by him and to swear allegiance to him by taking the oath of baiat. He ordained Syed Muhammad Husain, head of one of the three families, as his first vice-regent, set up a five-man council in Patna also drawn from the three families, and appointed a number of his leading supporters to be regional caliphs and collectors of religious taxes. Once this machinery was in place a highly sophisticated campaign was launched to promote Syed Ahmad's theology, which he himself named the Path of Muhammad (*Tariqa-i-Muhammadia*).

From an account of his mission left by Shah Muhammad Ismail we know that Syed Ahmad's first disciple was only one of many preachers who were now sent out to spread Syed Ahmad's gospel. Shah Muhammad Ismail writes of journeying 'from town to town preaching the sermon of jihad. Emissaries were likewise sent into the interior to prepare the minds of the Muhammadens for a religious war. Such was the powerful force of the orations of Maulvie Ismail [Shah Muhammad Ismail] that in less than two years the majority of respectable Muhammadans were in his favour.'

The theology preached by Syed Ahmad and his missionaries was based on five articles of faith. As summarised by T. E. Ravenshaw, these were:

1. reliance on one Supreme Being [the doctrine of *tawhid*];
2. repudiation of all forms, ceremonies, and observances of the modern Mahomedan religion, retaining only such as are considered the pure doctrines of the Koran [*bidat*];
3. the duty of Jehad or holy war for the faith against infidels generally;
4. blind and implicit obedience to their spiritual guides or *Peers* [*pirs*];
5. expectation of an *Imam* who will lead all true believers to victory over infidels.

The first four of these articles fell comfortably within the tenets of revivalist Sunni Islam as promoted by Al-Wahhab in Nejd and Shah Abdal Aziz in Delhi, but the last was a quintessential Shia belief, albeit deeply entrenched in Sunni tradition in India. There can be no doubt that both Al-Wahhab and Shah Abdal Aziz would have considered it heretical. Its inclusion as a basic article of faith appears to have been a deliberate bid by Syed Ahmad to raise the stakes by taking advantage of a belief widespread in all sections of the Muslim community in India. It has also enabled later commentators to argue, with some cause, that Syed Ahmad's 'Path of Muhammad' had little in common with Al-Wahhab's Wahhabism.

The fact is that Syed Ahmad and his first disciple Shah

Muhammad Ismail arrived in Mecca predisposed to accept Al-Wahhab's vision of tawhid through their spiritual apprenticeship at Delhi's Madrassah-i-Rahimiya – which reflected in large part the teaching acquired by Shah Waliullah in Mecca almost a century earlier. When Syed Ahmad returned to India he took with him a distinctly more hard-line, less tolerant and more aggressive Islam, directly inspired by the Wahhabi model, than he had imbibed at the feet of his first master Shah Abdul Aziz of Delhi. But because he was backed by several widely respected members of Shah Abdul Aziz's family, and because he carried out all religious ceremonies and observances according to the rules of the Hanafis, Syed Ahmad could present himself as the natural heir to this distinguished line of Hanafi reformers.

Due account must also be taken of the nature of the bonds that developed between Naqshbandi Sufi teachers in India and their students, bonds that demanded absolute devotion and loyalty. It will be remembered that Syed Ahmad's two closest disciples were respectively the nephew and son-in-law of his first master. With Shah Abdul Aziz's death in 1823 leadership had passed to his eldest son, SHAH MUHAMMAD ISHAQ, and he too appears to have been personally devoted to Syed Ahmad, if not to his cause. In consequence, Amir Syed Ahmad's teaching seems initially to have been embraced with enthusiasm by all the followers of the school of Shah Waliullah. Very soon, however, differences began to surface, probably disputes over matters of interpretation and emphasis, in which petty rivalries and jealousies must also have played a part. The outcome of these differences was the dividing of Syed Ahmad's Way of Muhammad movement into two factions held together only by the strength of personality of their leader. These two parties could well be termed the 'Delhi-ites' and the 'Patna-ites': the former made up of those such as the two first disciples who conformed to Sunni custom as already pushed to the limits by Shah Waliullah and Shah Abdul Aziz; the latter led by younger men such as Wilayat Ali of Patna who saw themselves as Wahhabis in all but name – and as committed jihadis. Syed Ahmad's first disciple

Shah Muhammad Ismail appears to have started out as a 'Delhi-ite' before his more extreme position forced him into the Patna camp. By his own account, he preached in Delhi's great Jamma Masjid every Friday and Tuesday, as a consequence of which thousands were reclaimed from 'the darkness of blasphemy in which they were plunged'. But his success attracted the jealousy of his contemporary divines, and a public debate was held to determine whether his preaching was in accordance with sharia. It broke up in disorder and Shah Muhammad Ismail was subsequently prohibited by the city authorities from public speaking. From that time Amir Syed Ahmad and his followers were proclaimed 'Wahabees'. According to an observer, 'The followers of the reformers are nicknamed "Wahabees" by their opponents, while the latter are called [by their opponents] "Mushriks", or associates of others with God.'

In December 1825 the mighty walls of Bharatpore were finally breached by British artillery and the fortress taken with great slaughter. It was a further demonstration of the ascendancy of the Nazarenes. Syed Ahmad now wrote to a friend in Hyderabad about his plans for holy war: 'During the last few years fate has been so kind to the accursed Christians and the mischievous polytheists that they have started oppressing people. Atheistic and polytheistic practices are being openly practised while the Islamic observances have disappeared. This unhappy state of affairs fills my heart with sorrow and I am anxious to perform *hijrat*. My heart is filled with shame at this religious degradation and my head contains but one thought, how to organise jihad.'

It had become clear to Amir Syed Ahmad that the time had come to emulate the Prophet, who had begun his conquest in the name of Islam by leaving the domain of enmity of Mecca and migrating to the dar ul-Islam of Medina: it was now incumbent on Syed Ahmad to follow suit, and to leave British territory for a secure base in God-fearing territory from which to wage jihad. There were also good military reasons for making this *hijra* or withdrawal. What had worked so well in the Arabian deserts, where the Wahhabi movement had expanded from a secure, isolated base at the centre, could not be applied in India. Patna's destiny would be to serve as his movement's recruiting base, a clandestine clearing-house through which funds, supplies, men and arms would be despatched to the front line. But the jihad itself had to be waged from secure territory on the periphery. For a while it seemed that the Muslim principality of Tonk in Rajasthan might serve, but a visit to Syed Ahmad's old patron Nawab Amir Khan quickly put paid to that idea; not only was Tonk surrounded by hostile Hindu rulers who had good reason to remain on friendly terms with the British, but the Nawab was himself under pressure from the British authorities to toe the line or risk losing his ruling privileges. He was prepared to support the movement secretly with funds and volunteers, but no further. The only safe option was the Afghan border area – perhaps the mountain region where Nawab Amir Khan had himself originated: the mountains of Buner. No doubt Syed Ahmad also had at the back of his mind the old belief that the Imam-Mahdi would make his first appearance from the west as the King of the West.

Various qualifications were required of the Imam-Mahdi. He would be an imam and a caliph, bear the name Muhammad, be a descendant of the Prophet through his daughter Fatima, arise in Arabia and be forty years old at the time of his emergence. Syed Ahmad fulfilled the most important of these qualifications: he was a Saiyyed, had been raised as 'Muhammad' (of which 'Ahmad' was a diminutive), and he became forty in 1826. In January of that year he began his hijra accompanied by a band of some four hundred armed and committed jihadis. These included members of his own family, his two leading disciples and others from the family of the late Shah Abdul Aziz of Delhi, and several members of the three Patna families, among them three of the four sons of Elahi Bux. Their retreat took them first to the Maratha state of Gwalior in central India, where Syed Ahmad hoped to win support for his jihad from its Hindu ruler, Daulat Rao Scindia. 'It is obvious to your exalted self', he wrote to the maharaja's brother, 'the alien people from distant lands have become the rulers of territories and times . . . They have destroyed the dominions of the big grandees and the estates of the nobles of illustrious ranks, and their honour and authority have been completely set at nought.'

Scindia of Gwalior had recently been forced to surrender a large slice of hard-won territory to the East India Company. He was now assured that if he joined Syed Ahmad in the forthcoming struggle against the British he would regain his lost lands 'as soon as the land of Hindustan is cleared of the alien enemies'. This remarkable letter has been cited as evidence that Syed Ahmad was an Indian nationalist at heart, happy to work in alliance with Hindus to throw off the British yoke. But it has to be set against half a dozen other surviving letters from Syed Ahmad, written to Muslim rulers such as the Emir of Bokhara, all making it plain that his ultimate goal was nothing less than the restoration of pure Islam throughout the whole of India. Syed Ahmad was indeed reacting to British and Sikh imperialism, but he was equally and unashamedly bent on Islamic imperialism – as were a number of alleged freedom fighters who came after him. No one can fault Syed Ahmad's courage, but the freedom he sought was that of a fundamentalist sect from India's Muslim minority to impose its religious will on the Hindu, Sikh and Jain majority.

In the event, the ruler of Gwalior ignored Syed Ahmad's overtures and his letter was buried in the state's archives. The jihadis then moved on to the Muslim state of Tonk, where they were warmly received by the Nawab and his heir apparent, Mohammad Wazir Khan. The latter became an enthusiastic convert to Syed Ahmad's cause and the two subsequently began a correspondence that continued to the time of Syed Ahmad's death. 'My motive in accepting the leadership', wrote Amir Syed Ahmad in one of the earliest of these letters, 'is nothing more than that of arraying forces of jihad and maintaining discipline among the army of the

Muslims. There are no other ulterior selfish motives . . . To my mind the value of the crown of Faridoon [a prophet of ancient Persia] and the throne of Alexander [the Great] is tantamount to a grain of barley. The kingdoms of Kasra [a ruler in the Persian epic *Shahnamah*] and Caesar are immaterial and insignificant to my eyes. I do, however, aspire to promulgate the orders of the Creator of the worlds called the principles of Faith among the entire humanity of the world without any subversion.' As a first step in this world conquest he would establish himself in a country of Faith west of the Indus. Once he had purged it of 'the impurities of polytheism and the filth of dissonance' he would then launch his main jihad: 'Then I will set out with my followers for India with a view to purifying the country from polytheism and infidelity, because my real motive is to launch an attack over India.'

To avoid the Sikh territories of Maharaja Ranjit Singh in the Punjab, the Amir and his Hindustanis marched from Tonk across the Thar desert into Sind and then across Baluchistan – a journey of about six hundred miles through some of the harshest terrain in the world, undertaken at the height of summer. Although both these last two regions were ruled by Muslim chiefs, neither offered any support. The jihadis then crossed over the Bolan Pass into Afghanistan. According to the hagiographies, they were welcomed in Kabul with open arms. However, the evidence suggests that they were asked to move on, for when the band of holy warriors finally emerged from the Khyber on to the Vale of Peshawar in November 1826, its numbers were greatly reduced. One text put them at no more than forty.

But at this point Amir Syed Ahmad's luck turned. The Yusufzai and the other Pathan tribes in and around Peshawar were smarting from a defeat recently suffered at the hands of a Sikh punitive column. In consequence, the Amir and his Hindustanis were warmly received as potential allies against the Sikhs. Syed Ahmad was, after all, a descendant of the Prophet and a Hajji, and he had made it known that he had been charged by God to liberate the trans-Indus lands from the yoke of the infidel oppressor. The elders of a number of Yusufzai clans and sub-tribes gathered for a *loya jirga* and concluded this inter-tribal assembly by offering the Hindustanis their hospitality and their armed support.

The Hindustanis settled initially at Nowshera, twenty miles east of Peshawar, but soon afterwards their leader was offered a permanent home in the Mahabun massif, the great mountain promontory that bulges out southwards from the mountains of Buner. It was a secure fastness into which the Sikh columns had never penetrated. Here Syed Ahmad found himself among friends and admirers, for not only was this the tribal homeland of his former patron the Pindari freebooter turned nawab, Amir Khan of Tonk, but also the home of a hero with ambitions not so very different from his own. Generations earlier a Saiyyed saint named Pir Baba had established himself in these mountains and had been granted a patch of land in perpetuity at Sittana, on the eastern slopes overlooking the Indus valley. In 1823 one of the pir's descendants, SAYYED AKBAR SHAH, had led the massed *lashkars* or tribal armies of the Yusufzai against the Sikhs. The battle, fought out in the plains near Nowshera, and the subsequent sacking of Peshawar had cost hundreds of Pathan lives but established Sayyed Akbar Shah as a champion of the Faith. He now invited Amir Syed Ahmad to make camp on his land in the Mahabun Mountain. Although it was some time before Sittana became established as the notorious 'Fanatic Camp' of the British, the Mahabun Mountain was even then (in Surgeon Henry Bellew's words) 'a noted nursery for saints, a perfect hot-bed of fanatics'. Now it became the movement's spiritual fortress. This was to be the Wahhabis' dar ul-Islam from which the jihad on India was to be launched and from which the King of the West and Imam-Mahdi would proclaim his long-awaited arrival. Sayyed Akbar Shah became Syed Ahmad's local patron, and in recognition of his importance was appointed the movement's treasurer.

Once established on the mountain, the Amir and his two closest disciples drew up a formal summons calling on all Muslims to join the holy war. In the late autumn of 1826 this document, passed from hand to hand and copied many times over, was carried to all the frontier tribes and to every corner of the Punjab where Muslim communities were to be found. Its call to arms must have made heady reading:

> The Sikh nation have long held sway in Lahore and other places. Thousands of Muhammadans have they unjustly killed, and on thousands they have heaped disgrace. No longer do they allow the Call to Prayer from the mosques, and the killing of cows they have entirely prohibited. When at last their insulting tyranny could no more be endured, *Hazrat* [Honoured] Sayyid Ahmad (may his fortunes and blessings ever abide!), having for his single object the protection of the Faith, took with him a few Musulmans [Muslims], and, going in the direction of Cabul and Peshawar, succeeded in rousing Muhammadans from their slumber of indifference, and nerving their courage for action. Praise be to God, some thousands of believers came ready at his call to tread the path of God's service; and on the 20th Zamadi-ul-Sani, 1242 AH [21 December 1826], the Jihad against the Infidel Sikhs begins.

Again the elders of the Pathan tribes who had first rallied to his standard met in grand council, this time joined by others who had previously held back. Amir Syed Ahmad was now formally chosen as the movement's imam. In Arabia, the title signified religious leadership and little else, but in Hindustan it carried significantly more weight, due to the influence of Shia teaching which acknowledged the imam as a supreme religious authority whose judgements were considered infallible. But there were also other reasons for assuming the title: under the rules of Hanafi jurisprudence jihad could only proceed by order of an imam; and it was a further qualification required of the Imam-Mahdi. As Syed Ahmad himself acknowledged in a letter to a friend written at this time: 'It was accordingly decided by all those present – faithful followers, Sayyids, learned doctors of law, nobles and generality of Muslims – that the successful establishment of jihad and the dispelling of belief and disorder could not be achieved without the election of an Imam.'

Syed Ahmad was also proclaimed *Amir ul-Momineen,* Commander of the Faithful. This echoed the titles of the early caliphs and amounted to a public declaration of his ambition to take the war of religious liberation a lot further than the Vale of Peshawar. Amir ul-Momineen Imam Syed Ahmad was now presented to the entire Muslim community on the Indian frontier as their long-awaited saviour.

The holy war began in earnest in the spring of 1827 with a massed attack on a Sikh column sent out from Peshawar. It was a disaster for the jihadis. According to Dr Henry Bellew's informants, the Sikhs held their ground and counter-attacked: 'In the first onset the Sayad's undisciplined rabble were panic struck and were easily dispersed with great loss. The Sayad himself escaped with only a few attendants.' All but their most loyal tribal allies deserted them and the Hindustanis were forced to flee to the safety of the Mahabun Mountain. Despite this near-annihilation, Syed Ahmad held to the hard line that characterised his vision of Islam, as demonstrated by his response when one of his most influential local allies, Khadi Khan of Hund, switched sides after suffering heavy losses among his tribesmen. To the Amir ul-Momineen Imam this was an act of apostasy. He immediately rallied his remaining friends and marched against Hund. After an untidy mêlée which neither side could claim as a victory, a much-loved Sufi hermit, revered on all sides as a saint, stepped in to act as an intermediary. This was a young man of humble origins named ABDUL GHAFFUR, known then as 'Saidu Baba' but later to achieve great eminence among the Pathans as the Akhund of Swat. Abdul Ghaffur duly interceded and persuaded Khadi Khan of Hund to come into the Hindustani camp under flag of truce, whereupon he was separated from his companions and had his throat cut – an act of treachery justified by Syed Ahmad on the grounds that under sharia the crime of apostasy was only punishable by death.

Because of his role in the affair, Abdul Ghaffur was driven from his hermitage into exile. Already alienated by the Amir's attempts to impose the Wahhabi version of the law upon them, a number of villages in the plains now publicly expressed their disquiet. This, too, was interpreted as apostasy – the worst of all sins in the Wahhabi book – and orders went out for the twin villages of Hoti and Mardan to be looted and fired as an example to other waverers. A decade later, when Hoti Mardan was chosen as the base for the new border force to be known as the Guides, this outrage was still remembered. It helps to explain why the irregulars who joined the Guides Cavalry and Infantry in later years regarded the Hindustanis in the hills to the north as their inveterate enemies.

Fortunately for the Hindustanis, a botched attempt by the Governor of Peshawar in December 1828 to poison the Amir ul-Momineen Imam sheltering among the Yusufzai brought an end to the dissent. The attempt on the life of their guest impugned their honour, and the Yusufzai tribes in the mountains reacted by setting aside their differences and again rallying to Syed Ahmad. They swept down from the hills and overwhelmed a Sikh army many times their superior in numbers and fire-power. The Governor of Peshawar was killed and his forces scattered.

This surprise victory was followed by a third loya jirga, held in February 1829, at which many of the khans agreed not only to levy special tithes on their people to pay for the holy war but also to implement the Wahhabi version of sharia among their people. Over this same period many new adherents to the cause began arriving from every corner of the frontier, until eventually the Hindustani camp in the mountains contained more than six thousand fighting men –

who from this point onwards began to refer to themselves by a word hitherto unused on the Punjab frontier: *mujahedeen*, 'those who undertake *jihad kabeer*', a word popularly translated as 'holy warriors'.

Under the direction of their Commander of the Faithful and Imam these mujahedeen received both military training and religious instruction. Syed Ahmad had always been a keen sportsman, and by instituting fitness training he saw to it that the new recruits followed his example. He organised wrestling, archery and shooting competitions, and held 'field days' in which his troops fought each other in mock battles across the hillsides. In between their religious studies and their military training the mujahedeen learned marching songs that extolled the virtues of their leader and his cause; a number of them survived to be presented as evidence in court cases in later years. The most popular was the *Risala Jihad*, the Army of Holy War, written by Syed Ahmad's first disciple, Shah Muhammad Ismail. Part of it went as follows:

> War against the Infidel is incumbent on all Musalmans;
> make provision for all things.
> He who from his heart gives one farthing to the cause, shall
> hereafter receive seven hundred fold from God.
> He who shall equip a warrior in this cause of God shall
> obtain a martyr's reward;
> His children dread not the trouble of the grave, nor the last
> trump, nor the Day of Judgement.
> Cease to be cowards; join the divine leader, and smite the
> Infidel.
> I give thanks to God that a great leader has been born in
> the thirteenth century of the Hijra [1786–1886, the 'great
> leader' being Syed Ahmad, born 1786].

In response to this new spirit of revolt the Sikh ruler of the Punjab, Ranjit Singh, ordered his generals to take sterner measures against the insurgents. A brutal war now began in which neither side gave any quarter, sowing the seeds of a hatred between the Sikhs and the frontier tribes that continues to this day. As the Victorian historian Sir William Hunter later put it, 'the Muhammadens burst down from time to time upon the plains, burning and murdering wherever they went. On the other hand, the bold Sikh villagers armed en masse beat back the hill fanatics into their mountains, and hunted them down like beasts.'

In spite of setbacks Syed Ahmad's army of mujahedeen continued to grow. Wherever possible direct confrontation with the Sikhs in open battle was avoided in favour of guerrilla tactics, using ambushes and night attacks. In the course of a year and a half the rebels came to control the entire countryside as far east as the Indus, leaving the Sikhs as masters of Peshawar city but little else. Finally, in October 1830 the new Governor of Peshawar concluded a private treaty with the rebels that allowed him to withdraw from the city unharmed, leaving Peshawar and the surrounding Vale in the hands of the Wahhabis and their allies.

To mark this great victory Syed Ahmad declared himself *Padshah*, or Great King, and had coins struck bearing the inscription 'Ahmad the Just, Defender of the Faith; the glitter of whose scimitar scatters destruction among the Infidels.' It was another step in the process of assuming the mantle of the King of the West, the longed-for Imam-Mahdi.

After appointing Mullah Muzhir Ali as his local caliph and chief judge in the city of Peshawar, the newly proclaimed Padshah returned to his mountain stronghold with his closest companions, leaving it to Muzhir Ali and his fellow Hindustanis to impose Wahhabi sharia on the inhabitants of the Vale of Peshawar. This lasted no more than two months before the Pathans had had enough. The tribesmen had been happy to pay the religious war tithes, but the strict imposition of sharia as meted out by a Hindustani judge soon came into conflict with their own tribal laws of *Pakhtunwali*. The two final straws appear to have been a ruling that the Pathans must abandon their un-Islamic custom of selling their daughters in marriage – followed by an equally ill-advised edict announcing that any single girls of marriageable age who were not married within twelve days should be made over to the Hindustani mujahedeen to become their wives.

This last edict struck at the very heart of the Pathan honour-code, *nang-i-Pukhatna*, a code as inflexible as anything devised by the Wahhabi jurists, and one which required that any personal injury or insult, however slight, be answered with blood. Again a loya jirga was held, but this time in secret, and a plan of retaliation was hatched with the objective of killing the Padshah and every other Hindustani along with him. In a Pathan version of the St Bartholomew's Eve Massacre, it was agreed that this strike should take place at the hour of evening prayer, the signal being the lighting of a beacon on the top of Karmar hill, a peak in the Malakand range overlooking the Vale of Peshawar. The beacon was duly lit, and within an hour Mullah Muzhir Ali, his fellow judges and all the Hindustanis in the Vale had been dragged from their prayer mats and put to the sword.

Either by chance or because of a loss of nerve on the part of his hosts in the Buner mountains, Syed Ahmad and his closest companions survived the massacre and fled eastwards across the Indus River into Hazara. They then made their way north to the Khagan valley and sought refuge among the Khagan Sayyeds, who now found themselves bound by the Pathan law of *nanawati* to give the Hindustanis shelter and to protect them with their lives. As so often in Pathan history, this absolute interpretation of sanctuary cost the hosts dear, for the news of the massacre and the retreat of the survivors galvanised the Sikhs into action. Peshawar was quickly restored to Sikh rule, and once all opposition in the Vale had been silenced the Sikhs advanced on the Khagan valley in force.

On 8 May 1831 the remaining Hindustanis, together with the

more committed Sayyeds of Sittana and Khagan, made a last stand
at the little village of Balakot which guards the entrance to the
Khagan valley. Expecting the Sikhs to advance up the valley from
the south, they dug trenches and flooded the open ground below
the village, only to be thrown into disarray when their enemy
came down on them from the hills above. Ringed in on almost
every side, they chose death rather than surrender. Led by their
Amir Al-Mumineem, Imam and Padshah, the Hindustanis
charged as best they could up the slopes to meet the advancing
lines of Sikh infantry.

Quite remarkably, considering this was a battle fought hundreds
of miles from the nearest British territory, the closing stages of the
battle of Balakot were witnessed by an American: a vagabond and
soldier of fortune named Colonel Alexander Gardner, born on the
shores of Lake Superior in 1785. Mystery surrounds Alexander
Gardner's exact origins and movements; he may not after all have
been born in America, and half the extraordinary tales of his wan-
derings through Turkestan, Badakshan, Kafiristan and Afghanistan
in the 1820s and 1830s may not be true, but there is no doubt that
he was among the many foreign mercenaries who served in the
ranks of the Sikh army under Maharaja Ranjit Singh. Prior to joining the Sikhs, Gardner had led a squadron of horse in the service of
a contender for the throne of Kabul. He found himself on the losing
side and fled northwards into the Pamirs, after which he journeyed
southwards through Kashmir, Gilgit, Chitral and Kafiristan until he
came to the frontier region of Bajour, ruled over by a chieftain
named Mir Alam Khan.

At the beginning of May 1831 Gardner and a group of Pathan
tribesmen, whom he termed his 'trusty band of Khaibaris [people
of the Khyber]', were in the process of offering their services to
Mir Alam Khan when 'a certain Muhammad Ismail arrived from
the fanatic chief Syad Ahmad with a demand for aid from the *mir*
[chief], as from all neighbouring Muhammadan chieftains'.
Gardner's 'Muhammad Ismail' was none other than Syed Ahmad's

first disciple, Shah Muhammad Ismail, then engaged in making a desperate bid to win back some of the allies who had deserted his master. Gardner suggests that he and his fellow mercenaries were won over to Syed Ahmad's cause by 'an impassioned address which I heard Muhammad Ismail deliver to a large assembly of the wild Eusufzai mountaineers. The enthusiasms which he aroused suggested to me that I might do worse than join the Syad his master, as I saw a good opportunity of getting together such a body of followers as would make my services valuable to any ruler to whom I might subsequently offer them.' Some money may also have been promised, for Gardner, at this time masquerading as a Muslim and carrying a copy of the Quran suspended round his neck, agreed to fight for the Hindustanis.

Shah Muhammad Ismail then hurried on ahead to rejoin Syed Ahmad in the Khagan valley while Gardner and some two hundred and fifty Pathans, 'all burning with religious zeal', came on at a steadier pace. According to Gardner, they then lost their way, as a result of which they arrived at Balakot 'just an hour too late'. The battle was already under way and it was clear that it was turning into a massacre: 'I well remember the scene', Gardner later wrote,

> as I and my Eusufzai and Khaibari followers came in view of the action. Syad Ahmad and the maulvi [Shah Muhammad Ismail], surrounded by his surviving Indian followers, were fighting desperately, hand-to-hand with the equally fanatical Akalis [Sikh warriors] of the Sikh army. They had been taken by surprise, and isolated from the main body of the Syad's forces, which fought very badly without their leader. Even as I caught sight of the Syad and maulvi, they fell pierced by a hundred weapons . . . I was literally within a few hundred yards of the Syad when he fell, but I did not see the angel descend and carry him off to Paradise, although many of his followers remembered

afterwards that they had seen it distinctly enough.

Seeing which way the battle was going, Gardner held back his men until the fighting was done and then moved in to claim a share of the booty: 'The death of the Syad broke the only link that held the followers together, and in the retreat many of the parties from different regions fell upon one another for plunder. My Khaibaris and Eusufzai were equal to the best in this matter and cut down several of the Hindustani fanatics who had joined them for protection.' It is said that thirteen hundred Hindustanis and their adherents died at Balakot, but the real figure was probably closer to half that number.

On receiving the news of Syed Ahmad's death the Sikh ruler Ranjit Singh gave orders for gun salutes to be fired from every fort, and for the Sikh holy city of Amritsar to be lit up in celebration. Accounts differ as to what happened to the remains of the Amir, Imam and Padshah. In the final stages of the battle a group of Wahhabis tried to carry away the body but were dispersed by gunfire, whereupon a single Wahhabi hacked the head off with his tulwar and attempted to make off with it. He was then struck down, and the head and body were found separately by the Sikhs. According to one report, both parts were subsequently chopped into small pieces and thrown into the nearby river in order to prevent the grave becoming a place of pilgrimage. Another version has the Sikhs burning the body on the battlefield and carrying the head back to Peshawar to be impaled on the battlements of the city's fort.

4

The Call of the Imam-Mahdi

Those who would prevent others from *hijra* and *jihad* are
in heart hypocrites. Let all know this: in a country where
the predominant religion is other than Islam, the religious precepts of Muhammad cannot be enforced,
[therefore] it is incumbent on Musalmans to unite and
wage war with Kaffirs.

Part of a letter written by Maulvi Inayat Ali,
leader of the Hindustani Fanatics at Sittana, 1852–3

The catastrophic end to Syed Ahmad's campaign to bring about
dar ul-Islam in a distant corner of the Punjab did not go unnoticed
in the rest of India. For all that his teachings had offended Sunnis
and Shias alike, Syed Ahmad had become more than just a
preacher of reform. He had taken the struggle to the enemy, and
every scrap of news of his jihad against the Sikhs that filtered
down from the Punjab had excited interest. The reports of his
martyrdom in the summer of 1831 were received with dismay by
Muslims up and down the land. In Bengal it was the spur that set
off Titu Mir's Wahhabi revolt.

Titu Mir, it will be remembered, was the Bengali 'enforcer' who went to Mecca on Hajj at the same time as Syed Ahmad and his band of pilgrims. On his return to Delhi he quit the service of his royal employer and went back to Bengal to preach the message of Wahhabism through the countryside north and east of Calcutta. The name he gave his movement, *Deen Muhammad* or Way of Muhammad, suggests an affinity with Syed Ahmad's Path of Muhammad. In Bengal the countryside was largely owned by wealthy landlords whose oppression of the peasantry working their fields was legendary. Titu Mir exploited this discontent by recruiting peasants and weavers to his cause. By the time the news of the death of Syed Ahmad reached Bengal in the late summer of 1831 he had gained several thousand adherents, distinguishable from their fellow Muslim and Hindu neighbours by the long beards and plain dress worn by the men, the almost complete withdrawal of their women behind the folds of the purdah and the *burqa*, and their contempt for all forms of religion other than their own. In October 1831 their leader called all the members of his Wahhabi sect together in the village of Narkulbaria and ordered them to prepare it for a long siege. They laid in supplies and built a strong bamboo stockade round the village, which now became their constituted dar ul-Islam.

Two weeks later Titu Mir marched out at the head of a band some five hundred strong armed with clubs and farm implements and attacked a nearby village in the name of jihad. They killed a Brahmin priest, cut the throats of two cows and dragged them bleeding through a Hindu temple – acts deliberately intended to outrage Hindus. At the same time their leader proclaimed an end to British rule in Bengal, evidently in the expectation that Muslims throughout the countryside would rise up and join him. Over the next few days more attacks on nearby villages were carried out, deliberately intended to terrorise both Muslim and Hindu communities. As the magistrates later noted, everything was done according to a set plan: each morning the rebels marched out in ranks under a military commander to attack and plunder a particular target, and every evening they marched back with their booty.

At first the local district magistrate, a Mr Alexander, failed to grasp the nature of the outrages. Escorted by twenty-two sepoys and about twice that number of local policemen, he advanced on the rebel village believing that his appearance on the scene would be enough to cause the troublemakers to disperse. Indeed, so convinced of this was Mr Alexander that he ordered his men to load their weapons with the blank cartridges used for ceremonials. To his consternation he found himself faced by a small army between four and six hundred strong drawn up in ranks behind their military commander, one Ghulam Masum, mounted on a horse.

The unhappy Mr Alexander now attempted to parley, but before he could say a word Ghulam Masum gave the order to charge and himself bore down on him brandishing a tulwar. Mr Alexander fled, leaving his sepoys to fire a volley of blanks before being overwhelmed by Titu Mir's peasant army. Only after a long chase through the countryside did Mr Alexander, bedraggled and frightened, reach safety. Fifteen men were killed and many others either wounded or taken prisoner, but still the Calcutta authorities assumed they were dealing with a minor local dispute. Three days after the massacre a second British magistrate, a Mr Smith, repeated Mr Alexander's error, this time approaching the rebel village in the company of a number of local British indigo planters, all of them mounted on elephants – the armoured vehicles of their day and as effective in counter-insurgency as Russian tanks in Afghanistan or US humvees in Iraq. They had brought with them a large body of armed watchmen, but the closer they drew to the village of Narkulbaria the less enthusiastic these became. 'One by one,' notes the official report, 'the Bengalis dropped behind, and when the party arrived in the large plain in front of the village they found that, with the exception of twenty or thirty up-country *burkundazes* [watchmen], every native had disappeared. Here they found the insurgents about a thousand strong, drawn up in regular order.'

The magistrate and his party at once turned their elephants about and lumbered off, pursued by a howling mob that soon caught up with them and began to cut down the stragglers. A second humiliating chase across the Bengal countryside followed, leaving the insurgents utterly convinced of their leader's claims that they were under the special protection of God, and safe from the bullets of infidels.

Now at last the Governor-General of Bengal became involved, and no fewer than twelve infantry regiments together with the Governor-General's own cavalry bodyguard and some horse artillery took to the field. On the evening of 17 November this substantial force marched out from Calcutta with colours flying and drums and fifes playing and, on the following morning, disposed itself for battle before the stockaded village of Narkulbaria. More than ten thousand professional troops found themselves opposed by a peasant army scarcely a tenth of their number, largely armed with farm implements and staves, but paraded as before in well-ordered ranks. By way of a banner, they flew the body of a dead Englishman suspended from a pole.

A text-book frontal assault followed, with the infantry advancing in extended columns and halting to fire volley upon volley into the massed insurgents. Even so, Titu Mir's men held their ground for almost an hour before the survivors retired into their stockade. The two guns of the horse artillery were then brought into play before the village was stormed at the point of the bayonet. Titu Mir was among the fifty dead. Almost two hundred of his followers were subsequently tried in court. Eleven received life sentences for treason, and 136 earned themselves sentences of imprisonment ranging from two years to seven. Ghulam Masum, Titu Mir's second-in-command, was hanged. 'These people', recorded the presiding magistrate, 'pretend to a new religion, calling out "Deen

Mohummad", declaring that the Company's government is gone.
They are headed by fakirs, two or three, and the men who led the
attack on us were fine able-bodied fanatics apparently influenced
by the decision that they were charmed.' An enquiry followed and
duly reported to the Governor-General that 'the insurrection was
strictly local, arising from causes which had operation in a small
extent of country'.

Without the forceful leadership of Syed Ahmad the Wahhabi
movement in India began to splinter as sectarian differences
resurfaced. Since their leader had himself decreed that a jihad
could only proceed by authority of an imam, and since that imam
was now dead, the holy war had to be abandoned.

However, at the time of the last stand of the Hindustanis at
Balakot three local caliphs appointed by the dead leader had been
away on a diplomatic mission in Kashmir. They and a few other
others succeeded in recrossing the Indus to the Mahabun
Mountain, where they petitioned the Sayyids of Sittana to again
give them refuge. A jirga was duly held and some new land was
found for them outside the village. But so hostile were the surrounding Pathan tribes to their presence that at least one of the
caliphs, Maulvi NASIRUDDIN, decided it was time to move on. He
abandoned the mountains for the plains, leaving a mere handful
of Hindustani diehards at Sittana under the charge of Maulvi
Qasim PANIPATI. There they hung on, and over the months that
followed they came increasingly to see themselves as guardians of
the shrine of their lost imam and amir. Visitors arrived anxious to
know more about the fate of Syed Ahmad the Martyr and how
exactly he had met his death. Then it was discovered that no one
had actually seen the Imam-cum-Amir die, although several eye-
witnesses were prepared to swear that they had seen him and
his two dearest disciples fighting fiercely in the very midst of the
battle. A cloud of dust had then descended on all three figures, and
they had disappeared from mortal sight. So inspired was Panipati

by this revisionist testimony that he wrote letters to Patna giving a quite different account of the battle of Balakot. He urged his co-religionists to take heart – and, while they were about it, to send up funds and fresh supplies.

Panipati's revelations were eagerly seized upon by the new leadership of the Wahhabi movement in Patna. Four members of the original six-man council appointed by Syed Ahmad had died with him on the frontier. Of the remaining two, Fatah Ali had died of natural causes, leaving Shah Muhammad Husain of Sadiqpur as the senior caliph in Patna. The five vacant places on the council were now filled by a younger generation, all accorded the title of *Maulvi* (preacher). They included Fatah Ali's two eldest sons, Wilayat Ali and Inayat Ali; the two eldest sons of Elahi Bux, AHMADULLAH and YAHYA ALI; and an outsider, FARHAT HUSAIN, who had married into the three interlinked Patna families by taking as wife yet another of the daughters of Shah Muhammad Husain. These five younger men together became the guiding force behind the Wahhabi movement's restructuring in the late 1830s and 1840s and its re-emergence as a fighting force in the 1850s.

For some years Wilayat Ali served as Shah Muhammad Husain's *wazir* (chief counsellor) before succeeding him as the movement's leading imam. His brother Inayat Ali then became the movement's minister for war, Ahmadullah the new counsellor in succession to Wilayat Ali, Yahya Ali treasurer and bursar, and Farhat Husain the movement's recruiter and chief religious ideologue, running the movement's madrassah and acting as caliph during Wilayat Ali's frequent absences from Patna.

Wilayat Ali, it will be remembered, was almost certainly a convert to Wahhabism even before his first meeting with Syed Ahmad. His youngest brother Talib Ali had accompanied Syed Ahmad on his long march and had died as a martyr fighting the Sikhs, so perhaps it was no surprise that Wilayat Ali and the middle brother Inayat Ali should emerge as the most determined members of the Wahhabi council. It appears to have been Wilayat Ali who first grasped the significance of the doubts emerging about their leader's death, and who made the first public announcements of his survival. He then let it be known that he himself had heard Syed Ahmad foretell his disappearance some years earlier in a sermon. Now he could report the glad tidings that their beloved master was indeed alive and well, but that God, displeased by the faint-hearted response of the Muslims of India to His prophet's call to arms, had withdrawn him from the eyes of men. Their Imam and Amir ul-Momineen was even now hidden in a cave in the Buner mountains, waited on by his two faithful disciples. Only when his followers had proved their faith by uniting once more to renew the jihad would their lost leader reappear. He would then manifest himself as padshah and lead them to victory against the unbelievers.

This was, in essence, a retread of the Shia version of the Imam-Mahdi story, in which the Hidden Imam absented himself from the sight of man in a cave in the mountains, awaiting the summons of the faithful to make himself known as King of the West.

Absurd as this story now appears, it gave great heart to the disconsolate faithful in the plains and, just as importantly, it overcame the technicality of the imam required to authorise jihad. If Syed Ahmad was still alive, the jihad he had proclaimed could be continued. The immediate outcome was a second hijra (retreat) made under the command of Nasiruddin, the caliph who had earlier abandoned the Fanatic Camp. He was authorised to form a new group of volunteers and in 1835 marched them off towards Afghanistan with the declared intention of resuming the holy war against the Sikhs. Their arrival in Sind aroused the suspicion of the British Political Agent in nearby Kutch. Political pressure was applied and Nasiruddin's jihadis found themselves stranded in Sind, where they kicked their heels for months that became years as they waited for reinforcements to join them.

Syed Ahmad in his lifetime had exploited the concept of the

Imam-Mahdi to his movement's advantage, but had never openly declared himself to be the 'expected one'. Nor did his successors speak directly of him in these terms. Nevertheless, a cult was now formed around his person. Those who had been closest to him set down their recollections of 'Imam Saheb', as they referred to him, and collected his sayings, very much as the followers of the Prophet had gathered the material for the Hadith. Syed Ahmad was now credited with all manner of saintly virtues, and, in a further deviation from the dictates of Wahhabism, miraculous powers were attributed to him – one of which, seemingly, was the ability to rise from the dead.

At the same time old Sunni and Sufi prophecies were dusted down, re-examined and, where necessary, revised: 'I see', read part of one such prophecy, originally devised by the Madhawi followers of Sayyid Muhammad of Jaunpur some centuries earlier, 'that after 1200 years [750 years in the original text] have passed wonderful events will occur; I see all the kings of the earth arrayed one against the other; I see the Hindus in an evil state; I see the Turks oppressed; then the Imam will appear and rule over the earth; I see and read AHMD ['MHMD' in the original, thus 'Ahmad' replaced 'Muhammad'] as the letters showing forth the name of this ruler.' Shia texts were similarly employed, particularly a prophecy which gave the date of the forthcoming advent of the Imam-Mahdi as the year 1260 AH, corresponding to 1843–4 in the Christian calendar. When 1843–4 came and went without any divine manifestations a fresh text, entitled *Asar Mahshar* or Signs of the Last Day, was circulated. This foretold that after an initial defeat by the English on the Punjab Frontier the Faithful would begin a search for the Imam-Mahdi, culminating in an apocalyptic four-day battle, the complete overthrow of the Nazarenes and the triumphal appearance of the Imam-Mahdi to preside over the triumph of Islam in India. No exact date was given; but these events were to be heralded by an eclipse of both the sun and the moon.

A cult can be defined as a form of worship with specific rites and ceremonies in which excessive devotion is paid to a particular person or belief system, creating a closed group environment everything within which is deemed good and everything outside bad. In the case of Indian Wahhabism, as it now became under the aegis of Wilayat Ali, these cult-like characteristics can be summed up as follows:

1. belief in one man's reading of the Quran and the Hadith, and a determination to bring about a theocracy based exclusively on those beliefs accompanied by a rejection of all other interpretations;

2. absolute devotion, formalised by the swearing of an oath, to a single authority figure who is both religious leader and military commander, Imam and Amir, often accompanied by the belief that this leader has quasi-divine abilities;

3. a perception of that figure as the natural heir to the caliphs of early Islam, if not an Imam-Mahdi figure heralding the final great battle against Islam's enemies;

4. a belief in millenarianism – the notion that the end of the world is fast approaching, and with it the triumph of Islam;

5. an us-and-them mentality, whereby all who hold other religious views are seen as heretics and thus fair game for violent suppression;

6. a recognition of jihad as one's prime duty, but ignoring *jihad akbar* (the great jihad) in favour of *jihad kabeer* (the lesser jihad), interpreted as nothing less than holy war;

7. the making of a symbolic retreat before beginning the jihad, so replicating the Prophet's hijra from Mecca to Medina;

8. the wish to return to a past golden age of Islam, together with a rejection of modern learning and technology (except where this can be used to further jihad);

9. the recruiting of young male followers from among the poor and ignorant (preferably prepubescent orphans), subjecting them to long periods of intensive and exclusive religious indoctrination while keeping them isolated from other sources of ideas; and lastly,

10. the promotion of a death-wish mentality in which the status of *shahid* (martyr) is exhalted as the ultimate goal of every jihadi.

The leading promoter of the cult of Syed Ahmad, if not its originator, was Maulvi Wilayat Ali. Though he himself was short, fat and dark, and entirely without the good looks and charismatic qualities which had distinguished his predecessor, Wilayat Ali soon emerged as the movement's new ideologue. What he lacked in appearance and character he more than made up for with his tireless promotion of Syed Ahmad and his teaching. He became the movement's leading strategist and, over time, its most successful propagandist, travelling far and wide to preach his version of Syed Ahmad's Wahhabism.

But as the tenets and agenda of his revivalism became more widely known, so opposition began to grow. Some months after Titu Mir's abortive uprising in Bengal, Wilayat Ali appeared in Bombay to preach in the mosques. According to one of his critics, 'he prohibited the people from reading "Mowlood Shareef" [a text not contained in the Hadith], and paying reverence to our Prophet. Upon this the Moulvees of Bombay took him for an infidel, and turned him out.' A year later fourteen leading Sunni mullahs of Delhi put their names to a fatwa denouncing the Indian Wahhabis as 'a faithless, wicked, treacherous, and seditious people', declaring that they had been banished from Mecca and Medina; and that, 'with a view to gaining worldly riches, they had founded a new creed to cheat and impose upon the ignorant Mussulmans.' From this time onward repeated denunciations of the Indian Wahhabis were made by mainstream Sunni Muslim leaders in India, accompanied by the pronouncement of fatwas declaring them to be infidels and faithless.

The 'Delhi-ites' among Syed Ahmad's original followers now began to distance themselves from the 'Patna-ites', realigning themselves with the more acceptable teachings of the school of Shah Waliullah. After the death in 1823 of Syed Ahmad's teacher Shah Abdul Aziz the leadership of the Madrassah-i-Ramiyah had passed to Shah Abdul Aziz's son, SHAH MUHAMMAD ISHAQ. Following the martyrdom of Syed Ahmad and his cousin Shah Muhammad Ismail at the battle of Balakot in 1831, Shah Muhammad Ishaq and a number of his disciples migrated to Arabia, where they remained for some years. Little is known about the circumstances of this self-imposed exile, but Shah Muhammad Ishaq's departure seems to have been followed by a marked falling-off of support for Wahhabi teaching in the Delhi madrassahs. However, at some point in the late 1830s or early 1840s Shah Muhammad Ishaq returned to Delhi and began to gather about him a wide circle of outstanding young teachers and scholars from the East India Company's Delhi College who in later years became hugely influential as radical leaders, ranging from the Mughal aristocrat SYED AHMAD KHAN of Alipore at one end of the spectrum to SAYYID NAZIR HUSAIN Muhaddith of Delhi at the other.

Despite the hostility of the Sunni ulema, the message of militant jihad as now promoted by Wilayat Ali and the Patna-ites still found appreciative audiences, particularly among the Muslim nawabs who ruled over their states under the suzerainty of the British crown. Foremost among these was the Nizam of

Hyderabad, whose enormous wealth and extensive titles could not disguise the fact that he was no longer an independent power. In 1839 Wilayat Ali arrived in Hyderabad to preach accompanied by his wife, the daughter of a Hyderabadi nobleman. News of his missionary activities soon reached the court of the Nizam's younger brother Mubariz-ud-Daula, who went to hear him and was converted to his cause. It was said of his preaching that the women of the court, as they listened from behind their latticed screens of marble, were so overcome that they threw off their jewels and gold bangles and contributed them to his cause.

The East India Company was now preparing to launch its ultimately disastrous intervention in Afghanistan, with the intention of ousting the current ruler in Kabul and putting their man, Amir Shah Shuja, back on the throne he had lost many years earlier. For this purpose a vast contingent of troops drawn from the EICo's Bombay and Bengal Armies was assembled and given the grandiose title of the Army of the Indus. With so many of the Company's troops about to be committed in Afghanistan, Wilayat Ali and his allies in Hyderabad saw an opportunity too good to be missed. Plans were laid for a pan-Hindustan rising and carefully worded letters were sent out from Hyderabad to a number of rulers expected to offer support. In the event, the nawabs had too much to lose, and their responses were noncommittal. But whispers of Prince Mubariz-ud-Daula's plotting reached the ear of the British Resident at the court of the Nizam of Hyderabad, and he confronted the Nizam with clear evidence of his brother's treasonable activities. A secret trial was held and the prince was sentenced to spend the rest of his days confined in the melancholy grandeur of the ancient fortress of Golconda. Every suspected Wahhabi follower in Hyderabad was rounded up and either imprisoned or expelled.

To make matters worse, Nasiruddin and his army of Hindustani mujahedeen, having spent almost six years in limbo in Sind, now

got caught up in the British invasion of Afghanistan. Answering a
call to come to the aid of the Afghan defenders of the great citadel
of Ghazni, they arrived in time to play a heroic but futile role in its
defence. Fifty of their number survived, only to be taken in
chains before Shah Shuja, where, in the words of a historian of the
period, they were 'hacked to death with wanton barbarity by the
knives of his executioners'. For a second time, Wahhabism in
India appeared to have run its course.

The storming of Ghazni by the Army of the Indus was followed
by the occupation of Kabul and the installation of Shah Shuja as
Amir of Afghanistan. But then a fatal decision was taken to withdraw the bulk of the army, leading to the killing of the British
Resident and a number of his colleagues and the destruction of
the remaining British and Indian troops as they tried to make
their way out of the country. Six months later a self-proclaimed
Army of Retribution marched back up the Khyber to visit token
punishment on the Afghans before once more withdrawing to the
safety of Hindustan.

Whatever gloss they cared to put on it, the British received a
drubbing in Afghanistan, and the withdrawal of their troops acted
as a fresh spur to the Wahhabis. No sooner had the Army of
Retribution been disbanded than the Wahhabi faithful in the
Indian plains learned that their Hidden Imam in the mountains
had at last ended his self-imposed exile and was preparing to
resume personal command of the jihad from Sittana. It was
announced that letters had been received in Patna, written by
Syed Ahmad's first disciple Shah Muhammad Ismail but dictated
by his master. They summoned the faithful to join him in the
mountains of Buner so that the holy war might be resumed.
Those who were unable to come themselves were to participate
in the jihad by providing funds and food.

Whatever their origins – and the suspicion must be that they
were the work of Wilayat Ali – these letters had the desired

effect. The mystique of Syed Ahmad, both as martyr and as lost leader in waiting, had grown over the years and to many young men of faith he now came to be seen as a unique symbol of Islamic resistance and resurgence – very much as Osama bin Laden became in later years. Large numbers of mujahedeen volunteers responded to the call, among them a devout but unusually independent-minded mullah from Hyderabad named Maulvi Zain ul-Abdin, who had been converted to Wahhabism by Wilayat Ali during one of his visits to the city. Travelling across India in small parties to escape detection, Zain ul-Abdin and almost a thousand recruits from the Deccan made their way to Sittana to begin their military training. However, Zain ul-Abdin was determined to meet the Hidden Imam whose call he and his fellow Hyderabadis had answered. He demanded to see the Amir ul-Momineem and, after being repeatedly fobbed off with excuses, was finally led up into the mountains above the Hindustani camp to a point from where he and a number of other curious mujahedeen could make out a distant cave, at the entrance of which stood three figures dressed in white robes. These, he was told, were the Amir-ul-Momineen and the two disciples who attended to his daily needs. The spectators were then made to promise not to go any closer, because if they or anyone else did so the Hidden Imam would again disappear, and remain hidden from the sight of man for fourteen years.

Thrilled as he and the others were by this distant glimpse of their leader, Zain ul-Abdin found himself unable to contain his curiosity. Finally, he and a number of comrades bolder than the rest went back up into the mountains to take a closer look. They clambered right up to the cave and found, to their horror, that the three figures were nothing more than effigies. As Zain ul-Abdin later reported it, he examined the figure of the supposed imam 'and found that it was a goatskin stuffed with grass, which with the help of some pieces of wood, hair, etc. was made to resemble a man. The suppliant enquired from

Qasin Kazzab [Maulvi Qasim Panipati, the Wahhabi's caliph at Sittana] about this. He answered that it was true, but that the Imam Humam had performed a miracle, and appeared as a stuffed figure.'

Thoroughly outraged by this deception, Zain ul-Abdin promptly decamped from Sittana together with most of the thousand volunteers from Hyderabad. Thereafter he became a vociferous critic of the Wahhabis. 'This deception', he wrote, 'is only a small portion of the acts, idolatry and heresy of these people . . . Now the errors and falsity of these people are as clear as noon-day, and [by abandoning them] I have saved my soul from sin.' Other disillusioned volunteers also decamped from Sittana, claiming that they too had been deceived. They included a number of unemployed weavers from Bengal, priced out of the market by cheap imported cotton goods manufactured in the Lancashire mills. They had volunteered in the expectation that they would take up arms against the British, but on arrival at Sittana had been put to work as tailors, water-carriers, wood-cutters and mule-drivers. The camp's leaders had decreed that only the peasant farmers who made up the bulk of the recruits were fighting material, leaving the weavers and other artisans to fill the less congenial supporting roles.

From these and other accounts gathered as judicial evidence in later years, it is clear that the great majority of recruits who went to Sittana in order to fight were poor, illiterate and unskilled young men, while those who trained and indoctrinated them were almost invariably mullahs or maulvis, older and better-educated. The same pattern continues to this day.

In March 1849, following two fierce-fought wars against the Sikhs, the Punjab became a province of British India, administered for the British Government by the East India Company acting on the orders of a Governor-General in Calcutta and a Court of Directors in London. This was a time of innovation and change in

British India during which a great many reforms were introduced, including the promotion of education on English lines. In Britain Evangelical Christianity was on the rise and many of the civil and military officers who went out to India to make a career for themselves began increasingly to see it as their Christian duty to spread the good word. This increased religiosity went hand in hand with a growing sense of racial superiority, characterised by the absolute conviction of Herbert Edwardes, who stepped into Frederick Mackeson's boots as Commissioner of Peshawar in 1853 after his murder, that God had awarded India to Britain because 'England has made the greatest effort to preserve the Christian religion in its purest form'.

These reforms and changing attitudes led to increasing disaffection in many sections of Indian society. Muslims and Hindus began to feel that their religious customs were under threat, none more so than the infantry sepoys and cavalry *sowars* of the Bengal Army. A majority of the former were orthodox high-caste Hindu Brahmins and Rajputs, while a significant proportion of the latter were Muslim cavalrymen of Pathan–Afghan origin whose forebears had settled in Delhi and in Rohilkund, the fertile plains east of the Jumna. One such Muslim was a soldier named Sheikh HEDAYUT ALI, whose grandfather had joined the ranks of the Bengal Army in 1763 and had been followed in his turn by his son and grandsons. Hedayut Ali was later to prove his loyalty to the salt he had eaten, but in 1842, as an adolescent boy in barracks, he had watched the regiments return from the Afghan War to the military cantonment of Ferozepore, and had observed how discontented the soldiers had become:

> The Hindoo Sepoys who had returned from Cabul were
> not allowed by the Hindoostanees to touch the cooking
> utensils, being looked upon by them as outcastes . . . The
> Sepoys spoke that they [had] lost caste by going to Cabul,
> because, they said, they were obliged to wear skins of

animals, and because they could do there none of the acts prescribed by their religion in consequence of [the] intensity of the cold weather. The Moosulmen Sepoys also did not perform their work with loyalty, because, they said, the British Government forced them to fight with people professing the Islam creed, which is forbidden in the Koran. They also boasted among themselves, that they had always fired upwards and never took aim.

As well as the usual grumbles over pay, accommodation and promotion, the sepoys also felt themselves becoming increasingly distanced from their British officers. According to Shaik Hedayut Ali, the sense of comradeship that had once existed between the British officers and the Indians they commanded had all but disappeared.

The Wahhabis were able to turn such discontent to their advantage. Throughout the 1840s and early 1850s they continued to send their missionaries out into the towns, villages and military cantonments, preaching jihad and the imminent return of the Hidden Imam. To encourage jihadis to proceed to their mountain hideout, they printed and circulated notices declaring that it was incumbent on all true Muslims to do as the Prophet had done: 'At the present time in this country, *hijrat* is a stern duty,' reads part of a Wahhabi pamphlet from this time. 'Truly learned men have written this. Now he who forbids this, hear faithful, let him declare himself a slave to sensuality. He who, having gone away, returns leaving his conscience in the land of Islam and does not again depart hence, let him know that all his past services are in vain. Should he die without departing hence, he will in the end lose the way of salvation.' Other pamphlets spoke of the duty to wage holy war against the English, and on the traditions of the Prophet regarding jihad. The movement's debt to the founder of Wahhabism was explicitly acknowledged by its publication of a work variously entitled *Tawarikh Kaisar Rum* and *Misbah-us-Sari*, described as 'a history of Abdul Wahhab, his persecutions and wars against the Turkish apostates'.

The two Ali brothers, Maulvis Wilayat Ali and Inayat Ali, spearheaded the proselytising programme, both undertaking extended tours across the country. In April 1843 the Superintendent of Police of Murshidabad in Bengal reported that one Inayat Ali had been found acting in ways 'inimical to our government'. He was said to have used 'the topic of a religious war and the resurrection of Syed Ahmed as a pretext for calling for aid', and it was recommended that his movement should be watched. The Secretary to the Government of Bengal responded with a note that Government was 'disinclined to attach much importance to this preaching'. In 1847, as recorded earlier, the two Ali brothers were arrested in Hazara by Harry Lumsden, sent under custody to Patna and bound over to remain in the city for five years. Ignoring these restrictions, they continued to travel freely throughout northern India.

Meanwhile, another Ali on the Wahhabi Council in Patna, Yahya Ali, youngest son of Elahi Bux, was focusing his efforts on restructuring the organisation. Under his aegis, which lasted right through into the mid-1860s, the Path of Muhammad movement became increasingly sophisticated and increasingly covert. As evidenced in testimony presented in trials two decades later, it continued to expand its organisation until a network of interlinked provincial, regional and district groups had been established across much of Bengal, Bihar, the North-West Provinces and Punjab – all unknown to the authorities.

A district network was usually initiated by a Wahhabi missionary seeking out a suitable base where he could establish himself, often marrying into the local Muslim community. He then set himself up as a schoolmaster or religious teacher and, having gained a following in the district, appointed three lay figures to act as tax-gatherer, postmaster and general manager. Once established, these four local representatives acted

independently of each other: the mullah taught and proselyt-
ised, the tax collector gathered funds, the postmaster arranged
the transmission of messages and the movement of recruits, and
the general manager co-ordinated. By this compartmentalising
of duties the Wahhabis avoided the attentions of the British
authorities. A mullah might be called before the district magistrate to account for his seditious preaching, but was almost
always allowed to carry on because he appeared to be working in
isolation. As Sir William Hunter put it, 'An English Magistrate in
India had all the reluctance of a Prefect of the Augustan Empire
to intermeddle with the various beliefs and superstitions of the
races over whom he rules. Treason can thus safely walk under a
religious habit.'

Every local group was linked to Patna through a number of
regional centres, while Patna itself was linked to the frontier by
the movement's own *dak* or posting system of safe houses, which
enabled messengers, supplies and recruits to be moved up and
down the line in secrecy and safety. To maintain confidentiality
the movement adopted a number of security measures. Its leading
members all used aliases, its communications were so written as to
appear to be innocuous business letters, and a code was devised
for key words. God was always spoken of as the *mukhtar* or 'agent',
jihad was termed a 'lawsuit', recruits for jihad were called variously *beoparis* (merchants), *musafirs* (travellers) or *khitmutgars*
(servants), bands of recruits being sent up the line were called
kafilas (caravans), money orders were referred to as 'white stones',
money as 'books' or 'merchandise', gold coinage as 'rosaries of
red beads', and the coins themselves as 'large Delhi gold-
embroidered shoes' or 'large red birds'.

During this period of expansion the house and attached caravanserai of Shah Muhammad Husain's family in Sadiqpore Lane
in Patna was greatly enlarged and fortified. A mosque was built in
its inner courtyard, with a madrassah attached. It was given the
code name of *chota godown* or small warehouse, while the moun-

tain camp up at Sittana was henceforward referred to as the *burra godown* or big warehouse.

Within a decade the Wahhabi movement in India was transformed from a minority preaching sect into a highly effective organisation for Islamic revival and revolution, with branches throughout northern India and the support of a large popular constituency drawn mainly from the labouring classes. It was an extraordinary achievement, one that even its most trenchant critic was forced to acknowledge. 'Indefatigable as missionaries,' wrote William Hunter in his polemic *Our Indian Mussulmans*, 'careless of themselves, blameless in their lives, supremely skilful in organising a permanent system for supplying money and recruits, the Patna Caliphs stand forth as the types and exemplars of the Sect. Much of their teaching was faultless, and it had been given to them to stir up thousands of their countrymen to a purer life and truer conception of the Almighty.'

In February 1850 Inayat Ali was again arrested for preaching sedition in Bengal. He absconded and fled to Patna, where he was re-arrested, the British magistrate noting that this was the second time he had broken the terms of the original order requiring him to keep the peace. Released on a bond of a thousand rupees, he concluded nevertheless that the authorities were on to him. He left secretly for Sittana to assume military leadership of the burra godown as its amir. Towards the end of that same year his elder brother Wilayat Ali decided that the time had come when he too should make his retreat. In December he appointed Farhat Husain to be caliph in his absence, and left him in charge of the chota godown at Patna. He then set out to join his brother in the mountains, accompanied by his family and an entourage that included Yahya Ali and his two younger brothers. Yahya Ali's responsibilities were taken over by his brother Ahmadullah, oldest of the four sons of Elahi Bux.

The party wintered in Delhi, where Maulvi Wilayat Ali was

invited by the Emperor, Bahadur Shah, to deliver a sermon
before him in the Red Fort's famous Hall of Public Audience.
According to court protocol, preachers avoided controversial subjects in the presence of the last of the Mughals, but Wilayat Ali,
in line with Wahhabi teaching, regarded the Emperor as an apostate for having submitted to the authority of the British.
Accordingly, he launched into a fiery speech on the pains of hell
awaiting those who failed to heed the commands of God.
Midway through his sermon the Emperor interrupted him to
declaim some verses he had composed on the transitory nature
of life. The maulvi's response was to recite a verse from the
Quran criticising those who interrupted sermons. Despite this
rebuke and the maulvi's breach of protocol, the Emperor enter-
tained his guest to a magnificent banquet and invited him to
stay at the Red Fort. However, the British Resident at Delhi was
also present at the Emperor's audience, and he now began to
question Wilayat Ali so closely about his background and his
intended movements that the maulvi grew alarmed. Making his
excuses, he led his entourage out of the fort and left the city as
soon as he could.

Shortly afterwards the two Ali brothers met by arrangement in
Ludhiana and continued their withdrawal from the domain of
enmity together, reaching Sittana early in 1851. Only once on
their journey through the Punjab did the local authorities attempt
to stop their progress, and even then they were soon allowed to
continue – after receiving a personal apology from the Deputy
Commissioner of Peshawar.

The two brothers had not been long established in Sittana
when it became clear that they differed on how the jihad was
now to be prosecuted. Officially the dead Syed Ahmad was the
movement's imam and amir but as long as he remained hidden
the two brothers shared these two roles between them, Wilayat
Ali as imam and Inayat Ali as amir. The problem was that the
former believed they should wait until the movement had gained

The British prepare to invade Afghanistan for the third time: a fanciful engraving from the *Illustrated London News* in November 1878 as British and Indian troops gathered to launch three armies into Afghanistan. Pathan and Afghan hostility was largely due to fears of British occupation and the threat to their religion (Illustrated London News)

Pathans in ambush: an early lithograph from the 1840s by Lieutenant James
Rattray, from his *Costumes of the Various Tribes of Afghaunistan* (British Library)

Elephant-drawn artillery and commissariat column pass a mosque in
Peshawar city: an engraving from 1878 (Illustrated London News)

'Abdallah Ebn-Souhoud, Chief of the Wahabys, beheaded at Constantinople in 1819': an engraving of the captured Wahhabi Emir Abdullah ibn Saud, from Sir Harford Jones Brydges' *Account of the Transactions of His Majesty's Mission to the Court of Persia* (British Library)

Four armed Bedouin on horseback *c.* 1900 (George Eastman House)

Maulvies or learned teachers of religion in the courtyard of an old-style madrassah, northern India, late nineteenth century (Charles Allen)

A street in Patna city showing Fakir Dowlah's mosque: a pen and ink sketch drawn in 1824 by Sir Charles D'Oyly of the Bengal Civil Service (Oriental and India Office Collection, British Library)

'The Warning or the "inoffensive Wahabee gentlemen"': William Tayler's caption to his cartoon, which shows Sir Frederick Halliday ('the Bengal Giant') racquet in hand, restraining William Tayler ('the Behar Chicken') from attacking the three Wahhabi mullahs he had interned, Maulvi Ahmadullah in the centre (Oriental and India Office Collection, British Library)

Another of William Tayler's cartoons, drawn by him in 1857 after his dismissal, captioned 'Lootf Ali's release' and 'Martyred Victim of the Commissioner's Cruelty'. The gold-braided Lieutenant-Governor Sir Frederick Halliday watches as Tayler's three leading critics in Patna (from left to right, Messrs Elliott, Farquharson and Samuells) come to the aid of one of the suspected rebels detained by Tayler (Oriental and India Office Collection, British Library)

A. Original position of the British force in the Umbeylah Pass.
B. Eagle's Nest picket.   C. Crag picket.
C. D. Front of Chamberlain's second position, 18th Nov.r
E. Scene of General Garvock's victory, 15th Dec.r
L. Laloo.   U. Umbeylah.   K. Kooria.   H. Bonair.

'The Umbeylah Pass and Chumlah Valley': the scene of the Ambeyla Campaign disaster of 1863. The Wahhabi stronghold of Malka was sited on the distant mountain peak at the head of the valley. A sketch by Major John Adye, reproduced in his book *Sitana: A Mountain Campaign*

'Storming the heights of Laloo, 15 December 1863': the final engagement of the Ambeyla Campaign: a sketch by Major John Adye, reproduced in Lord Roberts, *Forty-One Years in India*, 1897

Saiyyeds of the Black Mountains, drawn by Lockwood Kipling of Lahore, father of Rudyard Kipling. The Saiyyeds provided a haven for the Hindustani Fanatics and three expeditions were mounted in the 1880s to expel them from the Black Mountains (Sue Farrington)

The banners of jihad: a band of ghazis or 'religious fanatics' advance towards their enemy waving banners, banging drums and firing their jezails in the air. A watercolour by Lieutenant Dixon, 16th Lancers, 1898 (Sue Farrington)

The murdered Viceroy, Lord Mayo, 1872. His public declaration that he would destroy the Wahhabis made him a target for assassination

(Illustrated London News)

Shere Ali Khan, assassin of the Viceroy Lord Mayo, photographed in chains prior to his hanging. Although it was never proved, Shere Ali was widely believed to have been put up to it by the Wahhabis in revenge for Lord Mayo's persecution of their cult

(The Andaman Association)

more support, while the latter saw it as their religious duty to resume Syed Ahmad's jihad without further delay. Inayat Ali was very different from his brother, in both appearance and personality. He was physically taller and stronger, he possessed a violent temper, and he was a man of action rather than a thinker. It is said of him that he bore a great hatred of the British. Having assumed leadership of the camp a year before the arrival of his elder brother, he may well have been reluctant to relinquish any authority – but he also needed Wilayat Ali's permission as imam to commence jihad. So strained did relations between the two become that Inayat Ali finally left Sittana to set up his own camp at Mangalthana, deeper and higher in the Mahabun Mountain massif. Here he built a stone fort on land donated to him by Sayyed Akbar Shah, leader of the Saiyyed clan at Sittana and the late Syed Ahmad's old patron and admirer.

Since Syed Ahmad's demise a new political phenomenon had appeared in the mountains of Swat and Buner in the person of the Akhund of Swat, who was none other than Abdul Ghaffur, the saintly hermit who had been expelled from the mountains after his unwise intervention in Syed Ahmad's vendetta against a local chieftain. In 1834, at the age of forty, Abdul Ghaffur had returned to Swat in triumph as an acknowledged man of God and had been accorded the local title of *Akhund* or saint. Since then he had become increasingly influential as the religious leader of the mountain Yusufzai, and as a peacemaker. In 1850, in an attempt to bring an end to the inveterate feuding among the tribes, he had anointed Sayyed Akbar Shah as padshah and leader of the law (*amir-e-sharia*), effectively making him king of the Swatis and Bunerwals.

Although a Naqshbandi Sufi, the Akhund was resolutely opposed to the violent and exclusive creed of the Hindustani Wahhabis, which makes it hard to understand why he should have chosen the patron of the Hindustani Fanatics to be padshah. According to Abdul Ghaffur's grandson, Miangul Abdul

Wadud Badshah Sahib, the Akhund acted in response to a call from the tribes for a leader who would prevent the British from taking them over. To have selected a Pathan would have led to inter-tribal jealousy, whereas Sayyed Akbar Shah was both a Saiyyid and greatly respected for his leadership in the first insurrection against the Sikhs back in 1823 – to say nothing of his subsequent support for Syed Ahmad in his fatal campaign against the same enemy in 1830–1. So Sayyed Akbar Shah had been made king of Swat in the hope that he would command respect from all sides.

However, the effect of the Akhund's appointment of a king from the Saiyyed clan had one consequence that he may not have anticipated, for it gave further credence to the Wahhabi claim that here in the mountains of Swat was the dar ul-Islam from which the great jihad should be launched. Yet at the same time the Akhund's moderating influence over Sayyed Akbar Shah acted as a brake on the Hindustanis' warlike ambitions – until the death from natural causes of Wilayat Ali at Sittana in the late autumn of 1852. This event coincided with Lord Dalhousie's writing of his Second Minute on the Wahabees, in which he declared the Hindustani Camp at Sittana to be insignificant and best left alone.

Wilayat Ali's death left his brother Inayat Ali free to act as he judged fit. He at once descended on Sittana, assumed the imamship of the Fanatic Camp and ordered the Hindustanis on to the offensive – their first aggressive act being the seizing of the fort at Kotla from the Khan of Amb.

Despite the alarms raised in Patna a year earlier by the discovery of Inayat Ali's letters, the Wahhabi network was still untouched. In concert with his colleagues at the chota godown the movement's new amir-cum-imam now stepped up his plans for the great jihad against the British. As the Bengal magistrate James O'Kinealy later put it: 'He laboured to organise his followers and fire them with a hatred of the English *Kafirs*. The crescentaders [Muslim jihadis] even drilled daily, sometimes twice a day, and on parade were taught to recite songs extolling the glories of *jihad*, and on Fridays after the *jumma* prayers they listened to sermons descriptive of the joys of paradise, and exhorting them to wait patiently until the time appointed for the subjugation of British India would arrive.'

News of the Wahhabi build-up in Sittana eventually reached the ears of the British authorities in Peshawar and Lahore, who complained to Lord Dalhousie that the fanatics were 'trying to seduce poor and ignorant Mohammadens to join them, by false accounts of security and abundance'. The Governor-General's response was to issue an amnesty. The Hindustani Fanatics at Sittana were given one month to turn themselves in. If they did so, they would be given ten rupees each to cover their expenses and a safe-conduct back to their homes. If, however, they failed to surrender, they could expect no mercy: 'After this notice any Hindustani or other British subject found in arms, or otherwise attached to the Moulvis, will be treated as a *Moofsid* [enemy], and the least punishment he will receive will be three years on the road in irons. This circular is issued in mercy to the poor and ignorant, who have been deluded. Woe to those who neglect the warning! Their blood will be upon their own heads.'

The Wahhabis' response to Lord Dalhousie's amnesty was a redoubling of their propaganda campaign. Large numbers of printed prophecies and ballads now began to circulate in Delhi and other towns in Upper Hindustan. One of these was the *Ode of Niyamatulla*, purportedly written in the twelfth century, which concluded with the following lines:

> Then the Nazarenes will take all Hindustan.
> They will reign for a hundred years.
> There will be a great oppression in their reign.
> For their destruction there will be a King in the West.
> The King will proclaim a war against the Nazarenes.
> And in the war a great many people will be killed.

The King of the West will be victorious by the force
of the sword in a holy war.
And the followers of Jesus will be defeated . . .
In 570 AH [AD 1174-5] this ode is composed.
In 1270 AH [AD 1853-4] the King of the West will
appear.

This dating clearly demonstrates that Inayat Ali planned to launch
his great jihad against the British in India in the cold weather
months of 1853–4. That he failed to do so was almost certainly a
result of the disruption caused by Colonel Mackeson's raid in
January 1853 and the Hindustanis' humiliating expulsion from
Sittana (as described in the Introduction).

The consequence of Mackeson's raid was that the jihad had to
be rescheduled and the prophecies revised. Inayat Ali knew now
that he had found an enemy. Colonel Mackeson's assassination
nine months later can be seen as Inayat Ali's revenge, and the
Hindustani Fanatics' first telling blow against the hated Nazarenes.

British rule in northern India had officially begun in 1765, when
the East India Company received a royal order from the Mughal
emperor appointing it *Diwan* or local administrator of Bengal,
Bihar and Orissa. However, the popular understanding was that
the *Nasrani Raj* dated from the battle of Plassey, fought in Bengal
on 23 June 1757. It now began to be put about that British rule in
India would last for a hundred years and no more. Because it had
begun in June 1757, so it would end in June 1857, the centenary
of Plassey.

In 1855 printed copies of the Wahhabis' war song *Risala Jihad*
(The Army of Holy War) began circulating in the streets of Delhi
along with rumours of a great awakening. Such rumours and
prophecies fell on receptive ears. When asked to explain why his
fellow Muslims had joined in the Sepoy Mutiny, the soldier Shaik
Hedayut Ali had this to say:

It is said in the Koran that the British administration will once extend as far as Mecca and Medina, after which the Imam Mahdee will be born and wrest the kingdom from them. But some of the Moulvies have declared that the British dominion in India will continue for one century, and then disturbances will arise in the land. The Moosulmen learning this, imagined in their ignorance that the British administration was now to go away, and they therefore joined the Sepoys in the mutiny.

5

The Early Summer of 1857

The tenets originally professed by the Wahabees have
been described as a Mahomedan Puritanism joined to a
Bedouin Phylarchy, in which the great chief is both the
political and religious leader of the nation . . . With the
Soonnees the Wahabees are on terms of tolerable agreement, though differing on certain points, but from the
Sheahs, they differ radically, and their hatred, like all
religious hatred, is bitter and intolerant. But the most
striking characteristic of the Wahabee sect, and that
which principally concerns this narrative, is the entire
subservience which they yield to the Peer, or spiritual
guide.

William Tayler, *Our Crisis: Or Three Months at Patna
during the Insurrection of 1857*, 1858

The ancient city of Patna extends for several miles along the
southern bank of the Ganges some four hundred miles upstream
from Calcutta and a hundred and fifty miles short of Benares. In
the summer of 1857 a railway line linking these three cities was in

the process of being laid, but until its completion the only comfortable way to travel up-country was by river. The less comfortable alternatives were to travel by palanquin, carried on the shoulders of relays of porters, or to go by *dak*, a coach-staging system which involved travellers staying overnight in dak-bungalows.

Like most large towns in northern India with a British presence, Patna in 1857 was divided into three areas: the old city, which the British knew as the native town, with a population of three hundred thousand predominantly Muslim inhabitants; the civil station laid out on its western outskirts, consisting of government offices and the homes of the city's small population of European 'civilians' in government employ; and, further west again, the military cantonment of Dinapore, with a garrison of three regiments of Bengal Native Infantry together with one British infantry regiment. Patna was the collection centre for Bengal's most important cash-crop, opium, and the headquarters of a region of local government known as the West Bihar Division, an area comparable in size and shape to Ireland, made up of six sub-divisions or districts. Each of these districts was administered by a British member of the Bengal Civil Service known as a Collector, whose duties included acting as the local magistrate, supported by a deputy who was usually a learned Muslim. The collectors reported to the Commissioner, based in Patna, who was himself supported by a junior assistant and a city magistrate. The division also had its own sessions judge, also based in Patna, to whom all judgments by the district magistrates were referred. In all, the division's administrative and judicial systems were in the hands of scarcely more than a dozen Europeans. To maintain law and order they could call upon a locally raised police force known as the Nujeebs and, in times of civil disturbance, upon the troops stationed at Dinapore.

This was the region that became the charge of William Tayler when he was appointed Commissioner of Patna in April 1855.

Bill Tayler was then aged forty-seven and, in the words of a later champion, 'in the prime of life ... a gentleman and a scholar, possessing great natural abilities which he had lost no opportunity of cultivating, an elegant mind, and a large fund of common sense'. Before his commissionership Tayler had spent over a quarter of a century in Bengal in the service of the East India Company. As he worked his way up the civil service ladder in a variety of administrative posts he had shown himself to be a good all-rounder. But he was not the most tactful of men, and in the course of his career he had made a powerful enemy of a fellow member of the Bengal Civil Service, his senior by two years. This was Frederick James Halliday, whose talent for secretariat work had taken him up the promotional ladder with remarkable speed. By the age of thirty Halliday had secured his first secretary-ship, and within a decade had become the *éminence grise* of the Government of Bengal, so much so that it was said of him that he 'exercised all the powers, though not bearing the responsi-bilities, of Governor'. Not for nothing had he acquired the nicknames the Big Fiddle and the Bengal Giant. As Secretary to the Home Department, it was Frederick Halliday who guided Lord Dalhousie's hand and pen during the first six of his eight years as Governor-General. Then in May 1854 Bengal ceased to be a presidency under the direct control of the Governor-General of India and became a province under a lieutenant-governor. Halliday became its first Lieutenant-Governor.

The contrast between Tayler and Halliday could hardly have been greater: the one a small man of slight physique, with wide-ranging interests extending from poetry and sketching to field sports and antiquarian collecting; the other a big man in every sense, described by Buckland in his *Dictionary of Indian Biography* as 'of lofty stature and splendid physique ... the embodiment of great power, an impression which was strengthened by whatever he said or wrote'. Halliday was single-minded and ambitious, causing even his great admirer Lord Dalhousie to remark in private that 'he has so managed that I believe he has not in Bengal a single influential friend but myself'. He was also a bully, and never hesitated to use his forceful personality to get what he wanted. Tayler and Halliday had first come into conflict when the latter blocked Tayler's appointment to a post already allocated to him and gave it to his own choice, a Mr Edward Samuells. Later there had been a second brush when Halliday had dismissed Tayler's allegations that the police in his district were conniving with local robbers to conceal their crimes. A third and more serious difference between the two men occurred in April 1855, soon after Bill Tayler's appointment as Commissioner of Patna, when he wrote to warn the Government of Bengal that reforms being pushed through by Halliday were contributing to local unrest: 'I brought to the notice of Government . . . that there was a deep and growing dissatisfaction and excitement throughout Behar, particularly among the Mahomedans, arising from the suspicions with which several measures of the Bengal Government, and especially those connected with education, were contemplated.'

Among all sections of the populace there were deep-rooted fears that Government was interfering in their caste-practices and religion, but at the back of Tayler's mind was the Wahhabi conspiracy uncovered in Patna by his predecessors in 1852, which had resulted in the two dismissive Minutes from Lord Dalhousie. At the time of the writing of the second of these, Frederick Halliday was on home leave. However, as Secretary to the Home Department he had undoubtedly played a guiding role in the drafting of the first. Now, three years on, all those Wahhabis named as conspirators in the original reports dismissed by Dalhousie were still in residence behind the high walls of their caravanserai at Sadiqpore, and as active as ever.

One year later the Government of India added further fuel to the general discontent when Lord Dalhousie, as his last act before leaving India in 1856, sent in troops to annexe the Kingdom of

Oude on the grounds of 'barbarous government'. Oude was the last surviving Muslim kingdom in northern Hindustan, and its swallowing-up by the East India Company angered Muslims and Hindus alike. The annexation also brought many demobilised sepoys from Oude to Patna in search of new employment, exacerbating the tension in a city that was already, in Tayler's view, 'a very sink of disaffection and intrigue'.

To add further to Tayler's worries, he had on his doorstep a powerful Rajput aristocrat by the name of Kumar Singh of Jagdishpur. The elderly Raja Kumar Singh owned extensive estates in Shahabad district west of Patna but had become so debt-ridden that the Bengal Government's board of revenue had stepped in to manage his affairs on behalf of his creditors. Early in 1857 Halliday ordered the board of revenue to stop bailing out Kumar Singh, effectively ruining him. Up to this point Kumar Singh had been a good friend to Bill Tayler and, for all his troubles, had always professed his loyalty to the British Raj. Although required to carry out the order against Kumar Singh, Tayler wrote to Halliday to protest, and to warn him that this move would alienate Kumar Singh and his many fellow Rajputs in the region. Halliday's response was to initiate proceedings to have the troublesome commissioner transferred down-country to Burdwan.

In January 1857 the first of a series of disturbances occurred among the sepoys at the military depot of Barrackpore outside Calcutta, fed by rumours that new cartridges being introduced to the infantry were greased with cow and pork fat. Despite assurances from Halliday and from Lord Dalhousie's successor as Governor-General, Lord Canning, that the Government would continue to treat 'the religious feelings of all its servants, of every creed, with respect', these rumours spread up-country.

A year earlier the sepoy Hedayut Ali had transferred from the regiment in which he and several of his brothers were serving, the 8th Bengal Native Infantry, based in Dinapore, to join a new Sikh

Bengal Police Battalion being raised in Lahore by a battle-hardened frontiersman named Captain Thomas Rattray. In January 1857 Rattray's Sikhs began the long march south to Calcutta to take up their new responsibilities in Bengal. Riding at their head beside Rattray-Saheb as his second in command was Hedayut Ali, now promoted to *subedar*, the most senior Indian officer in the battalion. In the months that followed these two strong-minded men became a formidable double act. 'A rare specimen of an Oriental soldier' was how one of their admirers chose to describe Subedar Hedayut Ali. 'His physique was splendid, and the sight of him, with his drawn sword, running at the head of the Sikhs by the side of Colonel Rattray, was one the enemy never cared to stay very long to contemplate.'

On the road to Calcutta the Sikh column met units from the Bengal Army going in the opposite direction, and Hedayut Ali learned from them that the troops in Barrackpore were on the verge of mutiny: 'They spoke to our men of the new cartridges, as having been made up with the fat of cows and pigs, and that in consequence of these cartridges, the Sepoys of Barrackpore were ready to make a disturbance, and that the chief people of Calcutta and Barrackpore were promising to aid them with money.' Hedayut Ali had no doubts as to where his own loyalties lay: 'I have my home always with my Regiment, and know none for my patron except Government. It was for this reason that when the country began to rise against Government, I informed my Commanding Officer with all the circumstances connected with this insurrection.' He went directly to Rattray, recounted everything he had heard – and was told that he must be mistaken. In mid-February the Sikh battalion halted at Ranigunge, 120 miles short of Calcutta, where the subedar learned from sepoys of the infantry regiment stationed there that plans were now well advanced for the mutiny at Barrackpore, and they themselves were standing by to join in. This time Rattray believed Hedayut Ali, and immediately spoke to the commanding

officer concerned. The colonel responded just as Rattray had earlier, but the latter was now sufficiently troubed to send forward a
written report to the military authorities in Calcutta.

At this juncture Rattray's Sikhs received fresh orders: to report
to Arrah, the headquarters of the Shahabad district west of Patna.
Rattray and Hedayut Ali duly turned their men about and
marched back the way they had come, reaching the little country
station of Arrah in late February 1857. Here all the bazaar talk was
of the indignities heaped on their local raja, the elderly landowner
Kumar Singh, who was said to be so angry with Government that
he was plotting an uprising. This, too, was duly passed on to
Captain Rattray, who informed Shahabad's twenty-five-year-old
Collector and magistrate, Herewald Crauford Wake. The obser-
vant Mr Wake was well aware of the danger Kumar Singh now
presented, and in passing on Rattray's information to William
Tayler in Patna added that 'should these districts be ever the
scene of a serious outbreak, he [Kumar Singh] may well take it
into his head that it is time to strike a blow for his own interests,
and his feudal influence is such as to render him exceedingly
dangerous in such an event'.

A month later, on 29 March, a sepoy ran amok on the parade-
ground at Barrackpore, and in doing so pre-empted a general
mutiny planned for June. After two hangings and the disbanding
of one regiment the incident was considered closed. Governor-
General Lord Canning professed himself 'rather pleased with the
way in which it has been dealt with' and his Home Secretary
wrote to reassure Tayler and other local officials that it had been
no more than a 'passing and groundless panic'.

Letters and other papers seized during the suppression of what
the British termed the Sepoy or Indian Mutiny of 1857 show that
there was no overarching conspiracy to free India from a foreign
yoke. The uprising was sepoy-led and rose out of a combination of
grievances among the troops. But first among these grievances
were religious fears, fuelled in part by the insensitivity of the

British Government in India but also stoked and fanned by the activities of religious zealots travelling from one military base to another. Among the latter, the Wahhabis can be counted in a class of their own, due to the size of their network and the extent of their propagandising. However, they were far from alone in wishing to see an end to British rule in Hindustan. In Lucknow, former capital of the annexed Kingdom of Oude, there was widespread support for the restoration of the deposed Nawab – support that extended to large numbers of sepoys and sowars in the Bengal Army, many of whom were originally from Oude. In and around Delhi, too, there were just as many who wished to see the old emperor restored to his former glory, and an end to the humiliations heaped on him by the British. But in Delhi the links with the army were fewer, and the feebleness and irresolution of Emperor Bahadur Shah – eighty-two years old, part-Rajput by blood, a Sufi by faith and an opium addict – prevented the plotting from developing much beyond the stage of wishful thinking. Nevertheless, in Patna, Lucknow, Delhi and elsewhere groups of idealists sought the overthrow of the Company Raj and exchanged cautiously-worded correspondence.

Had these various conspirators acted together, the outcome of the 1857 Mutiny would have been very different. That they failed to do so was in some measure due to the Wahhabis, who alone had a well-thought-out plan to overthrow the British and the links to co-ordinate its execution. But theirs was a plan that called for an exclusively Sunni Muslim jihad, and for the strike against the British to come not from a city in Hindustan but from Sittana, and in alliance with the Afghan border tribes. The surviving evidence suggests that the Wahhabi council in Patna, under the leadership of Muhammad Hussain as the movement's senior imam, with Ahmadullah, eldest son of Elahi Bux, acting as his counsellor, held themselves aloof when approached by other non-Wahhabi conspirators from Lucknow.

On Sunday 10 May 1857 the long-awaited cataclysm finally

burst at Meerut, with mobs of soldiers and civilians rampaging through the military cantonment, firing the bungalows and killing every European they encountered. According to the survivors, the shouts most commonly heard were 'Deen! Deen!' ('The Way! The Way!') and 'Allah-i-Allah! Mare Feringhee!' ('Kill the British'). No one among the British officers took charge and the mutineers were allowed to set out for Delhi unhindered, leaving fifty dead in their wake. Despite the presence in Meerut of a large British force, the military commander failed to order a pursuit and initially refused even to allow a messenger to ride to Delhi with a warning. The result was that next morning the mutineers' cavalry rode into the city unopposed, again murdered every European they encountered, and forced Emperor Bahadur Shah to receive them with the demand that 'unless you, the King, join us, we are all dead men'. Although the emperor's sons were given nominal command of the rebel units it was the mutinous regiments' own Indian officers – the subedars, *risaldars* and *jemadars* – who gave the orders, including the fatal instruction to murder their European and Christian prisoners.

Garbled telegrams sent up and down the line before the wires were cut meant that the news of the fall of Delhi to the mutineers was received in all the larger stations of Hindustan within thirty-six hours of the uprising. Remarkably, the mutiny itself spread almost as quickly, again pointing, if not to co-ordination among the plotters, at least to well-established lines of communication.

As soon as news of the outbreak had been confirmed, emergency councils were held in divisional headquarters all over upper Hindustan and the Punjab. In Patna this meeting took place at the home of the commander of the locally recruited police battalion, the Nujeebs. Here the first signs of a serious split among the Europeans in Patna appeared when the sessions judge, Mr Farquharson, proposed that they all should move at once to the safety of the military cantonment of Dinapore, taking the station treasury with them. This was intemperately dismissed by

Commissioner Tayler on the grounds that it would induce a 'fatal panic'. He then made a vigorous address to all the Europeans present, telling them to stand firm, advice that was 'applauded to the echo'. Mr Farquharson's response was to abandon his bungalow and move himself and his family into the opium godown in the city, where he was joined by the Government's Opium Agent, Mr Garrett, who happened to be the brother-in-law of the Lieutenant-Governor of Bengal, Frederick Halliday. For the next two weeks these two and Mr Garrett's assistant, Dr Lyell, were, in Tayler's words, 'incessant in their representations of the danger anticipated'. Their alarm communicated itself to others, leading the workmen employed on building the new railway to down tools and join them in their refuge. Garrett then refused Tayler permission to store in his godown money brought in from the district treasuries of the two nearest district headquarters, Arrah and Chuprah, on the grounds that this would increase the danger to those who were sheltering there. He afterwards informed his brother-in-law Frederick Halliday that he had offered to hold the treasure, but that Mr Tayler had refused his help.

During this confused early phase of the Mutiny the Commissioner did what he thought necessary to maintain order in the division, while at the same time gathering as much intelligence as possible – a process greatly aided by the support of Patna's deputy magistrate, Dewan MOWLA BAKSH. From Mowla Baksh and a number of petitions sent in anonymously Tayler learned that 'conferences were held at night, both in mosques, and private houses, though with such secrecy and cunning that proof or capture was impossible. Particular individuals were named again and again by different parties, who concealed their names, but uttered emphatic warnings.' It seemed quite clear to him that 'mischief of some sort was brewing' and that it came from three separate quarters: 'Firstly, from the Wahabees of the city and the neighbourhood. Secondly, from the Lucknow immigrants and partisans . . . Thirdly, from the thieves and scoundrels of the city.' Of the three, Tayler judged the Wahhabis to present the most serious threat, concentrated in the persons of their leaders – 'several well-known Moulvees of this sect, little shrivelled skin-dried men, of contemptible appearance, and plain manners, but holding undisputed sway over a crowd of tailors, butchers, and low-born followers of every description'. Without hard information Tayler felt unable to act, but he quietly set about turning the house and grounds of his official residence into a fortified defensive position.

Late on 7 June Tayler received the news he had been dreading, contained in a letter handed in by one of the Nujeeb policemen. It had come from the nearby military cantonment of Dinapore and it spoke of the sepoys and the Nujeebs as being of *ek-dil* or 'one heart'. It gave notice that the three Bengal Native Infantry regiments stationed at Dinapore planned to rise against their officers that very night, and instructed that when this happened the Nujeeb police battalion should seize the Patna treasury.

Tayler at once implemented the emergency plans he had prepared, sending warning messages to each of his six district headquarters and summoning Captain Rattray to bring his Sikhs in from Arrah. Further summonses went out to every European in Patna telling them to come at once to his residence with as much food and bedding as they and their servants could carry. 'In less than an hour,' Tayler recorded a year later, 'almost every man, woman and child were hurrying helter skelter to our house, followed by a phalanx of beds, clothes, pillows, mattresses and other domestic impedimenta.'

Tayler was a good story-teller and his account of what followed, afterwards published as *Our Crisis; Or Three Months at Patna during the Insurrection of 1857*, is as lively as the best of the many personal narratives of the Mutiny. 'It was a lovely night,' he wrote of this first day of their crisis, 'and by the time that all were assembled, the moon had risen, and the grounds and garden were lit almost as day.' Every room in his house was filled with occupants:

In one, a bevy of children of every size, age and
disposition, the sleepy, the cross, the silent and the
squalling, were stretched in every conceivable attitude on
the floor; in another a group of nervous ladies scarcely
knowing what to apprehend; strange Ayahs [maidservants]
were stealing to and fro with noiseless step, and bearing
unintelligible bundles; agitated gentlemen, cool
gentlemen, and fussy gentlemen, gentlemen with guns and
swords, and gentlemen without guns and swords, were
holding consultation in groups; outside the house, a body
of the Nujeebs, or local Police Battalion were assembled
under the command of Major Nation, while a small party of
Holmes's Troopers were ready mounted near the door; the
rattling of carriages, the screaming of children, men's
hoarse voices, servants shouting – all formed on one side of
the house a Babel of confusion.

Just before dawn the tramp of marching feet was heard and the
alarm was sounded, but it turned out to be Rattray's Sikhs. Their
march had taken them past the military lines at Dinapore, where
they had been taunted by the sepoys, 'accused of being rene-
gades to their faith, and asked whether they intended to fight for
the "kafir", or for their "deen"'. However, the Sikh battalion's
unexpected appearance had also unnerved the conspirators
among the sepoys, to the extent that they failed to carry out their
planned uprising. The Sikhs took up positions outside the
Commissioner's compound and began to patrol through the city.
The immediate crisis appeared to be over.

The one action that Tayler had failed to take was to inform the
Lieutenant-Governor of Bengal, Frederick Halliday, of his plans.
However, first thing on the morning of 8 June he wrote a report of
the steps he had taken. Since the telegraph line to Calcutta was
operating only intermittently, he sent this despatch by rider. He
then himself rode over to Dinapore accompanied by Rattray and

his subedar, Hedayut Ali, to call on Major-General George Lloyd, the commander of the Dinapore cantonment. Lloyd had spent all his adult life in a sepoy regiment. In the words of the first historian of the Indian Mutiny, he 'had witnessed the fidelity of the native soldier under trying and difficult circumstances, and, fortified by the opinion of the several commandants of regiments, he still clung to his belief in their loyalty'. Despite the evidence of the seized correspondence, Lloyd had just reported to Halliday that his regiments were quiet and would remain so 'unless some great temptation or excitement should assail them'. He now informed Tayler and Rattray that their fears were groundless, and that the three Bengal Native Infantry regiments under his command were beyond suspicion. One of these three corps was Hedayut Ali's old regiment, the 8th BNI, in which no fewer than four of his younger brothers were still serving. When he called in on them to renew old acquaintances he found the atmosphere highly charged, and was warned that if he stayed overnight in Dinapore he would pay for it with his life.

The Sikhs guarding the civil lines in Patna now came under intense pressure to desert. 'The Mahomedans who came to our regiment', recorded Hedayut Ali, 'used to say "Thanks be to God that our king has been reinstated on the throne of Delhi." When I heard them speak so, I immediately informed my Major and Mr W. Tayler, the Commissioner ... I then ordered some of the sepoys that if any Hindoo or Mahomedan spoke to them such seditious words they should apprehend him instantly. The townsfolk, learning this, ceased their visits to the Regiment.' The subedar now set up his own network of informers and learned from them that a number of outsiders had arrived in Patna 'with the intention of making a row and that they were engaged in hiring men at 2 annas per diem and in polishing and mending their arms. On the 13th June I informed my Commanding Officer of this.'

Hedayut Ali's intelligence only reinforced what Commissioner

Tayler had learned from his own intelligence network. However, this dependence on spies and informers did not go down well with some of Tayler's civil service colleagues. One of the most critical was the Patna magistrate, J. M. Lewis, who wrote to Tayler on 21 July complaining of his methods: 'I had come to distrust spies and underhand information, not only from being myself approached by one of your goindas [informers], armed with a perwannah [warrant] from you . . . but also from what I learned afterwards of this spy . . . Much mischief resulted from such powers being placed in the hands of unscrupulous persons.' The commissioner's response to these and other concerns was to brush them aside. The situation demanded firm action, and he was not to be deflected from taking such steps as he deemed necessary for the maintenance of law and order in his division. This arrogance cost him dearly.

On 19 June Tayler received the Lieutenant-Governor's response to his report sent to Calcutta eleven days earlier. To his astonishment, instead of congratulations he received a rebuke. 'My letter was written on the 8th,' he afterwards explained:

> To my utter bewilderment I received his [Halliday's] reply,
> dated the 13th, saying that he 'could not satisfy himself
> that Patna was in any danger', and that 'the mutiny of the
> sepoys was inconceivable'. I leave my readers to conjecture
> what my sensations were on the receipt of this letter. I did
> not, however, waver for a moment. Mr Halliday was 400
> miles distant, telegraphic communication had become
> uncertain, every Christian life was at stake, and moments
> were too precious to be wasted in remonstrance or
> argument.

Over the previous two weeks every post had brought news of further mutinies in Upper Hindustan. Bengal Army regiments had turned on their officers in Benares, Allahabad and Azimgargh, and in Oude the troops in half a dozen outlying districts had followed suit, isolating Sir Henry Lawrence and a small garrison in the British Residency at Lucknow. In the Punjab, sepoys were said to be deserting in droves to join the mutineers in Delhi; a score of Bengal Army regiments were in the process of being disarmed and disbanded before they too followed suit. Meanwhile, in Patna itself it had been reported to Tayler that 'an intimacy' had developed between the 'saintly gentlemen' who led the Wahhabis and a rich banker named Lootf Ali Khan. The latter was a Shia and thus a natural enemy of the Wahhabis, which made him, in Tayler's eyes, 'an unnatural subject for such a connexion'. Fearing that the Wahhabis had finally put aside their religious scruples to join forces with the Lucknow rebels, Tayler decided to make a pre-emptive strike. As he himself put it, 'I came to the determination in my own mind, to take the initiative against the town, and deprive the disaffected, as far as I might, of all power of mischief.'

Among those now living in the Commissioner's bungalow were two junior assistants, the youngest of whom was twenty-year-old Edward Lockwood. He had only recently arrived in Patna on his first posting, and he now slept on Tayler's front veranda with a revolver under his pillow and a gun beside his bed. In later years Lockwood remembered his Mutiny days in Patna as the most exciting and 'joyous' period of his life. To begin with, however, their prospects appeared very bleak: 'Truly there was no lack, most days, of news which was qualified to make one's hair come out of curl . . . but we soon got used to it. The calm confidence felt by the Commissioner communicated itself to all the others, and with Tayler and Rattray at the head of affairs, I felt comfortable enough.' On 19 June Lockwood was told by the commissioner that he had issued an invitation to 'all the respectable natives' in the city to meet in his house on the following day, and that he would need his help. Among those asked to attend were three Wahhabi leaders, described by Tayler as 'three Puritan Moulvees,

Shah Mahomed Hossein [Syed Muhammad Hussain], Moulvee Ahmad Oollah [Ahmadullah], and Moulvee Waiz-ool-Huq'.

'Next day,' wrote Lockwood, 'when the Wahabee Chiefs arrived by invitation, I received them, and bowed them, with all due ceremony, into the large room in which we all used to dine.' When all the local dignitaries were present, Tayler entered flanked by Captain Rattray and Subedar Hedayut Ali. After some perfunctory discussions the meeting was declared over, but then, as all got up to leave, the three Wahhabis were asked to stay behind. They were then informed by Tayler that he had decided to hold them 'in safe keeping until matters had settled down'. They were to be conveyed in their palanquins to the Patna circuit house where a guard of Rattray's Sikhs would be placed over them. To all intents, they were under arrest – but without any charges being laid against them.

The three took the news remarkably calmly, Ahmadullah responding 'with a politeness of manner worthy of all admiration' that whatever the commissioner ordered was best for 'your slaves'. Young Lockwood was less impressed: 'An old fellow [probably Muhammad Hussain] who sat next to me was the only one who appeared uneasy, for he looked at me slyly through the corners of his eyes as though he could not understand our little game; but I calmed his fears, and said: "Your Reverend, in your new abode . . . you will enjoy peace with honour whilst these troubled times remain; and you can tell your beads and study your Koran at leisure."'

Tayler's action was inspired by what he called 'the most striking characteristic of the Wahabee sect . . . the entire subservience which they yield to the Peer, or spiritual guide'. He had taken the trouble to study the Wahhabis' beliefs, and had been struck by the fact that once a follower had committed himself by taking the oath of allegiance to the leader of the movement he 'henceforward abandons himself mind and body to a state of utter and unreflecting slavery to his saintly superior'. By removing the head,

Tayler hoped to render the rest of the body incapable of independent thought or action. He believed he had now placed under house arrest two of the three most important leaders of the movement: Muhammad Hussain – 'the Peer, or spiritual chief, to whom the entire body of converts of the last generation owe their admission to the fraternity' – and Ahmadullah, considered by Tayler to be 'the principal "Mureed", or disciple, and . . . said to possess greater influence than his superior'. In this supposition he was entirely correct.

Following the death of Wilayat Ali at Sittana, Muhammad Hussain and Ahmadullah had assumed what was essentially joint command of the Wahhabi organisation in the plains. Both were men of influence. As well as senior imam, Muhammad Hussain was the head of one of the three founding families of the Wahhabi movement in Patna, while Ahmadullah, besides filling the role of deputy and chief counsellor to Muhammad Hussain, was also one of Patna's leading public figures. He too was effectively the head of his family, for his father Elahi Bux was now a frail seventy-one-year-old and no longer played any significant role in the movement's affairs. Tayler had in fact hoped to apprehend Elahi Bux in this same coup, but the old man had failed to attend the meeting in the commissioner's bungalow. Balked, Tayler went out of his way to threaten Ahmadullah that his father's freedom depended on his own good behaviour, using the phrase 'His life is in your hands, yours in his.'

Tayler's enemies subsequently chose to interpret these words as a threat to kill the old man, just as they chose to portray his tricking of the three mullahs as an act of treachery on a par with the seizing and murder of the British envoy Macnaghten during the Afghan War. Edward Lockwood and others present saw Tayler's action in a very different light: 'There appears to me', argued Lockwood, 'a vast difference between inviting a man to my house, in order to kill him when he gets there; and inviting him, in order that his followers shall not kill me, so long as I keep him handy.' Tayler himself had no doubts as to the rights and wrongs of the case: 'To this day I look at the detention of these men as one of the most successful strokes of policy which I was able to carry into execution.' It was, however, a detention lacking the approval of the Lieutenant-Governor of Bengal, for Frederick Halliday was notified by Tayler only after the event.

Having safely secured the three Wahhabi mullahs, the Commissioner next issued a proclamation calling on all Patna's citizens to surrender their arms within twenty-four hours. This was backed up by a curfew, under which no one was allowed to leave his home during the hours of darkness. Shortly afterwards a Muslim magistrate suspected by Tayler's right-hand man Dewan Mowla Baksh of being in league with conspirators in the city was also arrested. These measures had the desired effect: Patna and the surrounding districts remained relatively calm, and Farquharson and others who had taken refuge in the opium store were persuaded to return to their posts.

Tayler's pre-emptive strike in Patna also had other effects that he could never have anticipated. Deprived of the direction from the top that was such a marked feature of their organisation, almost the entire Wahhabi network across the plains of northern India entered a state of paralysis. And with the chota godown at Patna effectively closed, the movement of caravans of much-needed supplies of men, arms and money to the burra godown in Sittana came to a halt.

By mid-June the city of Delhi had become the focal point of anti-British resistance as increasing numbers of Muslims, soldiers and civilians alike, answered what they believed to be a call from their emperor, and rallied to his cause.

It will be remembered that after the martyrdom of Syed Ahmad at Balakot divisions had opened up between the Wahhabi 'Patna-ites' led by Wilayat Ali and the Wahhabi 'Delhi-ites'. For many years the latter were led by Shah Waliullah's grandson,

SHAH MUHAMMAD ISHAQ, whose cousin and brother-in-law were Syed Ahmad's first two disciples. Following the death of his cousin with Syed Ahmad in 1831, Shah Muhammad Ishaq and a group of his disciples had migrated to Arabia. After an absence of many years he and his followers returned to Delhi, where Shah Muhammad Ishaq placed himself at the head of a radical circle of scholars working within the traditions established by his grandfather. After Shah Muhammad Ishaq's death in 1846 the Madrassah-i-Rahimiya broke up into a number of interlinked schools, of which the most obviously Wahhabi was that led by Maulana SAYYID NAZIR HUSAIN of Delhi.

Born in 1805, Sayyid Nazir Husain had begun his religious studies in Patna at the Sadiqpore house of one of the heads of the three Patna families, Muhammad Hussain, and it was there that he first heard Syed Ahmad speak in the 1820s. He later moved up to Delhi to sit at the feet first of Shah Abdul Aziz and then of his son and successor, Shah Muhammad Ishaq, becoming in time a highly respected teacher of Hadith. The degree to which Sayyid Nazir Husain participated in the 1857 Mutiny can only be guessed at. He afterwards denied that he was one of the thirty-seven ulema of the city who in July 1857 put their seals to a declaration calling for jihad against the Nazrani – but there are grounds for believing that he did just that.

The circumstances of the signing of the Delhi fatwa are surrounded in obfuscation and claims of forgery; understandably so, since to have admitted any support for the mutineers in the dark days that followed the suppression of the uprising would have been tantamount to signing one's own death warrant. The undisputed facts are that on 19 May 1857, eight days after the arrival of the mutineers from Meerut, a group of mullahs erected a green banner on the roof of the city's greatest mosque, the Jama Masjid, and published a fatwa proclaiming jihad. As soon as he heard of it, the Emperor ordered the banner to be removed and denounced the jihad fatwa as a great folly because it would alienate his Hindu supporters. His actions were supported by the Wahhabi 'Delhi-ites', but for very different reasons. Sayyid Nazir Husain is said to have considered this declaration of jihad to be 'faithlessness, breach of covenant and mischief', and to have pronounced that it was a sin to take part in it. But his reasons for doing so were essentially doctrinal: he and other Sunni fundamentalists viewed the emperor as 'little better than a heretic' on account of his insistence on working with Shias and Hindus; and he did not consider Delhi to be a dar ul-Islam, making it unlawful to proclaim jihad from there. All the evidence suggests that the 'Delhi-ites' and other Sunni hard-liners in the city initially remained aloof from the mutineers and kept their own counsel.

However, everything changed with the arrival in Delhi on 2 July of a large contingent of sepoys accompanied by 'three or four thousand *ghazis* [warriors of the Faith but, in British eyes, fanatics]'. A significant number of these ghazis, led by one Maulvi Sarfaraz Ali, were Wahhabis. They had come from the town of Bareilly (not to be confused with Syed Ahmad's birthplace in Oude, Rae Bareli), capital of Rohilkhand, which in earlier days had been an Afghan–Pathan stronghold in the plains. Ever since Syed Ahmad's day Bareilly had been an outpost of Wahhabism on a par with that other Pathan bastion, Tonk. The Bareilly brigade was led by a senior officer of artillery, Subedar Muhammad Bakht Khan, whose first act on arriving in Delhi was to go straight to the Emperor and offer to take command of the mutineers – an offer gratefully accepted by the bewildered old man. Bakht Khan and two senior cavalry officers at his side were afterwards named as Wahhabis and the charge may well have some truth in it, because from this point onward the dominant group among the mutineers in Delhi became increasingly insistent that Emperor Bahadur Shah should lead them in a religious war, to the great disquiet of the many high-caste Hindus in their ranks. Bakht Khan assembled all the mullahs in the city and called on them draw up and put their seals to a second fatwa, 'enjoining upon Mahomedans the duty of making religious war upon the British'. Initially, many refused to do so, but in mid-July a further six hundred ghazis arrived in the city, this time from Tonk. Again the presumption must be that many of them were Wahhabis – and that they came with the blessing of Syed Ahmad's former devotee, Mohammad Wazir Khan, now the Nawab of Tonk. It was then put to the mullahs that the presence of all these warriors of the Faith – now said to number seven thousand in total – had, together with that of their Muslim brothers-in-arms in the Bengal Army, transformed Delhi into a land of Faith. This time thirty-seven divines put their seals to the jihad fatwa, and it was duly published.

6

The Late Summer of 1857

Mutiny is like smallpox. It spreads quickly and must be
crushed as soon as possible.

John Nicholson in a letter, Peshawar, June 1857

The ruthless crushing of the Sepoy Mutiny on the Punjab frontier
by Nicholson and others has been recounted in *Soldier Sahibs*,
but it should be remembered that it was prompted by the discovery of a number of damning letters, some from mullahs, others
from Muslim conspirators in the ranks, but all calling for an uprising against the Nazarenes. One of these letters specified the
fourth day of the Muslim festival of Eid, 22 May, another directly
implicated the Hindustani Fanatics gathered under Maulvi Inayat
Ali on the eastern slopes of the Mahabun Mountain.

Despite the successful disarming and disbanding of the suspect
units on the Peshawar parade ground on 21 May, one regiment of
Bengal Native Infantry, the 55th, mutinied at Hoti Mardan and
marched off towards the nearby mountains. Following a hot pursuit by John Nicholson and others in which about half the
regiment perished, some five hundred men survived to reach the

safety of Swat. Unfortunately for them, the Padshah of the Swatis and local patron of Syed Ahmad, Sayyed Akbar Shah, had died of natural causes on 11 May and his brother, SAYYED UMAR SHAH, had failed to win the backing of the tribal elders that his father had enjoyed. Despite this lack of support Sayyed Umar Shah offered the mutineers his protection and agreed to take them on as his standing army. But a majority of the sepoys were high-caste Hindus and they very soon found they were not welcome. The Swatis' revered religious leader, the Akhund of Swat, then inter-vened and all the sepoys were ordered to remove themselves from Swat – along with their protector Sayyed Umar Shah. They made their way eastwards over the mountains to the Sayyeds' homeland in Buner and there divided into two groups: the larger party, mostly composed of Hindus, crossed the Indus in the hope of finding refuge in Kashmir; the remainder proceeded south to join Maulvi Inayat Ali and his Hindustanis.

At this time Inayat Ali had no fewer than four camps in the Mahabun massif: a lower camp at Sittana, two fortresses higher up in the mountains at Mangalthana and Narinji, and a village over-looking the Vale of Peshawar at Punjtar. This last had come to the Wahhabis through an alliance Inayat Ali had formed with the chief of Punjtar, Mokurrub Khan. Inayat Ali's role in the subversion of the 55th BNI, previously based at Nowshera before they mutinied at Hoti Mardan on 23 May, remains unknown. But the arrival in his camp some five weeks later of more than a hundred armed and uniformed sepoys, nearly all Muslim, must have given him and his Hindustani mujahedeen a powerful fillip. Due to the disturbed state of Upper Hindustan at this time it is unlikely that Inayat Ali received news of the arrests of the Wahhabi leadership in Patna until after he had launched his first strike against the infi-dels in mid-July. This took the form of a raiding party, led by his cousin Meer Baz Khan, which swept down on to the Yusufzai plain, seized two villages, and there 'raised the standard of the Prophet'. Perhaps the hope was that the surrounding tribespeople would rally to their banner. In the event, the jihadis failed to take the most basic military precautions, and early next morning were caught off-guard. Herbert Edwardes, Commissioner in Peshawar, afterwards set down a summary of the events of 2 July: 'Major Vaughan (then commanding the fort at Mardan) fell upon them with about 400 horse and foot and two mountain guns, killed Meer Baz Khan, took prisoner a Rohilla leader named Jan Mahomed Khan, hanged him and Mullik Zureef, the headman of the rebels, burnt two villages which had revolted, fired others and extinguished this spark of mischief. Nothing could have been better than the promptness of this example.'

This setback forced Inayat Ali to pull back from Punjtar to a more secure position in the hills: his fortress at Narinji, on the end of a long ridge overlooking the western slopes of Mahabun Mountain. 'This mountain village', recorded Edwardes, 'was so strongly situated that the police scarcely dared to go near it, and it became a refuge for every evil-doer. Its inhabitants, about 400 in number, welcomed the moulvie with delight. The holy war seemed auspiciously opened with every requisite: a priest, a banner, a fastness, a howling crowd of bigots and several days' provisions.' But here too the Hindustanis were caught by surprise, being woken at dawn on 21 July by the crash of artillery as four mountain guns opened up on their village – the prelude to an assault by a combined force of eight hundred horse and foot. They and the rebel sepoys with them took to their heels, leaving behind a banner and sixty dead.

By all accounts the summer of 1857 was exceptionally hot, and Major Vaughan's men were too exhausted by the climb to continue the chase. This gave Inayat Ali the chance to regroup. He gathered his reserves from Sittana and Mangalthana and reoccupied Narinji, where he rebuilt and strengthened the defences of his eyrie. There he settled down to await the arrival of the first of many waves of mujahedeen from Patna and elsewhere in Hindustan that he and the other leaders had confidently

predicted would flock to their banner in the wake of the
Wahhabis' calls for hijrat and jihad. As a result in large part of the
measures taken by Commissioner Tayler in Patna, those reinforcements never came. Instead, at sunrise on 3 August a British
force twice as large as the first began a fresh assault on Narinji:

> The *Ghazees* had thrown up some formidable
> entrenchments, and danced and yelled as they saw a small
> column advancing on their front. Their shouts were
> answered by British cheers from a second column under
> Lieutenant Hoste, which had gained the heights by a bye-
> path and now appeared above Nowrunjee. A general fight
> took place, 30 of the *Ghazees* died fighting stoutly, and
> three were taken prisoners, amongst whom was a moulvie
> from Bareilly who was summarily hanged. The village was
> then knocked down by elephants and its towers blown up
> by engineers. Nowrunjee was at last destroyed.

In this engagement Elahi Bux's youngest son Akbari Ali became
a martyr; he may well have been the moulvi referred to above who
was summarily hanged.

The fate of the surviving members of the mutinous 55th was a
melancholy one. Having crossed the Indus on rafts of inflated
animal skins they entered Hazara with letters from the unrecog-
nised Padshah of Swat directing all good Muslims to help them
and denouncing all who did not. This cut no ice with the
Hazariwals, who not only informed Major Becher, the British
Assistant Commissioner, of the sepoys' movements but harried
them every foot of the way, hurling down boulders on them and
picking off the stragglers. 'The Mahomedan women', recorded
Becher, 'were shocked by these strange, dark men cooking and
bathing almost naked; they were most of them armed with muskets, or rifles and swords, but had little clothing and no cover
from the rain and night dews . . . Every step of their advance now

brought new embarrassments; the knapsacks and bayonets and many of the muskets were cast down the rocks, and a large payment of silver could scarcely procure a seer [kilo] of flour.'

The ever-dwindling band struggled on through this wild country until in early July they surmounted the ridge that divided Kohistan from the Khagan valley. They then made their way up the Kunhar River and entered a deep *nullah*, or ravine, which they knew led to Kashmir and safety. At the head of this nullah was a high mountain pass, but it was blocked with snow. Trapped, they had no option but to stand and fight as the Sayyeds, Kohistanis, Gujars and other local tribesmen moved in for the kill: 'It was a rainy day, and as they appeared through the mists on the hills beating their drums and flaunting their pennons the hearts of the mutineers despaired. Checked everywhere, there seemed no hope, and after a faint resistance and a slaughter of a few of their number, they surrendered their arms, and 124 more prisoners were afterwards made over to the escort which I had despatched to receive them.' The prisoners were tried by Becher, found guilty of mutiny and executed in different parts of the district of Hazara. 'They met their deaths', concluded Becher, 'with the calmest bearing. Those who were hung spoke only to request that they might be blown from the guns instead . . . Thus hunted to the last like wild beasts was consummated the miserable fate of the 55th Regiment.' The Kunhar gully is still spoken of locally as *Purbiala nar katha* – 'the ravine of the killing of the plainsmen'.

Meanwhile in Patna, Commissioner Tayler had once again appealed to Major-General Lloyd in Dinapore to disband two of his three Bengal Infantry regiments, and had again been assured that there was no need. He then concentrated his efforts on reducing the threat posed by the other suspected conspirators linked to the rebels in Lucknow and Delhi. A police officer named Waris Ali, with ties to the royal family at Delhi, was found with a bundle of incriminating letters showing that he and a prominent mullah named Ali Kareem were in contact with the Delhi rebels. The letters were coded: one referred to a major commercial enterprise with many partners from the east and west in which extensive profits were to be made; another spoke of a savoury *pullao* now ready for eating, and urged the recipient to bring all his friends to enjoy it, even if it meant making sacrifices. Ali Kareem was forewarned and initially evaded arrest, but Waris Ali was tried and found guilty of conspiracy to overthrow the Government. Much to young Edward Lockwood's horror, he found himself in sole charge of Waris Ali's public execution. 'When I mounted my man upon the gallows,' recorded Lockwood, 'he appealed to his compatriots to rescue him. But the sight of my rosy cheeks and awful European hat, had such a terrifying effect upon the crowd that no one stirred, and when the Surgeon came, the man was dead. I always thought the natives a very tractable, pleasant set of fellows after that.'

For a while it looked as though Tayler's measures had succeeded in damping down talk of revolt in Patna, but on 27 June virtually the entire garrison at Cawnpore, three hundred miles up-river, was massacred beside the Ganges after vacating their defences under a truce. Three days later Sir Henry Lawrence and his beleaguered garrison at the Lucknow Residency suffered a defeat so severe that it appeared they too were on the brink of destruction. Within days the news of these two reverses had reached Patna, and on 3 July a large mob waving banners, banging drums and chanting 'Deen! Deen!' attacked the Roman Catholic Mission in the heart of the native town. Word of the rioting was quickly brought to the Commissioner, and Rattray's Sikhs were despatched to restore order. The riot was swiftly broken up, but not before Dr Lyell, assistant to the opium agent, had been set upon and killed. A wounded rioter was seized and taken to the hospital to be treated. There Subedar Hedayut Ali, Rattray's second-in-command, gained his confidence and he began to talk. This led to the arrest of thirty-one alleged conspirators, including a bookseller named PIR ALI KHAN, 'noted for his enthusiasm for his religion and his hatred of the English'. Tayler already had information suggesting that Pir Ali was the leading member of a cell taking its orders from the rebels in Lucknow, and now a bundle of letters found in his possession confirmed this. They had come from a fellow bookseller in Lucknow and contained instructions as to how Pir Ali was to further the cause of the *Futteh ooper Nasara* or Victory over the Nazarenes. Pir Ali had also been charged with the task of persuading the leaders of the Wahhabis in Patna to join the revolt, but in this he had failed, probably because the Lucknow correspondent had urged that the rebels should join forces with all religious groups in India, even if that meant working with Shias and Hindus.

All those arrested were tried before an emergency tribunal set up by Tayler, and were found guilty on various counts, Pir Ali and sixteen others being sentenced to death. Shortly before his execution Pir Ali was taken before Tayler to be questioned further. 'He was calm, self-possessed and almost dignified,' wrote Tayler later. 'He taunted me with the oppression I had exercised, and concluded his speech by saying, "You may hang me, or such as me, every day, but thousands will rise in my place, and your object will never be gained".'

With this last round of arrests Bill Tayler severed Patna's links with the rebels in Delhi and Lucknow.

The immediate threat lifted, the Europeans quartered in the commissioner's bungalow felt able to take life less seriously. The open ground in front of the circuit house holding the Wahhabi leaders was turned into a recreation area upon which, in Edward Lockwood's words, 'we challenged the Sikhs to cope with us in feats of agility and strength . . . The Wahabees used to sit in the verandah of their house telling their beads, and viewing what doubtless they called our antics unworthy of sober men. But it was quite impossible to judge from their Fagin-like faces, in which low cunning was mingled with ferocity, whether they were pleased or not, for they never laughed or even smiled.'

In the evenings Lockwood and his colleagues applied themselves to keeping up their spirits in other ways:

> Occasionally we would have a dance – the Lancers being most affected – in which all were obliged to join. We wore no coats, but Garibaldi jackets of gaudy colours, and leather belts, in which our revolvers, hardly ever laid aside, were stuck, and high untanned leather boots, of native make. These in time were wont to draggle down, giving us the appearance of ruffians on the stage. Every one was obliged to do what, I believe, is called the steps, and when the fiddle struck up and we all went round, old and young together, those who smoked being armed with churchwarden pipes, which someone had procured somehow, the effect was so very comical, and we looked such awful idiots, that I could hardly stand for laughing.

To those sharing his quarters Bill Tayler was now the hero of the hour. 'The Commissioner was daily receiving congratulations from all parts of India regarding his successful policy,' recorded his youthful assistant. 'Indeed some of us went so far as to address Mrs Tayler as "My Lady" in anticipation of the decoration we supposed in store for her gallant husband.' However, a serious breach had now opened between Tayler and the Collector of Patna, Mr Woodcock, on the one hand, and the sessions judge, Mr Farquharson, and the two magistrates, Mr Lewis and Mr Elliott, on the other. The first party felt that the second were failing in their duties to uphold the law and were showing marked signs of pusillanimity, while the second considered that Tayler had cut too many judicial corners in arresting and sentencing on the basis of suspicion rather than proof. Furthermore, Tayler had acted without proper consultation with Calcutta and in some instances against the advice of his colleagues, so providing further ammunition for his critics. Both in Calcutta and in Patna Tayler's enemies were already working to bring about his downfall.

Despite Major-General Lloyd's assurances, the loyalties of the Bengal Native Infantry regiments in the military cantonment at Dinapore continued to trouble Tayler. His fears were at last realised when just after midday on 25 July Subedar Hedayut Ali appeared at his office 'in a state of excitement' and told him that the sepoys there were showing unmistakable signs of a 'mutinous spirit'. Still unwilling to take the drastic step of disarming his BNI regiments, Major-General Lloyd had compromised. A battalion of British infantry, towed in barges by a steamer, had recently arrived at Dinapore on their way up-river to Benares. Heartened by their presence, he had ordered a general parade at which the sepoys were to be required to surrender the percussion caps of their muskets. Quite inexplicably, however, this parade was held while the British troops, HM 10th Regiment of Foot, were having their dinner in a mess-hall and while he himself took lunch aboard the steamer moored off Dinapore. The moment the first company of sepoys were commanded to hand over their percussion caps they broke ranks, ran for their weapons, and began firing on their officers.

Tayler immediately put out a general alarm: 'I barely had time to summon the different residents to our house, and make all necessary arrangements for protection and defence, before the two signal guns were heard, and we knew that the ball had commenced.' The rattle of musketry followed, which Tayler and those gathering at his bungalow took to be the British regiment suppressing the mutineers: 'As we listened to the firing, which could be plainly heard from Patna, we calculated how many mutineers would be destroyed. Some said 600, others 800, some perhaps not more than 500!'

But at Dinapore one disaster had been followed by another. On hearing the firing the British troops in the mess-hall had run out on to the parade ground, but no senior officer appeared to give them any orders, Major-General Lloyd having decided that he 'should be most useful on board the steamer with guns and riflemen etc.' Astonished to find themselves at complete liberty, the mutineers loaded themselves with arms and ammunition and marched unimpeded out of Dinapore.

Fortunately for Patna, the three regiments headed westwards, away from the city and the civil lines and towards the sub-division of Shahabad, with the intention of joining the Rajput landowner Raja Kumar Singh. He now put himself at the head of a local army of Rajputs numbering some seven thousand men, and both armies then converged on the Shahabad district headquarters: the little town of Arrah. Here a local railway engineer named Boyle had long put up with the jeers of his friends as he converted what was intended to be the station billiard hall into a fortified redoubt. This now became the refuge of Arrah's official staff, consisting of the Collector, Herewald Wake, his Muslim deputy, and fourteen other Britons and Eurasians. With them was a contingent of fifty Sikhs from Rattray's police battalion, which Tayler had providentially sent back to Arrah from Patna only a few days earlier.

Early on 27 July the three rebel regiments marched into Arrah in good order, won over the local Nujeeb police, released the prisoners from the local jail, and then began to pour down musket fire on what afterwards became celebrated as 'the little house at Arrah'. That same afternoon they were joined by Kumar Singh, who immediately took command of a combined force in excess of ten thousand men. Every effort was made to induce the Sikhs defending the billiard hall to change sides, including bribery and threats. Those Sikhs could, in the words of one of those besieged, 'have eaten the [European] men up for breakfast', but they chose to stay and fight.

In Patna it was taken as a foregone conclusion that their friends in Arrah were lost. 'We thought they would all be massacred,' wrote Edward Lockwood, 'but, in case they should be able to hold out for a time, HM 10th Regiment was sent to their relief, and Ross Mangles, Wake's cousin, who was living with me, joined the force as a volunteer. I volunteered also, but the Commissioner would not let me go.' This bald statement conveys nothing of the tension and drama that followed as Tayler, on hearing from Major-General Lloyd that he proposed to hold back the British troops in Dinapore for the defence of Patna, did his best to make the general change his mind and send troops to relieve Arrah. 'I deprecated the measure,' was how Tayler put it, 'and strongly urged an immediate and active pursuit of the rebels.' Finally Lloyd relented, to the extent of allowing him two hundred soldiers from HM 10th Foot. These were loaded on to the steamer's barges and despatched up-river, only for the steamer to run aground on a sandbank. The general now called off the relief expedition – until a second steamer quite unexpectedly hove into view. After further delays and arguments Tayler again succeeded in making Lloyd change his mind, so that late on the afternoon of 29 July the second steamer, towing the original two hundred British soldiers from the stranded steamer plus an additional two hundred men, at last set off for Arrah. 'The intense anxiety for the deliverance of this brave little band may be easily conceived,' wrote Tayler, 'and the feelings which swelled the hearts of all who saw the relieving force depart, full of hope and confidence, with smiling faces, and cheers of anticipated triumph, may perhaps be imagined.'

The next afternoon, 30 July, Bill Tayler drove his wife and daughter in a carriage down to the river-side to welcome the steamer bringing the relieving force back to Dinapore. To their dismay the vessel sailed straight past the usual mooring and anchored opposite the cantonment hospital. 'Never have I witnessed so harrowing a scene,' wrote Tayler afterwards:

too dreadful to forget, far too dreadful to attempt to
describe, with any minuteness. Of the gallant band of 400

men which had left the shore in bright array, and in
assurance of victory, but a few hours before, 180 had been
left for dead on the field, several officers were no more,
almost all the survivors were wounded. The scene that
ensued was heart-rending, the soldiers' wives rushed
down, screaming, to the edge of the water, beating their
breasts and tearing their hair, despondency and despair
were depicted on every countenance.

Tayler returned to Patna with 'the fearful conviction that the
Arrah garrison was lost, irremediably lost! ... The crisis, as far as
Behar was concerned, had now evidently arrived.' That same
afternoon Edward Lockwood was seated on the veranda of
Tayler's bungalow taking Urdu lessons from an Indian *munshi*
when he saw a 'tramp-like figure' staggering up the driveway. It
proved to be his fellow assistant, Ross Mangles, 'who briefly said,
"We have had an awful licking; the 10th is pretty well annihilated,
and I am one of the few to come back to tell the tale."' The
relieving force had been ambushed in the dark by Kumar Singh's
forces and then pursued all the way to the steamer, Mangles carrying a wounded soldier on his back for the last five miles – an act
of gallantry for which he subsequently received the Victoria Cross.

Soon after Mangles' reappearance the commissioner drew up in
his carriage. 'My Munshi', continues Lockwood, 'then retired to
spread the news like wild-fire through the town; and I went to the
Commissioner, who I found had also heard of the disaster. But he,
as usual, seemed to take the matter very coolly, although he did
not dissent, when by way of opening the conversation, I said, "It
seems we shall have hot work here presently ... Surely you will
call in the out-lying Europeans, and not let them be massacred in
detail like the Arrah Garrison."' By Lockwood's account, Tayler
then replied that he was issuing orders 'commanding or inviting –
I forget which, but the point appears immaterial – the Europeans
at the outlying stations to come in and rally at Patna'.

When he set down his recollections of this conversation many years later Lockwood added the observation that 'if I could have peeped ahead and seen the events which occurred during the next few hours, I would joyously have committed an act of treachery, equal to that which I was supposed to have played on the Wahabees. I would have persuaded the Commissioner to entrust his orders of recall to me for delivery, and then, when no one was looking, slyly flung them all into the Ganges.'

After the near-massacre of the force sent to relieve it, Tayler had concluded that Arrah must fall, leaving Kumar Singh free to redirect his ten-thousand-strong force on Patna and the surrounding districts. He himself had barely enough troops left to defend Patna, let alone offer protection to his outlying sub-divisions. 'It seemed to me evident', he wrote, 'that no out-station was in a position to protect itself against the force, which at any moment might be sent against it.' The most endangered of these outstations was Gaya, sixty miles to the south, which besides being threatened by Kumar Singh from the north-west was also in danger of being attacked by three battalions of mutineers approaching from Bengal. To defend his station and his treasury the magistrate, Alonzo Money, had just fifty-five British soldiers and a hundred of Rattray's Sikhs. 'Under this appalling combination of dangers', wrote Tayler, 'I directed the withdrawal, and instructed the Magistrates [of Gaya and Tirhut] to come to Patna, as quickly as possible . . . *bringing the treasure with them, unless, by so doing their personal safety was endangered.*'

A quite unexpected turn of events now came about that later cast this order of withdrawal in the worst possible light. Tayler had been told that a relief force was planning to set out from Buxar, forty miles west of Arrah, in an attempt to relieve the besieged officers in their billiard hall, but this was no more than a handful of gunners commanded by a passed-over artillery major named Vincent Eyre plus an escort of barely a hundred and fifty fighting men. 'It was the opinion of all,' wrote Tayler, 'that this small force would have but little chance of success against so large a body as was then under the command of Kooer Singh [Raja Kumar Singh].' Accordingly, he wrote to the civil officer accompanying Major Eyre advising him that he should postpone his advance until more troops could be sent up-river to join them. This letter he sent open to Major-General Lloyd in Dinapore, 'to be forwarded with such instructions as he should think fit to give. What orders he gave I do not precisely know.'

But before Tayler's letter could be delivered Major Eyre had won a quite stunning victory, routing Kumar Singh's forces with a desperate bayonet charge and so relieving the defenders at Arrah.

Meanwhile, in Gaya the local magistrate Alonzo Money was behaving in a most irrational manner. He had earlier reported to Tayler that Gaya was in a 'ferment' and that the local Nujeeb police could no longer be trusted. Within hours of receiving Tayler's order to withdraw he set out for Patna with all the other Europeans on the station – but without the money in the subdivisional treasury, amounting to £80,000. After travelling only a few miles he was persuaded by someone in his party to return to Gaya to collect the treasure, leaving the rest of the party to carry on to Patna. At midnight on 2 August William Tayler received a letter from Mr Justice Trotter, now leading the Gaya party on the road, 'representing the dilemma in which Mr Money's "vacillation" had left him and the other officers, and asking whether I adhered to my former order'. Tayler replied that Trotter should stick to his instructions and proceed to Patna.

Having returned to Gaya, Money was joined, providentially, by a party of reinforcements from HM 64th Foot. With their help he emptied the Gaya treasury and then left the town with his new escort, to proceed at a great pace – not to Patna, as ordered, but down the Grand Trunk Road to Calcutta. Here he was duly received as a hero: the man who, disobeying orders to cut and run, had gone back to Gaya to save the treasury. 'Mr Alonzo Money,' wrote Colonel G. B. Malleson, the first authoritative chronicler of the Indian Mutiny, 'first disobeying then half obeying the directions of his commissioner, was, by his vacillating and impulsive action, converting a plain act of duty into a sensational drama, of which he, for a few brief moments, was the star-spangled hero.'

Alonzo Money's unexpected appearance in Calcutta and his self-serving account of his actions coincided with the arrival of a batch of letters from Patna addressed to Frederick Halliday, the Lieutenant-Governor of Bengal. They included the first account of Eyre's sensational relief of Arrah – but also copies of Tayler's order to Alonzo Money directing him to withdraw to Patna, and his letter advising that Vincent Eyre should wait for reinforcements before moving on Arrah. There was, additionally, a letter from Major-General Lloyd stating that he himself had ordered Eyre to advance – although, curiously, the actual letter containing that order appeared to have miscarried.

This was all the ammunition Halliday needed. On 5 August he informed the Governor-General that 'it appears from a letter just received from Mr Tayler, that, whilst apparently under the influence of a panic, he has ordered the officials at all the stations in his division to abandon their posts and fall back in Dinapore . . . Under these circumstances I have determined at once to remove Mr Tayler from his appointment of Commissioner of Patna.'

On the basis of Halliday's report, which cited Tayler's withdrawal order but omitted the sentence (set in italics on page 151) instructing his two assistant commissioners to bring the treasure with them unless to do so would endanger their personal safety, Lord Canning confirmed William Tayler's removal on three grounds: 'showing a great want of calmness and firmness'; 'issuing an order quite beyond his competency'; and 'interfering with the military authorities'.

William Tayler received the news of his dismissal from one of his most persistent critics, Mr Justice Farquharson, now appointed acting commissioner pending the arrival of Tayler's replacement. It coincided with news of a second great victory secured by Major

Eyre in his pursuit of Kumar Singh's army – a victory that to all intents put the Patna Division and most of Bihar out of danger. 'My friends were congratulating me that the crisis had passed, that success had at length crowned my exertions,' wrote Tayler. 'In the midst of these congratulations, and, at the moment when I thought that, without presumption, I might look, if not for reward, at least for acknowledgement, I was dismissed from the Commissionership; by a singular coincidence, the appointment was made over for a time to the officer who had suggested the abandonment of Patna.' To further salt Tayler's wounds, his replacement as Commissioner of Patna turned out to be Edward Samuells, the placeman to whom Halliday had a decade earlier awarded a post allocated to Tayler.

With the revolt still raging in Delhi, Lucknow and elsewhere, there was little Tayler's many friends and supporters could do other than grit their teeth and continue to carry out their duties. Mr Samuells duly arrived, bringing with him his own deputy to replace William Tayler's right-hand man, Dewan Mowla Baksh, dismissed on the grounds that he and a Muslim banker who had also rendered great assistance in the house-arrest of the Wahhabi leaders had both been motivated by jealousy. Among the first acts of this new administration was to order the release of the three detained Wahhabis. This was accompanied by the profuse apologies of the Government of India and a proclamation that they were 'innocent and inoffensive men', against whom there was 'no cause for suspicion', but who had, on the contrary, shown 'exceptional and unprecedented loyalty'. This was done at the express instruction of the Lieutenant-Governor of Bengal, Frederick James Halliday.

To his dismay, Edward Lockwood was among the officials then ordered to attend a 'conciliatory, let bygones be bygones pic-nic' on the river organised by the new Commissioner to honour the Wahhabis. As he made his way down to the steamer he met the now disgraced assistant magistrate Mowla Baksh: 'I asked him if he also had received an invitation to the pic-nic, but he, in melancholy tones, which made me laugh heartily, said, "Alas! Dear sir, a new king has arisen here who knows not Joseph."'

The river picnic itself was a subdued affair. 'If those little rascals had possessed any sense of the ridiculous', declared Lockwood of the Wahhabi leaders,

> how they would have roared with laughter at all this
> humbug. But when I found them assembled on the
> steamer which was to take us on our pleasure trip down the
> Ganges, they looked as good as grace in their priestly
> petticoats, as though a joke was neither here nor there to
> them. Directly I arrived, however, they one and all gave
> me a sly look through the corners of their eyes, and
> although they said nothing, I knew very well they meant to
> say, 'Aha! My fine fellow, you and your Governor [Tayler]
> have had your combs pretty closely cut, we guess!'

The pusillanimity of the Government of Bengal in failing to order the disarming of the sepoys in Dinapore and in turning its back on Commissioner Tayler's actions has to be set against the shared determination of the Governor-General of India and the Lieutenant-General of Bengal not to further alienate the Indian public, which for the most part had watched the Mutiny unfold from the sidelines, waiting to see which way the struggle went before coming forward to profess loyalty to the winning side. In this they succeeded admirably, and the Government of Bengal in particular was quick to congratulate itself in an official report on its conduct, written by none other than Frederick James Halliday.

Once released, the leaders of the chota godown in Patna behaved with circumspection, doing nothing that might attract the attention of the authorities, and so apparently justifying the trust placed in them by Halliday. The replacement Commissioner, Mr Samuells, was able to report to him that

Maulvi Ahmadullah, the Wahhabis' acknowledged leader, bore no grudges, and that he and his fellow-Puritans in Patna were in every respect model citizens.

Banished to a subordinate post in Bengal, Tayler fought furiously for his reinstatement and the recognition he regarded as his due. Finding the doors of Government closed to him, he went into print, setting out his case with chapter and verse but also claiming that his dismissal was due to the 'covert machinations' of the Lieutenant-Governor of Bengal, inspired by an 'intense political, perhaps personal dislike' of him. This was a mistake, for the Governor-General, Lord Canning, had only just declared Halliday to have been 'the right hand of the Government' during the dark days of the Mutiny – which was indeed the case in almost a literal sense, as Halliday had moved out of his own residence, Belvedere Lodge, and into Lord Canning's Government House for the duration. Canning's response was to suspend Tayler and threaten a judicial enquiry to examine the charge that Tayler had condemned men to death on insufficient evidence. Such an enquiry would only have drawn attention to the high-handed measures adopted by many other local magistrates and judges besides Tayler, but it was enough to force Tayler to back down. He resigned the service and set up his own legal firm in Patna, while continuing his fight to clear his name. He found many champions among the Anglo-Indian community, but Sir Frederick Halliday, KCB – as he became in 1859 – was too powerful to be moved. Despite the support of *The Times* and many influential public figures both in India and in Britain William Tayler remained, in the words of the historian Colonel G. B. Malleson, 'in the cold shade of official neglect'.

It has always been argued that the Indian Wahhabis played only a peripheral role in the Sepoy Mutiny and the several local uprisings that followed; that the Hindustanis in the Fanatic Camp on Mahabun Mountain alone took up arms against the British. But

there is convincing evidence, long suppressed and never discovered by the British authorities in India, that a small group of
Wahhabis associated with the 'Delhi-ites' also took up arms and
made a determined bid to replicate the jihad of Syed Ahmad.
Not only did they survive, but they went on to set the Wahhabi
movement in Hindustan on an entirely new course.

This group of Wahhabis came from the faction led by Sayyid
Nazir Husain, leader of the 'Delhi-ites' after the death of Shah
Waliullah's grandson Shah Muhammad Ishaq in 1846. As noted
earlier, the Sayyid was a noted teacher of the Hadith and had
many students, but first among them was his disciple Hajji
IMDADULLAH, who had been among those who acompanied Shah
Muhammad Ishaq on his long exile in Arabia in the 1830s. Hajji
Imdadullah was a declared devotee of the martyred Syed Ahmad,
and had written of how he had once beheld him in a vision standing beside the Prophet and holding his hand: 'I, out of respect,
stood afar. And Hazrat Sayyid Sahib [Syed Ahmad] took my hand
and put it in his.'

For all his denials, Sayyid Nazir Husain was widely believed to
have been one of the Delhi mullahs pressured into putting their
seals to the jihad fatwa in mid-July. At that time both sides,
British and mutineers, were handicapped by indecisive leadership, but in the weeks that followed it was those camped out on
Delhi Ridge who came together, while the much larger force
gathered inside Delhi's walls fell into increasing disarray as its
leaders squabbled among themselves. Although the sepoy mutineers and their allies fought with courage, their attacks against
the British positions were poorly co-ordinated, and as each was
repulsed so the revolutionary fervour that had inspired the
sepoys in the first weeks gave way to fatalism. The atmosphere
inside the city became increasingly doom-laden as citizens and
insurgents alike watched the small British force encamped below
their walls grow in both numbers and confidence. No one was in
charge, least of all Emperor Bahadur Shah or his sons – and the

belief that Delhi was a domain of Faith wherein great things might happen soon evaporated.

It was probably at this low point in early August that Sayyid Nazir Husain's disciple Imdadullah and three of his students – MUHAMMAD QASIM Nanautawi, RASHID AHMAD Gangohi and RAHMATULLAH Kairanawi – decided to make their own jihad. For reasons that are unclear but were most probably linked to their doubts about Delhi's religious status as a seat of jihad, these four left the city and with a number of supporters made their way along the river Jumna to the district of Thana Bhawan, about fifty miles due north of Delhi. Here they raised their own green banner and proclaimed holy war. The town of Thana Bhawan and the surrounding area fell to them without a fight, the British civil authorities having abandoned their posts long before.

Hajji Imdadullah and his jihadis now set about transforming the district into a theocracy modelled on that first tried in Peshawar by Syed Ahmad thirty years earlier. Imdadullah acted as the group's imam, but it was twenty-four-year-old Muhammad Qasim who emerged as the real leader of the group. He appointed himself its military commander, with twenty-eight-year-old Rashid Ahmad serving as his lieutenant and judge, and the slightly older Rahmatullah acting as the link-man between their group and the rebels in Delhi.

This second Wahhabi dar ul-Islam was as short-lived as the first. On 12 September the walls of Delhi were breached and stormed, and the city was taken after a week of vicious house-to-house fighting. The British general directing the assault had ordered that no quarter was to be given, and this order was implemented to the hilt. As the rebel Mainundin Hassan Khan afterwards recorded: 'The green as well as the dry trees were consumed; the guiltless shared the same fate as the guilty. As innocent Christians fell victims on the 11th of May, so the same evil fate befell the Mahommedans on the 20th September, 1857. The gallows slew those who had escaped the sword.'

Even before Delhi was fully secured, the surrounding country was being purged of rebels. As part of this process a squadron of Afghans and Sikhs of the 1st Punjab Cavalry led by Mr Edwards, Collector and Magistrate of Muzaffurnugur, set out for Thana Bhawan in mid-September. It met with unexpectedly fierce resistance, and was forced to retreat with the loss of one trooper and a camel-load of ammunition. It regrouped and again advanced on the town, only to have its baggage train attacked from the rear. Whether it was Muhammad Qasim or some other, whoever led the rebels showed courage and initiative. Unable to take Thana Bhawan, Mr Edwards moved on to the town of Shamlee, where he left a number of subordinates in charge with a detachment of eleven troopers before moving south to assault a fortress held by a separate group of rebels. He returned to Shamlee to find the officials and soldiers massacred by the insurgents from Thana Bhawan. A last stand had been attempted in the local mosque, whose inner walls Edwards found 'crimsoned with blood'.

Edwards and his demoralised cavalrymen rode back to Thana Bhawan, which was now occupied by more than a thousand insurgents. A further assault was attempted and driven back with heavy losses, leading Edwards to conclude that his safest course was to return to Muzaffurnugur. But his force now found itself pursued by the insurgents, leading fourteen Muslim troopers to desert. 'I attribute their defection', afterwards wrote Edwards' deputy, Mr Ward, 'partly to the loss of the detachment murdered at Shamlee, and partly to the hoisting of the green flag at Thana Bhawan.' Their situation soon became so desperate that Mr Edwards finally ordered his men about and called them to follow him in a cavalry charge. As so often in those desperate times, decisive action saved the day: the charge put the insurgents to flight, leaving a hundred dead. 'Amongst the slain', recorded Mr Ward, 'were several men of importance, who had acted as the leaders of the insurgents.'

However, it seems that the true leaders of the revolt at Thana

Bhawan were not among the dead: they were on the run. Imdadullah and Rahmatullah both fled to the coast, from where they eventually made their way to Mecca. The two younger men went into hiding. Two years later Rashid Ahmad was arrested as a suspected rebel, but was released after six months' detention for lack of evidence. In due course he and the man who may well have commanded the rebels at Thana Bhawan, Muhammad Qasim, went back to Delhi to resume their religious studies under their old teacher Maulana Sayyid Nazir Husain.

7

The Ambeyla Disaster

In our ancient capitals once so well-known, so rich, so great and so flourishing nothing is now to be seen or heard save a few bones strewn among the ruins or the human-like cry of the jackal.

Syad Ahmad Khan of Aligarh, in an address to the
Muhammadan Literary Society of Calcutta, 1862

By the end of September 1857 Delhi was a ghost town, entirely cleansed of Muslims, who were now increasingly viewed by the British as the real enemy. 'There has been nothing but shooting these villains for the last three days,' wrote a young British officer in a letter home from the Delhi camp, 'some 3 or 400 were shot yesterday. All the women and children are of course allowed to leave the city and the old men. I have seen many young Mussulmen, who no doubt had a hand in murdering our poor women and children, let pass through the gates, but most of them are put to death.' Areas of the city believed to have given aid and succour to the rebels were flattened, including several mosques. Even the city's great Jumma Masjid was threatened with demolition. For a time it served as a barracks for Sikh troops, and two years passed before it was finally released to a body of Muslim trustees.

Up on the Punjab frontier the British authorities were equally ruthless. Apart from those rebels killed in the field, quite a number were found guilty of mutiny or sedition and executed: 20 hanged, 44 blown away from guns and 459 shot by musketry. Then in October 1857, just as order appeared to have been restored, a night attack was made on the camp of one of Herbert Edwardes' assistant commissioners. The raiders were identified as Hindustani Fanatics. Against all the odds, they had regrouped under Inayat Ali and had once more joined forces with a local ally, Mir Alam Khan of Punjtar. Edwardes decided that they must now be finished off once and for all.

In mid-April 1858 five thousand fighting men gathered under cover of darkness near Hoti Mardan and set off across the plain towards the Mahabun Mountain. They were led by the local military commander, Major-General Sir Sydney Cotton, accompanied by Edwardes as his political adviser. Despite his advanced age, Cotton had learned in his five years as the area commander that frontier warfare demanded very different tactics from those he had employed as a cavalry officer in the plains. 'Protracted warfare in the mountains has proved to be fatal to success,' he afterwards wrote. 'There is a sporting phrase which is very applicable to this description of mountain warfare, "In and out clever." The proper mode of punishing the hill tribes, and that which is attended with the least risk, is to go in upon them suddenly and unexpectedly, without affording them time to assemble, or otherwise make preparation.'

Despite their considerable numbers, Cotton's troops moved fast and succeeded in penetrating deep into Mahabun Mountain before their presence was discovered. Soon after dawn the first column passed the village of Punjtar unopposed and started the long climb up to the main Hindustani stronghold at Mangalthana. 'The advance reached the height about eleven a.m.,' wrote

Cotton. 'Not a shot had been fired at us, as we laboured up the steep and wooded road, and on entering Mangul Thana we found the fort abandoned, and every sign of a hasty and recent flight.'

Cotton was not to know that the Hindustanis' amir, Inayat Ali, had died of fever just days earlier. The mujahedeen were leaderless and seemingly unable to offer any resistance. At Cotton's approach they scattered into the surrounding hills and ravines. All Cotton could do was mine and blow up all the buildings at Mangalthana and return to his camp on the edge of the plains. It was put about that the raid was over, but this was a bluff. Two weeks later Cotton struck again, acting on the reports of his scouts that the Hindustanis had regrouped at Sittana together with their Sayyed allies under Sayyed Umar Shah, brother of the late Padshah of the Swatis, Sayyed Akbar Shah. This time Cotton divided his force and advanced on the Hindustanis' lower camp at Sittana from three sides. Once in position, the three columns began to fan out until their enemy was in effect surrounded. Unable to break through this tightening ring, the Hindustanis gathered on the crest of a ridge to make a last stand. Cotton's official report gives no numbers, but comments that their fight to the death was 'marked with fanaticism; they came boldly and doggedly on, going through all the preliminary attitudes of the Indian prize ring, but in perfect silence without a shout or a word of any kind. All were dressed in their best for the occasion, mostly in white; but some of the leaders wore velvet cloaks.' Sayyed Umar Shah was very probably among the dead.

Had Cotton's troops held their positions, every last mujahedeen could have been finished off the next day. But with night approaching and all objectives taken, Herbert Edwardes decided that it was time to withdraw. Cotton was the senior officer and the military commander, but it was customary to heed the advice of the political officer present, and so he did – a decision both he and Edwardes came to regret. When Cotton later set down his account of the action he chose his words carefully: 'The Commissioner', he wrote, 'considered that adequate punishment had been inflicted on them, and called upon me to withdraw the troops, not deeming it expedient to raise against the British Government, by further pursuit of the enemy in the hills, the Judoon and other independent hill tribes who had naturally become excited by the presence of so large a British force in and amongst their mountains.'

Sydney Cotton could at least congratulate himself on having showed how it could be done. The hitherto impregnable mountains of Swat and Buner had been penetrated successfully by a large military force, and what had been done once could be done again – provided the force came 'in and out clever'. It was a lesson that his successors signally failed to learn.

But when Cotton's army marched down from the Mahabun Mountain it left behind alive ABDULLAH ALI, twenty-eight-year-old eldest son of the late Wilayat Ali, and his three small sons. He was subsequently chosen as Inayat Ali's successor as amir of the Hindustani Fanatics. It appears too that a number of sepoys, most likely remnants of the mutinous 55th BNI, survived. They and a handful of mujahedeen who had also escaped Cotton's net hid out in the mountains until given sanctuary by the new leader of the Sayyeds of Sittana, SAYYED MUBARIK SHAH, son of the late Padshah of Swat. The sanctuary was an abandoned settlement named Malka, just a few miles to the north-east of Mangalthana on the northern slopes of the Mahabun Mountain, looking down on the Chumla valley and the mountains of Buner beyond. Here this last core of the Hindustani Fanatics remained in hiding, cut off from the Indian plains and entirely dependent on the charity of their neighbours.

In November 1858 Lord Canning proclaimed an end to East India Company rule in India and the transfer of authority to the British Crown. The Company's Bengal, Madras and Bombay Armies were dismantled and the high-caste regiments replaced by mixed corps composed of different ethnic groups, castes and religions. At the same time, so-called 'martial races' such as the Sikhs and the Gurkhas who had proved both their loyalty and their fighting spirit in the Mutiny were recruited in increasing numbers. In March 1862 Lord Canning went home to die and was replaced as British India's second Viceroy by Lord Elgin, who himself sickened and died of heart failure in the Himalayas in November 1863. The office then went to John Lawrence, the hard-nosed administrator who had steered the Punjab through the Mutiny and its aftermath as its first Lieutenant-Governor. Unlike his predecessors, Lawrence knew the country and its people, but he was in England when Elgin died and it was eight weeks before he could be sworn in as Viceroy, too late to have any say in the political and military disaster that became known as the Ambeyla Campaign.

The road to Ambeyla began with a summons sent out in the late summer of 1863 by the Hindustanis' amir Abdullah Ali, calling on all the chiefs of the surrounding tribes to 'quit the friendship of the unbelieving and join the would-be martyrs of the Faith'. One of these letters was received by the Khan of Amb, who promptly forwarded it to Reynell Taylor, Herbert Edwardes' successor as commissioner in Peshawar. For some months the Hindustanis at Malka had been showing signs of renewed activity in the form of minor cross-border raids and the kidnapping of Hindus. Taylor consulted with Colonel Alfred Wilde, who had taken over the command of the Corps of Guides at Hoti Mardan from the legendary Harry Lumsden. Both agreed that action should be taken 'to effectually rid the frontier of the chronic cause of disturbance – the Hindustani fanatics'. For the future peace of the frontier, 'the destruction of this colony of priests and fanatics was a necessity ... They must be removed by death or capture from the hills, and a treaty made with the hill tribes not to allow them to reside in their territories.'

Colonel Wilde took the view that Brigadier Cotton had failed to

destroy the Hindustanis back in 1858 because the survivors had
been able to escape north. Wilde proposed using the same tactics
of surprise but this time encircling the Mahabun Mountain, 'the
military object being to attack the Hindustanis from the north,
forcing them to fight with their backs to the plains.' Once their
escape route had been closed, the Wahhabis and their Sayyed
allies could be driven down to the Indus and the plains. The only
means of achieving this encirclement was by way of the Ambeyla
Pass.

The Ambeyla Pass lay just over twenty miles to the north-east
of the Corps of Guides Headquarters at Hoti Mardan on the
Yusufzai plain (see Map 2, 'The Peshawur Valley'). The defile
leading up to the pass provided a natural gateway into the Buner
country and a back door to the Mahabun Mountain range, opening up beyond the pass on to the plain of the Chamla valley, some
twelve miles long and four wide. 'The only entrance to the
Chumla Valley is from Eusofzye,' explained Colonel John Adye, a
senior staff officer with the Royal Artillery, in his first-hand
account of the Ambeyla campaign, 'by a narrow gorge a few miles
in length called the Umbeyla Pass, being, in fact, the rocky bed of
a little stream, passing round the western side of the Mahabun.'

The only drawback to this plan was that it meant intruding on
the territory of the Buner tribes, the Bunerwals, whose lands
extended along the northern side of the Ambeyla Pass, and the
less numerous Chamlawals, who occupied its southern slopes and
the western end of the Chamla valley. Little was known about
these two tribes by the civil authorities in Peshawar, but they
were believed to be rather more peaceful than their fellow
Yusufzais in Mahabun. The Bunerwals, in particular, were followers of the Akhund of Swat, Abdul Ghaffur, now in his
seventieth year, who exercised a moderating influence over the
Swatis and Bunerwals and had always opposed the extreme views
promulgated by the Hindustani Fanatics. 'The Bonair [Buner]
people had no sympathy as a body with the Fanatics,' was John

Adye's view, 'being of different tenets, and forming part of the religious constituency of the Akhoond of Swat, who was known to be bitterly opposed at that time to the Fanatic body, the members of whom he denounced as Wahabees [and] whom his followers had not scrupled to stigmatise as Kaffirs.'

To Reynell Taylor, too, it seemed that 'nothing at that time was, to all appearance, so little probable as a coalition between the Akhoond of Swat and his adherents and the Hindostanees'. He therefore concluded that the proposed expedition could safely intrude on Buner and Chamla territory – so long as it was made quite clear to the tribesmen what the Government's objective was, and provided this was coupled with an undertaking that the troops would be withdrawn as soon as that objective had been accomplished. Taylor passed Wilde's plan on to Sir Robert Montgomery, the Lieutenant-Governor of the Punjab, who radically altered it by insisting that the numbers of troops involved should be doubled. The last word rested with the Viceroy, but Lord Elgin was too ill with his heart condition to play any part, so it was left to his commander-in-chief, Sir Hugh Rose, to express serious doubts about the wisdom of sending what was now a large force into unknown country without proper transport or reserves of supplies, and with winter approaching. He recommended that the expedition should be postponed till the spring.

It was precisely at this juncture that details of a remarkable supply chain linking the Hindustani camp with the plains were received by Montgomery in Lahore.

Five months earlier an unusually sharp Pathan *daffadar* or sergeant of mounted police named GHAZAN KHAN had been on duty on the Grand Trunk Road at Panipat north of Delhi when he observed four travellers whose unusually dark skins and small stature made them stand out. When questioned, they revealed that they were Bengalis returning to their homeland from the frontier. Puzzled by their answers, he went out of his way to appear friendly, and eventually discovered that they were

Wahhabis, and part of a supply chain smuggling men and guns up to the frontier. He promptly arrested them, whereupon the Wahhabis appealed to him as a brother Muslim to let them go, saying that a petition-writer named MUHAMMAD JAFAR from the nearby town of Thanesar would gladly pay whatever he demanded. Daffadar Ghazan Khan remained resolute, and next morning took his four prisoners before the local magistrate of Karnal – who dismissed the case, accusing his subordinate of bringing charges against the travellers in an attempt to extort money from them.

So outraged was the daffadar by this slur on his character that he decided to prove his case, and enlisted the support of his son. Where exactly this son lived is not recorded, but the assumption is that it was in Ghazan Khan's home village in Pathan territory. He now received a letter from his father asking him to collect evidence about the Hindustanis at Malka; in particular, how they received their supplies of men and guns. The son immediately set out on this strange quest, making his way into the mountains and presenting himself to the Wahhabis at Malka as an eager jihadi. Some months later he returned to his father in Panipat with the desired information.

Daffadar Ghazan Khan at once took his son to the magistrate and triumphantly presented his evidence: details of the supply chain by which the Wahhabi chota godown at Patna ferried men, money and guns across northern India to the burra godown at Sittana. Included in this evidence was the statement that 'Munshi Ja'far of Thaneswar, whom the men call Khalifa, was the great man who passed up the Bengalis and their carbines and rifles.' The British authorities at Karnal were now forced to act, which they did by seeking the advice of the recently appointed Commissioner of Amballa (not to be confused with Ambeyla) who, by a stroke of luck, happened to be Herbert Edwardes, the former Commissioner of Peshawar. Edwardes at once informed his old friend Reynell Taylor in Peshawar – who in turn informed

Sir Robert Montgomery. Fearing that the unrest the Hindustanis were provoking would spread if left unchecked, Sir Robert chose to ignore Sir Hugh Rose's advice and to order the launch of the now greatly enlarged expedition without further delay.

Command of the force was given to Brigadier Neville Chamberlain, another of that band of paladins who had made up the first wave of Henry Lawrence's political officers. His appointment was received with enthusiasm by the troops ear-marked for the expedition, for Chamberlain's standing in the Indian Army was second to none. He was said to bear more wounds on his body than any serving officer in India, and his gallantry at the taking of Delhi in 1857, when he had returned to the battlefield on a stretcher to rally the troops, was still talked of as a turning point in the Mutiny. Chamberlain was only forty-three, but like his old friends and former comrades in arms Herbert Edwardes and Reynell Taylor he was worn down by years of hard service and by the malaria endemic on the Punjab frontier. Although he accepted the command, he did so without enthusiasm. 'If duty requires the sacrifice I cannot repine,' he wrote to his brother, 'but . . . I have no wish for active service.'

On 18 October 1863 Chamberlain's force set off from its marshalling point outside Nowshera. To preserve the element of surprise Chamberlain had been ordered not to take up his command until the last moment, but when he arrived he found his troops already on the move – and hopelessly unprepared. 'I never before had such trouble or things in so unsatisfactory a state,' he wrote to his brother. 'Carriage, supplies, grain-bags, all deficient. Some of our guns and the five and a half inch mortars have to be sent back as useless.' Unlike the unencumbered and fast-moving force that had assembled under Brigadier Cotton five years earlier, this was a body twice as large and three times as slow. The column marching towards the Mahabun Mountain was swollen by 'long lines of elephants, camels, bullocks and carts, transporting huge tents, together with tables, chairs, bedsteads, carpets, crockery, and many other unwieldy and unnecessary items of officers' and soldiers' equipment; and to these impedimenta must be added the hordes of native followers, who, far outnumbering the fighting men, have been and still are the invariable appendage of an Indian army.' It took an entire day for this procession to reach the mouth of the Daran Pass, the point at which Cotton's army had entered the hills in 1858.

Reynell Taylor had handed over the commissionership of Peshawar to his deputy, Major Hugh James, so that he could accompany Chamberlain as the expedition's political officer. But after consulting with Montgomery he had taken the fateful decision not to give the Bunerwals advance notice of the invasion of their lands, on the grounds that 'our intentions would assuredly have been communicated'. Not until Chamberlain's army was encamped in full view at the southern foot of the Mahabun Mountains did Taylor despatch envoys to the chiefs of the Bunerwals, the Chamlawals, the Swatis and all the other Yusufzai tribes in the mountains with copies of a proclamation stating that his forces were about to enter the Chamla valley. His proclamation assured them that the intrusion was taking place 'with no intention of injuring them or of interfering with their independence, but solely because it was the most convenient route by which to reach the Hindustani fanatics, and to effect their expulsion from the Mahaban.'

That same night the army struck its tents and marched along the edge of the plains to the mouth of the Ambeyla Pass, which the head of the column reached at dawn the following day. The Guides Infantry then begin the climb to the head of the pass, the *kotal*, with the rest of the army following on behind. The response of the Bunerwals and Chamlawals was entirely predictable. As Major Hugh James, Reynell Taylor's successor as Commissioner of Peshawar, afterwards wrote, 'Was it likely that a brave race of ignorant men would pause to consider the purport of a paper they could not read, when the arms of a supposed invader were glistening at their doors?'

Chamberlain's plan was to have the bulk of his troops up and over the kotal and in occupation of the head of the Chamla valley by nightfall. Reynell Taylor's scouts had assured him that 'the pass presented no military obstacles', but they were wrong: the expected mule track turned out to be nothing more than the bed of a stream 'encumbered with boulders and large masses of rock'. Only by walking in single file was the advance guard able to reach the kotal, at which point they came under fire directed down on them from the crags above. The hills on every side were covered in low brushwood and jutting rocks and boulders – perfect cover for the tribesmen with their long-barrelled *jezail* flintlocks, clumsy to handle and load but remarkably accurate up to a quarter of a mile. However, the Guides and Punjab Frontier Force infantry who led the advance were adepts at just this style of mountain warfare and they skirmished forward, forcing the tribesmen back up the mountainside. By early afternoon the western end of the Chamla valley had been secured and picquets set up on all the surrounding spurs. But when night fell not a single baggage animal had reached their camp, and several thousand men were still stuck at the bottom of the pass.

After a night made sleepless by continual sniping Chamberlain met with his senior officers to take stock of the situation. He concluded that until the mule track through the pass had been improved by his engineers it was best to 'make no further movement in advance'. For two days his force did little but strengthen its existing positions.

This delay was to prove fatal. The Hindustani stronghold of Malka was twenty miles away at the far end of the Chamla valley. The latest intelligence suggested that it was now garrisoned by a combined force of more than a thousand Hindustanis and their Sayyed allies, convincing proof that the supply chain was back in operation with a vengeance. 'They were drilled in our system,' noted the official account of the campaign of the Hindustanis, 'and some were clothed like the sepoys of the old Indian Army.

Three of their *jemadars* [junior officers] were non-commissioned
officers of the late 55th Regiment Native Infantry . . . They numbered in the commencement about 900 men, most of whom had
been wrought up to a pitch of fanaticism, and were prepared to lay
down their lives.' The Bunerwals and the Chamlawals together
could muster up to twelve thousand fighting men, but they were
still in disarray and remained so until their chiefs had met to
decide how to respond to this armed incursion. In similar circumstances the younger, fitter Chamberlain who had shown such
'dash' in his earlier days would surely have pushed on with his
advance column of fast-moving Punjab Frontier Force troops, as
Cotton had on Mangalthana in 1858. But Chamberlain's preoccu-
pation with the difficulties of bringing supplies through the
nine-mile stretch of the Ambeyla Pass caused him to hang back.

It was not until the morning of 22 October that a small force of
mixed cavalry and infantry was sent forward to reconnoitre the
Chamla valley. At first it appeared deserted, and the scouting
party was able to push on down the valley for eleven miles before
turning back. But it then had to fight its way back to camp, and
was saved only by a moonlight cavalry charge. That same night a
letter was brought into camp by one of Reynell Taylor's spies: it
was addressed to the Buner chiefs and signed jointly by Amir
Abdullah Ali, leader of the Hindustani Fanatics, and Sayyed Umar
Shah, leader of the Sayyeds. Although it appeared to anticipate
Reynell Taylor's proclamation, it had in fact been written in
response to it:

> The evil-doing infidels will plunder and devastate the
> whole of the hilly tract – especially the provinces of
> Chumla, Bonair, Swat etc. – and annex these countries to
> their dominions, and then our religion and our worldly
> possessions would entirely be subverted . . . The infidels
> are extremely deceitful and treacherous, and will, by
> whatever means they can, come into these hills, and

declare to the people of the country that they have no
concerns with them, that their quarrel is with the
Hindustanees, that they will not molest the people, even
as much as touch a hair of their heads . . . They will also
tempt the people with wealth. It is therefore proper for you
not to give in to their deceit, for when they should get an
opportunity, they will entirely ruin, torment, and put you
to many injuries, appropriate for themselves your entire
wealth and possessions, and injure your faith.

Chamberlain's delay had allowed the Hindustanis and their
Sayyed allies to seize the initiative, giving them time to send
their call out not only to the Bunerwals but to every khan and
malik in the hills. The very next morning groups of armed tribesmen began to appear on the surrounding crests, coming from
almost every quarter, each group headed by standard-bearers carrying green and black flags and supported by drummers. Among
them were seen a large *lashkar* or war party of men whose distinctive black waistcoats and blue shirts identified them as
Hindustanis. With every passing hour more tribesmen joined
them, so when darkness came the mountains overlooking the
Ambeyla gorge and the valley beyond were ringed with camp
fires. It was now learned in Chamberlain's headquarters that the
Buner chiefs had met in jirga and had sent an appeal to the
Akhund of Swat, calling on him to come to their aid.

At this point Reynell Taylor still expected the Akhund, Abdul
Ghaffur, to intervene in his favour, for as John Adye put it, 'The
influence of the Akhoond of Swat over all the hill and plain tribes
of the Peshawur frontier is very great, and towards them he fills a
position which I can best illustrate by comparing it with that of
the Pope of Rome. If he declares against us, he will no doubt
bring an immense amount of material as well as moral strength to
the people of Bonair and the other tribes already in arms against
us.' But the Akhund was now facing his own internal challenge

with the appearance of Sayyed Mubarak Shah, pretender to the title of Padshah of Swat, at the head of the Hindustanis. If he allowed the British invasion to proceed, he would lose all claim to moral authority as defender of Swat and hand the advantage to his rival.

Three days later Reynell Taylor's worst fears were realised when a beating of massed drums was heard and a forest of waving banners crested the northern skylines, accompanied by a host estimated at four thousand strong. They were Swatis and in their midst was the Akhund himself, who now made camp on the hills overlooking the village of Ambeyla. According to the Akhund's grandson, the first Wali of Swat, his grandfather had set out for Ambeyla alone, but 'the news that Saidu Baba [the Akhund] was going for *jehad* spread like fire and hundreds of people joined him on the way, with the result that when he reached the battle-field at Ambeyla on October 26, there were four thousand volunteers on foot and one hundred and twenty five on horseback with him.'

Once it was known that their beloved Saidu Baba had lent his authority to the defence of Buner and Chamla, those who had previously wavered threw aside their scruples, seized their weapons and hurried over the passes to join in. By the end of October it was estimated that there were no fewer than fifty-five thousand fighting men gathered on the heights above Ambeyla, including ten thousand Swatis.

Chamberlain's only concern now was to prevent his position from being overwhelmed. His picquets on the slopes on the north and south sides of the Ambeyla Pass were most at risk, the one overlooked by the Guru mountain range, the other by a high conical peak known as Laloo. The land dropped from these two high points in a series of irregular steps that formed bluffs, of which the most prominent was a position on the north side that came to be known as the Eagle's Nest, and a sharp-pointed knoll on the south that was named the Crag Picquet. On the night of 24 October

Chamberlain's troops launched the first of a series of attacks to prevent these two positions from being encroached upon. Owing to the broken nature of the ground it was impossible to build continuous defensive lines or trenches, but wherever possible *sangars* were thrown up, loop-holed stone breastworks protected where possible by sharp-pointed sticks.

No sooner had these two strategic positions been secured than they were subjected to a succession of desperate assaults, with the Hindustanis almost invariably to be seen in the thick of the fighting. Thirty Hindustani dead were counted after the first attack, many of them young men of Bengali appearance. In the short truces that followed this and subsequent assaults it was observed that while the tribesmen came forward to collect their dead and wounded, the fallen Hindustanis were left untouched: 'Their allies seemed to look upon the Hindustanis as earthen vessels, to be thrown at our heads in the day of battle, but of which it was quite superfluous to think of picking up the fragments if they happened to get broken in the fray.'

Despite their superiority in weaponry, the defenders were unable to prevent the tribesmen from launching repeated attacks on the most vulnerable sectors of their perimeter. These were always preceded by heavy fire from concealed positions, which allowed assault parties to work their way forwards through the rocks and brushwood until they were massed before one section of the defences. The attackers would then rise from cover with cries of 'Allah-ho akbar' ('God is great'), raise their standards and charge: 'The bolder spirits of the mountaineers – men armed with short swords, and who had fully made up their minds to a hand-to-hand fight – then advancing rapidly and with great courage to the very foot of the work, and collecting under cover of the rocks, would pause for a while to regain their breath, and prepare for a final rush.'

In an attack launched just before dawn on 30 October on the Crag Picquet a company of the 1st Punjab Infantry was overwhelmed and the position seized by the Hindustanis. At first light several hundred tribesmen to the rear could be seen moving down to join the Hindustanis, and a desperate counter-attack was launched: 'A most exciting hand to hand fight ensued, in which Major Keyes was wounded, the enemy driven out at the point of the bayonet, the position recovered and three standards taken . . . The Hindustani fanatics lost 54 men killed on the spot, and 3 wounded.' This was the first of three occasions in which the Crag Picquet changed hands.

After a week of heavy fighting Neville Chamberlain sat down to write a despatch outlining the seriousness of his position:

> There is in fact a general combination of almost all the
> tribes, from the Indus to the boundary of Cabool, against us.
> Old animosities are, for the time, in abeyance; and under the
> influence of fanaticism, tribes usually hostile to each other
> are hastening to join the Akhoond's standard. The Akhoond
> has hitherto been opposed to the Sitana Moulvie [Amir
> Abdullah Ali], who represents an exceptional set of
> Mahomedans; but at present the two are understood to be
> on friendly terms, and it is certain that the whole of the
> Hindoostanee colony are either at, or on their way to,
> Umbeyla . . . We are engaged in a contest in which not only
> are the Hindoostanees and the Mahabun tribes, but also the
> Swatees, the Bajourees, and the Indus tribes north of the
> Burrendo, with a large sprinkling of the discontented and
> restless spirits from within our own border.

An advance on the Hindustani stronghold of Malka was now out of the question, but so too was a retreat: 'The only way to uphold the honour of our arms and the interests of the Government is to act on the defensive, in the position the force now holds, and trust to the effect of time, and of the discouragement which repeated unsuccessful attacks are likely to produce upon the enemy.'

So stand and fight became the order of the day, and for the next three weeks Chamberlain's army had to contend with repeated attacks by day and by night, with intermittent sniping in between. At many points along the perimeter the two sides were now so close that the men were able to exchange taunts and insults. 'The enemy', recorded Major Frederick 'Bobs' Roberts, one of half a dozen Mutiny VCs present at Ambeyla, 'used to joke with Brownlow's and Keyes's men [20th and 1st Punjab Infantry, both Muslim regiments] and say on these occasions, "We don't want you. Where are the men of the *lal pagriwalas*? [14th Sikhs, who wore red turbans] or the *goralog* [white people]? They are better *shikar* [sport]!"' Soldiers in all the Punjab Frontier Force units present found themselves fighting against men from their own tribes, and in several instances against brothers and other relatives. After one engagement a sepoy from Buner recognised his father lying among the enemy dead in front of his position. Remarkably, there was not a single desertion.

The first great crisis for Chamberlain and his troops began on 12 November as the Pathans made a new attempt to recapture the Crag, launching one attack after another throughout the night and the following morning. After forty-eight hours under constant fire the defenders of Crag Picquet broke and ran. In the confusion, sepoys manning sangars lower down the slope also panicked and joined in the retreat. Brigadier Neville Chamberlain was in the camp directly below but, because of the thick mists overhanging the mountainside and the clouds of black smoke from all the firing, was unable to tell what was going on. Alarmed by a stampede of camp-followers past his tent, he ran out and called for the 101st Royal Bengal Regiment. Quite fortuitously, this British regiment was about to take up new positions, and was already lined up before moving out. It was ordered to retake the Crag at all costs. The heights were stormed and the Crag reclaimed, but at such cost that a temporary truce was called to allow both sides to collect and bury their dead.

Chamberlain's positions on the slopes of Laloo on the south side of the pass had by now become extremely vulnerable. Reynell Taylor was anxious to make some gesture to the Bunerwals to show that the British had no designs on their territory, so on the night of 16–17 November all the troops on the heights of the Guru mountain range north of the pass were quietly withdrawn. This gesture went down well with the Bunerwals, who from this time onwards no longer played an active role in the fighting. But it failed to curb the fighting zeal of the Hindustanis. Interpreting the withdrawal as a sign of their enemy's weakening resolve, they responded with a near-suicidal rush on the camp's front breastworks in the valley itself, and were only repulsed after the fiercest hand-to-hand fighting. Shaken, Chamberlain despatched a blunt call for help to Montgomery: 'I find it difficult to meet the enemy's attacks . . . If you can give some fresh corps to relieve those most reduced in numbers and dash, the relieved corps can be sent to the plains and used in support. This is urgent.'

A day later the Pathans and Hindustanis made their third and last attempt on the Crag Picquet. As before, they attacked in repeated waves and, as before, the two hundred men holding the picquet finally lost their nerve and abandoned the position. But this time the enemy's capture of the Crag took place in broad daylight and was seen from every corner of the camp. Every field gun and rifle was brought to bear on the attackers, pinning the new occupiers down until a reserve corps could be brought up. Now it was the turn of the other British regiment present, the 71st Highland Light Infantry, to show its mettle.

Despite being warned by Reynell Taylor to stay out of harm's way, Neville Chamberlain chose to lead from the front: 'The prospect of failure pressed upon the mind and he could stand it no longer.' Both he and Taylor were at the head of the Highlanders as they retook the Crag at the point of the bayonet, and for his pains Chamberlain received a bullet in the arm, smashing the bones of his elbow. The surgeon who removed the bullet was his old friend Henry Bellew.

In Lahore Sir Robert Montgomery received Chamberlain's call for reinforcements with alarm. Not only did he have no troops to send but he had been warned by Major Hugh James in Peshawar that 'the excitement was spreading far and wide' along the Afghan border: 'The Momunds on the Peshawar border were beginning to make hostile demonstrations . . . Rumours were also reaching me from Kohat of expected raids by the Wuzeerees and Othman-Khail. Emissaries from Cabool and Jellalabad were with the Akhoond, who had been further reinforced by Ghuzzun Khan, the chief of Dher, and 6000 men.' The Pathans and Hindustanis had now suffered in excess of two thousand dead and perhaps three times that number wounded, but the British losses were proportionately just as severe: 18 officers and 213 men killed, and another 731 wounded.

Montgomery concluded that the only thing for it was to authorise Chamberlain to withdraw. He ordered Major James to Ambeyla to replace Reynell Taylor and to tell Chamberlain to pull out 'if it was desirable on military terms'. James found Chamberlain in too much pain to be able to discuss the situation in detail – but set in his belief that a withdrawal would be 'most unadvisable'.

The Commander-in-Chief, Sir Hugh Rose, now intervened, overruling Montgomery, and ordered troops from Amballa and elsewhere in the plains to proceed by forced marches to Peshawar. Major 'Bobs' Roberts, at that time attached to Rose's headquarters staff, was sent up to Ambeyla to report on the true state of affairs. He found Chamberlain confined to his tent but adamant that a withdrawal would only encourage the Pathans to extend the fighting along the Frontier. Furthermore, there were clear signs that the Bunerwals and Swatis were beginning to lose heart: 'They had borne the brunt of the campaign, and had lost many men, and they now found their valley overrun, and their limited supplies eaten up by crowds of hungry mountaineers from distant provinces.'

On 10 December a delegation of Buner khans and maliks approached the camp under a flag of truce, and an agreement was worked out by which they would allow the British to expel the Hindustanis from the Mahabun Mountain provided there was an immediate withdrawal thereafter. It seemed that the fighting was over – until the agreement became known to the Akhund of Swat. He had now come round to Abdullah Ali's view that the British were intent on conquest, and that what was at stake here was his religion. Setting aside his long hostility to the Wahhabis and their teachings, the Akhund called every Swati of fighting age to arms to protect his faith. For a second time the hillsides around became crowded with tribesmen and their encampments: 'Standards might be counted by the dozen, and the watchfires at night betokened the presence of many thousands.' By mid-December it was estimated that fifteen thousand Pathans were massed on the slopes of Laloo mountain alone.

Half the relieving force were now gathered at Nowshera, awaiting the arrival of Sir Hugh Rose and the remaining troops. But so critical had the situation at Ambeyla become that Major James asked General Garvock, commanding this first brigade of three regiments, to march without further delay. His troops reached Ambeyla on the morning of 15 December and were immediately thrown into action: 'General Garvock directed "the advance" to be sounded down the centre of the line. At that signal 5,000 men rose up from their cover, and, with loud cheers and volleys of musketry, rushed out at the assault – the regiments of Pathans, Sikhs, and Goorkhas all vying with the English soldiers as to who should first reach the enemy'. Their assault carried on up and along the Laloo mountain range, pushing the enemy down from the hills and into the Chamla valley, where they could be harried by the cavalry and dispersed.

Characteristically, the last to offer resistance was a large body of

Hindustanis, described by 'Bobs' Roberts as 'a band of *ghazis*', who made a desperate charge just when it appeared that the fighting was all over. 'At the critical moment,' wrote Roberts, 'Wright, the Assistant Adjutant-General, and I, being close by, rushed in among the Pioneers and called on them to follow us. As we were personally known to the men of both regiments they quickly pulled themselves together and responded to our efforts to rally them . . . We were entirely successful in repulsing the Ghazis, not a man of whom escaped. We counted 200 of the enemy killed; our losses were comparatively slight – 8 killed and 80 wounded.'

By the following day the dozens of Pathan tribes and clans who had gathered about the Ambeyla Pass were on their way back to their homes, leaving only the Bunerwals and the Amazais, whose lands extended along the southern edge of the Chamla valley and the hills above. The Bunerwals had taken no part in the most recent fighting, and their leaders now came to a new agreement with Reynell Taylor: if he promised to remove all British troops from their soil, they would themselves expel the remaining Hindustanis from the Mahabun Mountain and destroy their stronghold at Malka.

Taylor was now desperate to salvage something from the political disaster for which he himself was largely responsible. He accepted this compromise, with the proviso that the expulsion and destruction should be real and not merely nominal, and to this end it was agreed that he and a small escort should accompany the Bunerwals. The latter would send a force of two thousand tribesmen led by four of their chiefs, and Taylor would accompany them, together with an escort of seven British officers and four companies of Guides Infantry. 'Bobs' Roberts, who had a quite extraordinary knack of finding himself in the thick of the action, was one of the officers selected to accompany Taylor.

On the afternoon of 19 December Reynell Taylor and the officers mounted their horses and set off across the Chamla valley with their infantry escort and the four Buner khans. But instead of the two thousand flintlockmen promised by the Bunerwals, there were barely a hundred. Furthermore, the Bunerwals' private agreement had angered the several smaller Yusufzai tribes who had their homes in the Mahabun Mountains, particularly the Amazais, who had suffered heavy casualties defending their land on the Laloo ridge. 'The Amazais', Roberts later wrote in his autobiography, 'did not attempt to disguise their disgust at our being present in the country, and they gathered in knots, scowling and pointing at us.'

Despite the Amazais' hostility, Malka was reached late on 21 December. Inevitably, it was deserted. But it was also far more substantial than had been anticipated, 'containing several large edifices amongst which the Moulvie's hall of audience, barracks for the soldiers, stabling and a powder manufactory formed conspicuous objects. There was no regular fortification but the outer walls of the houses were connected and formed a continuous line of posterns.' The next morning the British officers watched as every building was set on fire, sending up columns of smoke visible for miles around. Also viewing this spectacle was a large and very angry crowd of Amazai, who became visibly more agitated with every passing minute, pressing forward until the British officers and their escort were hemmed in on every side.

All thoughts of pursuing the Hindustanis any further had to be abandoned. 'We were a mere handful compared to the thousands who had gathered,' wrote Roberts. 'Our position was no doubt extremely critical, and it was well for us that we had at our head such a cool, determined leader.' Reynell Taylor went over to the Amazai headman and told him in a firm voice that since the object of their visit had been accomplished, they were now ready to retrace their steps. But at this the Amazais became still further excited: 'They talked in loud tones, and gesticulated in true Pathan fashion, thronging round Taylor, who stood quite alone and perfectly self-possessed in the midst of the angry and dangerous-looking multitude.'

At this moment of crisis a grey-bearded Buner khan with one arm and one eye, ZAIDULLA KHAN of Daggar, forced his way through to Taylor's side, raised his one arm and called for silence. He then made what Roberts termed a 'plucky speech', telling the assembled Amazai that they could of course kill the Englishmen and their escort, but that to do so, '"You must first kill us Bunerwals first, for we have sworn to protect them, and we will do so with our lives."' It was a remarkable demonstration of the Pathan code of *nanawati*. As Zaidulla Khan's later conduct demonstrated, he regarded the British as his enemies; yet having agreed to accompany them to Malka and back, he felt honour-bound to protect them with his life.

Although the journey was frequently interrupted by 'stormy discussions' between the Amazais and the Bunerwals, Taylor and his escort returned safely to Ambeyla. The military camp at the head of the pass was at once broken up and by Christmas Day 1863 both the Ambeyla Pass and the Mahabun Mountain were free of the taint of the infidel. 'The colony of fanatics', wrote Major James in his final report, 'so perversely hanging on our borders, a blemish on our administration . . . has been half-destroyed, forced to retreat to more inhospitable and uncongenial regions, and will shortly, I trust, be eradicated for ever.' Army records indicate that in excess of seven hundred Wahhabi mujahedeen died in the fighting. Yet the fact was that Amir Abdullah Ali and perhaps as many as two hundred of his fellow Hindustanis lived to fight another day.

So too did an Afridi tribesman named SHERE ALI, a cavalry trooper who had served first Hugh James and then Reynell Taylor as his mounted orderly. Shere Ali was at Taylor's side throughout the Ambeyla campaign and was rewarded by him with a horse, a pistol and a certificate. As his personal orderly Shere Ali subsequently attended Taylor 'with eager zeal and devotion in rough work, and in peace he had been the playfellow of my children, one little girl having him entirely at her beck and call. In his rough *posteen* [sheepskin jacket] and boots, and armed always like men of his clan with sword and knife, he would carry her all over the place and attend her on her pony rides.' But popular as Shere Ali was among the European officers he served, he was nevertheless Afridi to the core: 'Like the rest of his tribe, he was constantly involved in blood feuds, and I well remember the look on his face when he informed me he had obtained a month's leave for the purpose of killing some hereditary enemies who taken advantage of his absence to shoot a woman of his family while drawing water.'

This blood feud had been maintained in Shere Ali's family for generations and it continued after Taylor's departure, when as their mounted orderly Shere Ali served two more Commissioners of Peshawar. However, in March 1867 he spotted a kinsman involved in his family feud walking near the house of the then Commissioner, Frederick Pollock, and killed him. He duly appeared before Pollock and was found guilty of murder, but because of the extenuating circumstances and his long record of service Pollock declined to sentence him to death, and instead ordered him to be transported for life. This was badly received by Shere Ali, who before his removal from the court begged that his sentence might be commuted to death. Pollock refused, so Shere Ali was sent away in chains to the Government of India's penal colony on the Andaman Islands in the Bay of Bengal. There, lost to the outside world and forgotten, he continued to believe that Pollock and the British Raj he represented had done him a great injustice.

8

The Wahabees on Trial

Our prison gates have closed upon batch after batch of unhappy misguided traitors; the Courts have sent one set of ring-leaders after another to lonely islands across the sea; yet the whole country continues to furnish money and men to the Forlorn Hope of Islam on our Frontier and persists in its blood-stained protest against Christian rule.

Sir William Hunter, *Our Indian Mussulmans: are they Bound in Conscience to Rebel against the Queen?*, 1876

In 1884 a remarkable autobiography was published in Delhi. It was entitled *Kala Pani: Tarikh e Ajeeb* (The Black Water: a Strange Story) and was the first printed memoir by an Indian Wahhabi, telling of his arrest, trial and transportation across the *kala pani* or black water – in this instance, the salt waters of the Bay of Bengal – to the Andaman Islands, where he spent sixteen years in exile. Its author was Muhammad Jafar of Thanesar, the petition-writer named by the mounted police daffadar Ghazan Khan in the evidence collected by his son and presented to the district magistrate at Thanesar in the late autumn of 1863: evidence suggesting that 'Munshi Ja'far of Thaneswar, whom the men call Khalifa, was the great man who passed up the Bengalis and their carbines and rifles.'

Muhammad Jafar's autobiography begins with a brief history of his early years: how after losing his father as a child he had lived like a vagabond until he taught himself to read and write, becoming a petition-writer at a magistrate's court. Then a chance meeting with a Wahhabi preacher changed his life and he came to regard his association with British infidel justice as highly corrupting. Muhammad Jafar glosses over any activity that presents him as anything other than a victim of injustice, but nevertheless implies that when the Sepoy Mutiny broke out in 1857 he headed a group of Wahhabis who went up to Sittana. He was then twenty-one years old. After General Cotton's break-up of the Hindustani Fanatics in 1858 he returned to Thanesar and resumed his former profession. This was 'by order of a Certain Person, and for a Hidden Object'. His work as a court petition-writer now became a front, for the 'Hidden Object' was jihad against the British Government and the 'Certain Person' was the Amir of the Wahhabis in Patna, Ahmadullah, one of the three Wahhabi mullahs detained by Commissioner William Tayler in the summer of 1857. Since the death of his co-detainee from natural causes Ahmadullah had assumed the leadership of the Wahhabi movement, while his younger brother Yahya Ali had become the movement's senior imam. Unknown to the British, these two brothers were now joint leaders of the Indian Wahhabis in plains India.

But then came the day in December 1863 when a friend with contacts in the judiciary in Thanesar arrived at Muhammad Jafar's house to warn him that the policeman Daffadar Ghazan Khan had made a 'false complaint' against him to the British authorities. Later that same night a party of policemen led by Captain Q. D. Parsons, Superintendent of Police in Amballa, raided his house and immediately found what Muhammad Jafar himself termed a 'dangerous letter', written but not yet sent. 'That letter', admitted Jafar, 'was addressed to the head of the Mujaheddin caravan and there was a coded message about the despatch of a few thousand coins.' The letter and other incriminating papers were seized, but no arrest was made. Next morning Muhammad Jafar gave out that he was going to Amballa, and fled. Captain Parsons, who can perhaps be best described as a rogue policeman with psychopathic tendencies that finally drove him to insanity, was furious. He had all the male members of Muhammad Jafar's household beaten up until his younger brother revealed that he had taken refuge in Delhi.

It was at this point that Sir Herbert Edwardes, the Commissioner at Amballa, grasped the full import of Muhammad Jafar and his letter. The military expedition against the Hindustani Fanatics was on the point of being launched under Neville Chamberlain's command, and here was the first hard evidence to show who was orchestrating the fighters in the Fanatic Camp in the mountains – and how. A reward of ten thousand rupees for information leading to Muhammad Jafar's arrest was authorised, and Delhi now became the scene of a major manhunt led by Captain Parsons. Jafar initially evaded the police net and fled with two companions in a phaeton to Aligarh. But Parsons got to hear of it, telegraphed ahead, and Muhammad Jafar was arrested on his arrival and brought back to Amballa in irons. Over the next few days the Wahhabi petition-writer was repeatedly roughed up by Parsons and his policemen in an effort to get him to reveal the names of 'the participants and supporters of the Jihad'. He was told that if he agreed to act as an 'approver' he would be released and given a high post, but that if he refused he would be hanged.

The use of approvers, miscreants who turned Queen's evidence against their fellow conspirators or partners in crime in return for a pardon, was a standard weapon in the British judicial armoury. In his autobiography Muhammad Jafar rails against these approvers and their lies, but the details he supplies show that it was the incriminating evidence he himself inadvertently provided, combined with his actions in leading the authorities to other branches of his organisation while on the run, which resulted in the series of arrests that destroyed the Wahhabi leadership in the 1860s and early 1870s.

Muhammad Jafar's letters led Captain Parsons to Patna and to Elahi Bux, aged head of one of the three Patna families and father of the two most important members of the Wahhabi council, Maulvis Ahmadullah and Yahya Ali. Acting on Parsons' telegraphed information, the Patna city magistrate arrested the old man in his own house and then released him on a surety of ten thousand rupees. Already forewarned by news of the arrest of Muhammad Jafar and his contacts in Amballa and Delhi, Elahi Bux's two sons set about burning all the incriminating documents stored in the Sadiqpore chota godown. This process appears to have been still incomplete when on 21 January 1864 Parsons himself arrived in Patna and, with the local magistrate and a large body of police, raided the Wahhabi headquarters. He was too late to catch Maulvi Ahmadullah, who had just left for Calcutta to attend a meeting with the Lieutenant-Governor of Bengal, but his younger brother Yahya Ali and two other members of the organisation were arrested and more papers seized. By Muhammad Jafar's account, Patna's disgraced former commissioner William Tayler was present at these arrests, which must have given him immense satisfaction.

The papers recovered mostly concerned money transactions and were not in themselves sufficient to build a case against anyone in the household at Sadiqpore, but they led the indefatigable super-intendent of police to a number of suspects in Bengal. Two of these were persuaded by Parsons – by means unknown but which may be guessed at – to testify that they had stayed in the small godown at Patna while on their way up-country from Bengal to the frontier to wage war against the British. There they had met the imam of the

Wahhabis, Yahya Ali, and had heard him preach jihad. When three of those arrested in Amballa after Muhammad Jafar's flight also turned approver, the cases against him, Yahya Ali, Elahi Bux and eight others were considered complete.

In the opinion of the Deputy-Commissioner of Amballa there was also sufficient evidence to charge Yahya Ali's elder brother Ahmadullah, but this was disputed by the Government of Bengal. Maulvi Ahmadullah was now held in high esteem by Government, he still had influential friends such as Sir Frederick James Halliday in England and, moreover, he occupied several important public positions in Patna, including that of Deputy Collector of Income Tax, and was a member of the Committee of Public Instruction. After the grave injustice he had suffered at the hands of William Tayler in 1857 it was was unthinkable that he should be arrested a second time except on the strongest evidence. So Ahmadullah was left untouched, no doubt greatly to the disappointment of Tayler, who was following these goings-on with the closest interest from his legal firm's offices in Patna.

Amid much general excitement and newspaper comment, the trial of eleven Wahhabis on the charge of waging war against the Queen opened at Amballa in April 1864 at the court of the Sessions Judge, Sir Herbert Edwardes, assisted by two Muslim and two Hindu Assessors. Yahya Ali refused to defend himself, so it was arranged by friends that he and his father should be represented by a young European barrister, persuaded to take on the case by a very large fee. Nevertheless, Yahya Ali remained aloof from the proceedings, endlessly reciting verses from the Quran and seemingly resigned to his fate. In his account of the trial Muhammad Jafar makes much of the way many of the several dozen witnesses called 'would look at us and weep bitterly' as they gave their evidence. He asserts that all were kept in police custody until the trial was over, and threatened with execution if they failed to testify as they had been coached to do. He cites the example of a boy who worked in his household and who at a preliminary hearing failed to give his evidence convincingly: 'On the same day he was beaten so brutally at night that he died before he could appear as witness in the sessions court. In order to avoid the embarrassment Mr Parsons announced that the boy had died of an illness.' The use of approvers' testimonies was always open to abuse, but it is hard to take Jafar's complaints of a mistrial too seriously when he himself acknowledges that there was indeed a conspiracy to make war against the Government of India and that he was part of it.

All eleven accused were found guilty. According to Muhammad Jafar, when the verdicts and sentences were pronounced not only the spectators in court but even the four Indian assessors had tears in their eyes: 'They wished our release at heart, but when they found the judge and the commissioner inclined on punishing us, they got frightened and wrote that the crime had already been proved.' Three of the prisoners were condemned to death and the remaining eight sentenced to transportation for life. In pronouncing sentence Sir Herbert Edwardes was in no doubt as to who was the most serious offender. 'It is proved against the prisoner Yahya Ali,' he declared,

> that he has been the mainspring of the great treason which this trial has laid bare. He has been the religious preacher, spreading from his mosque at Patna, under the most solemn sanctions, the hateful principles of the Crescentade. He has enlisted subordinate Agents to collect money and preach the Moslem Jihad. He has deluded hundreds and thousands of his countrymen into treason and rebellion. He has plunged the Government of British India, by his intrigues, into a Frontier War, which has cost hundreds of lives . . . He belongs to a hereditarily disloyal and fanatical family. He aspires to the merit of a religious reformer, but instead of appealing to reason and to conscience . . . he seeks his end in political revolution.

Muhammad Jafar was the next to receive the court's judgment. In his version of events, which conflicts in several material points with the official record, he declares that he heard with pride Edwardes' closing remarks about how he had used his great intelligence to conspire against the Government, and that Edwardes would be happy to see him hanged: 'I listened to the whole statement very calmly but in response to the last sentence I said, "It is God who decides about life and death. These things are not within your power. God has the power to finish you even before I die." He was very angry to hear my response.'

The Wahhabi trial was Sir Herbert Edwardes' last public duty before his early retirement, and he left for England as soon as it was over. His death from pneumonia three and a half years later was seen by Muhammad Jafar as God's punishment.

As soon as sentence had been passed the convicts had their heads shaven and their long beards cut off, and their white robes and turbans were exchanged for rough prison garb consisting of a saffron-coloured suit of coarse dungaree cloth – to all intents, orange overalls. By Muhammad Jafar's account, he and Yahya Ali rejoiced at their death sentences, the latter asserting that he felt as if he was 'in heaven and was watching heavenly nymphs'. They were placed in the condemned cell in Amballa Jail, where their continuing high spirits astonished their many visitors, European and Indian: 'Often they used to ask, "Soon you will be hanged. Why are you so happy?" We would only say that in our religion we attain martyrdom on being killed in this cruel way in the path of God and that was the reason for our happiness.'

However, the third prisoner sentenced to death was far from happy. He was Muhammad Shafi, a wealthy butcher in Delhi with contracts to supply meat to all the military cantonments along the Grand Trunk Road. Originally incriminated by Muhammad Jafar's letter, Shafi was shown to be the movement's main banker, using his agencies to move the Wahhabis' money from one place to another while making a considerable profit in the process. Deeply involved though he was in the conspiracy, Shafi was not a committed Wahhabi. Several months after sentencing he turned approver in a bid to save his own life.

Captain Parsons and others in Amballa had in the meantime continued their efforts to assemble a sustainable case against Maulvi Ahmadullah. Armed with the fresh evidence from Shafi and from a second approver, a Patna shoe-merchant named Elahi Baksh, they were finally able to bring him to justice. The revelation by Elahi Baksh in his testimony in court that three persons named in various letters as Ahmed Ali, Mohomed Ali and Ahmad Khan were all aliases used by Ahmadullah appears to have been a turning point. The identification proved beyond doubt that Ahmadullah was 'General Manager of the temporalities of the Kafilah [the name given to the Wahhabi's secret supply route]' and had abetted the waging of war against the Government of India 'by traitorously furnishing supplies of men and money to fanatics at Sittana engaged in warring against the Queen'.

On 1 January 1865 a new up-country newspaper named *The Pioneer** came into production and over the next three months charted not only the course of the trial of Ahmadullah Ali in Patna but also the public reaction to it, as the following extracts show:

2 January: The trial of Ahmud-oola, the chief Wahabee Moulvee of Patna, commences, we believe, today. The indefatigable Captain Parsons is now in Bankipore, assisting the Magistrate of Patna, Mr Ravenshaw.

11 January: Not deterred by the examples lately made in the case of the Patna and Umballa conspirators, some amiable gentlemen of the Wahabee persuasion have been getting up a minor conspiracy of their own in Purnea . . . A

---

* Founded and produced by my great-grandfather, George Allen: C.A.

Moulvee has been collecting money from the faithful in anticipation of the 'Jehad', which will be inaugurated by the Twelth Imam, who is about to make his appearance in a flood of light and glory!

13 January: Mahomed Shuffee [Muhammad Shafi] has turned Queen's Evidence, and the *Delhi Mail* says that his voluntary disclosures and the trial of Ahmad-oola at Patna, could lead to the hunting-up of the whole gang of traitors.

16 January: The Patna shoe-maker Iahee Buksh [Elahi Baksh] has been admitted as Queen's Evidence. His disclosures have been of a very important character, and bear strongly against the Moulvee.

1 March: The Judge of Patna has sentenced Moulvee Ahmed-oolla to be hanged. The case against him was complete. A miserable attempt at defence broke down at once; the only witness examined, we are told, simply perjured himself. The verdict of the assessors was unanimous. Thus ends the last act of the Wahabee drama . . . Ahmed-oolla, we suppose, will lose no time in telegraphing to Sir Frederick (James) Halliday.

In the event, the Government decided at the appeal stage that to hang the three Wahhabi leaders would elevate them to martyrs. Their death sentences were commuted to transportation for life, and with seven of the other co-defendants from the two trials they were shipped in chains to the Government of India's penal colony on the Andaman Islands. The banker Muhammad Shafi and the shoe-merchant Elahi Baksh were spared transportation because of the evidence they had provided. To Muhammad Jafar's great vexation the former was released after one year in jail, although his properties, said to be worth five million rupees, were never returned to him. The goods and properties of all those found guilty were confiscated, and the great serai in Sadiqpore Road which had for so long served as the Wahhabis' chota godown was demolished and the site converted to a public garden.

The proving in the law-courts that the chota godown in Patna was the centre of treasonable activity against the Government of India, and had been so for many years, was a very public vindication of Bill Tayler's conduct in detaining Ahmadullah Ali and the other leading Wahhabis back in 1857. There was now a great clamour, led by *The Pioneer* and other British newspapers in India, for Tayler's name to be cleared. Tayler himself was quick to reissue the defence of his actions that he had published in the wake of his dismissal, and again began to bombard the government authorities in India with intemperate letters accompanied by testimonials from the great and good. Finally in 1868 it seemed as if Tayler's name would at last be cleared when the Duke of Argyll, newly appointed Secretary of State for India, was prevailed upon to reopen his case. At this same time, however, William Tayler's nemesis, Sir Frederick James Halliday, former Lieutenant-Governor of Bengal, was appointed to the Council of India, which advised the Secretary for State for India. The Duke duly took the Council's advice – and opted to support the status quo.

Membership of the Council of India was for life, and Sir Frederick Halliday lived until 1901. William Tayler died in 1892 without ever clearing his name. 'To the hour of his death,' wrote Edward Lockwood, who had been Tayler's assistant in Patna in 1857, 'he thought and talked of nothing but the alleged injustice done to him, carrying on at the same time a hopeless war with those who had kept him from honour, by refusing to acknowledge him as the Saviour of Patna during the Indian Mutiny.' Lockwood compared Tayler to British India's first Governor-General, Warren Hastings, a small man but a great one, also brought low by his enemies: 'He was no bigger than Warren Hastings, and both like Virgil's bees *Ingentes animos augusto in pectore versant* [With mighty souls in little bodies present] ... They both would have saved themselves, and everybody else, a great deal of trouble had they used honey in the place of gall for ink.'

The Victoria and Albert Museum has in its South Asian collection 667 jewels and curios amassed by William Tayler during his years in India and bought from him in 1874. Among them is a seal ring in the form of an octagonal engraved carnelian set in silver. It carries the Quranic motto 'Verily He is the certain Truth' and is dated 1278 AH, corresponding to 1861–2. How it came into Tayler's possession is not known, but in the museum's inventory it is noted that the ring had formerly belonged to 'Ahmad-ullah, the Wahhabi rebel of Patna'.

The successful outcome of the Amballa and Patna trials greatly encouraged those in Government who regarded the Wahhabis as a major political threat. In their wake a somewhat shady Special Police Department, armed with extra-judicial powers of arrest, was set up under the leadership of J. H. Reily, the Deputy Inspector-General of Police in Bihar. Little is known about this special police unit but it is clear that a number of Wahhabi cells in eastern Bengal were turned over by its men, which led to further underground groups being uncovered. It soon became apparent that well-organised Wahhabi networks existed in many rural areas of Bihar and Bengal. By repeating the same successful tactics of inducing or forcing some of the accused to turn state's evidence, enough witnesses were found to bring the rest to court, resulting in a further series of high-profile trials in 1870 and 1871.

One of the many trails uncovered by Reily led his team to the Punjab. In October 1868 he visited Hoti Mardan, as close to tribal territory as he could safely go, and from there he sent an emissary to the Hindustani camp. Since the Ambeyla war five years earlier the Hindustanis under Abdullah Ali, son of Wilayat Ali, had been denied access to their traditional sanctuaries on the Mahabun Mountain and had been driven from one refuge to another on the Hazara side of the Indus. It was at one of these temporary camps that they were found by Reily's emissary, who reported back that the Hindustanis now numbered 362 fighting men, divided into eight units. They had seventy women and children with them and were living in very straitened circumstances. Reily then wrote to his superiors recommending pardons for all the Hindustanis – except for Abdullah Ali, their leader, and his deputy Faiyyaz Ali, a brother of Ahmadullah and Yahya Ali, both now in prison. Shortly afterwards Reily seems to have been visited in the Hazara hills by Abdullah Ali himself or by an emissary from the Hindustani camp – a mysterious meeting that may have been part of an unauthorised bid to bring about a peace deal with the Hindustani Fanatics. It evidently failed, and was subsequently hushed up, but at that meeting Abdullah Ali (or his emissary) made a statement of sorts, witnessed by the Assistant Commissioner of Rawalpindi, giving a great deal of information about the Wahhabi organisation, naming names of active members and supporters. Armed with this statement, Reily proceeded to Delhi, where an informant claimed to have seen a letter bearing the seal of Prince FIROZE SHAH, a nephew of the recently deposed last emperor, Bahadur Shah.

Prince Firoze Shah was the only member of the Mughal royal family to have participated actively in the 1857 uprising. With the collapse of the rebellion he had fled from Hindustan into Pathan tribal territory and, according to Reily's informant, subsequently used the Wahhabi supply chain to write to supporters in Delhi calling for jihadis to join him in the mountains. More arrests were made and statements were taken which pointed to the involvement of the leading *maulana* (learned teacher) of the school of Shah Waliullah: Maulana Sayyid Nazir Husain of Delhi, famous for his expositions of Hadith.

A mass of correspondence was subsequently seized from Sayyid Nazir Husain's home, including letters from Wahhabis convicted in the Amballa and Patna trials and from Abdullah Ali, the Wahhabi amir leading the Hindustanis on the frontier. These letters appeared to bear out a claim made by Abdullah Ali himself in his recent statement to Reily: that the respected maulana was the leader of the Wahhabis in Delhi and had been since before the Sepoy Mutiny.

Reily presented his case to the Punjab Government, under whose jurisdiction Delhi still came at this time, and Sayyid Nazir Husain was arrested. After six months' detention he was released without any charges being brought against him. Why the authorities decided not to proceed against the maulana remains a mystery; it may be that they were concerned about the circumstances in which Abdullah Ali's statement had been obtained, or it could be that Sayyid Nazir Husain's standing in Delhi was such that the authorities felt it best not to take the case against him any further. The maulana lived on to the venerable age of ninety-seven and always denied any links with the Wahhabis, just as he denied having played any active or supportive role in the Delhi uprising in 1857. One of his biographers states that of the hundreds of students who sat at his feet up to the time of his death in 1902, many were from Afghanistan and others came from as far afield as Kashgar, the Hijaz and Nejd.

Sir John Lawrence's successor, Lord Mayo, began his Viceroyalty by expressing his determination to 'put down Wahabeeism in India as he had put down Fenianism in Ireland'. A Special Commission was set up to examine the extent of the threat posed by the sect, one outcome of which was the first detailed report on the Indian Wahhabi movement and its origins, compiled by T. W. Ravenshaw, the City Magistrate at Patna. His report demonstrated the extraordinary extent of the movement's organisation, and its history of armed jihad. Then the whole Wahhabi issue came dramatically back to the boil with the murder of two of the highest officials in the land.

The first was the stabbing to death in Calcutta on 20 September 1871 of the acting Chief Justice, Justice John Norman, as he was on his way into court to preside over a Wahhabi trial. His assailant, a Pathan named Abdullah, went to the gallows without giving any coherent account of his motives. A visitor to India named James Routledge attended his trial and observed that the prosecutor soon abandoned 'any hope of discovering the motive of the crime'. But he further noted that 'a very uneasy feeling prevailed throughout India at this time . . . People saw in the murder the beginning of a system of warfare in which one man of a body of thugs of a new order would draw a lot which would condemn him to give his life, if need be, to destroy that of some distinguished Englishman. Looking at the circumstances of the case, with many notes before me, I have no doubt that the cause of the murder was the Wahabee trials.'

Routledge's fears appeared to be confirmed when less than five months after Justin Norman's assassination a second and even more sensational murder took place.

In September 1872 Lord Mayo began a tour of the Andaman Islands. Prison reform was one of the Viceroy's special interests, and he wanted to see for himself the conditions under which transportees served out their sentences on the several islands that made up the Andaman group. It is clear from Muhammad Jafar's account of his life in exile that he and his fellow Wahhabis were well treated by the British officials in charge of the penal colony. Because of his skills Muhammad Jafar worked as a chief clerk for the Chief Commissioner, and although he and the other leading Wahhabis were housed on different islands they were able to meet from time to time to pray and take food together. In Muhammad Jafar's eyes, what happened to Lord Mayo was a clear example of divine justice.

On 8 February the Viceroy, having inspected various utilities on the main islands, went ashore on the small island of Mount Harriet to view the sunset from its summit. Afterwards he descended in the gathering darkness to board his steam launch, preceded by two torch-bearers and surrounded by a small crowd of dignitaries, officials and armed guards. As Lord Mayo began to walk up the pier leading to his boat a man ran right through the party, jumped on him from behind and stabbed him twice. The assailant was immediately seized, but Lord Mayo fell over the side of the pier into the water. He got to his feet and was helped back on to the pier, and then into his carriage. But within minutes he was dead. His attacker was the Afridi Shere Ali, former orderly to Reynell Taylor and other commissioners of Peshawar, sentenced to transportation for a blood-feud killing in 1867.

Shere Ali was interrogated at length, but said nothing to link him with the Wahhabi convicts on the islands or their movement. Among those who gave evidence was George Allen, proprietor of *The Pioneer*, who had been standing close to Lord Mayo when he was struck. He reported that, when asked why he had attacked the Viceroy, Shere Ali had answered simply that 'God had ordered him to kill the enemy of his country, that he had no associate in his crime, but that God was the *shereek* [accomplice].' Allen described the Afridi as 'of middle height, brownish complexion, brown beard, and not at all a bad face, as far as one can judge – at least he does not convey the idea of a criminal', adding that 'the way in which he glories in the act with his harsh triumphant laugh is revolting to a degree. Hanging is a thousand times too good for him.'

After his sentencing Shere Ali was again interrogated by experienced police officers from the mainland. They too were unable to extract any hard information from him beyond the fact that 'he had heard of Abdullah having killed Justice Norman – that was a great deed, but that his was much greater than anything ever done before, as he had killed the greatest sahib in India . . . He hoped his name would be glorified in his country for the deed.' In his understandably triumphant rendering of the affair Muhammad Jafar has little to add, except to record that at his execution Shere Ali briefly spoke to those gathered to watch: 'He loudly addressed the prisoners: "Brothers! I have killed your enemy and you are a witness that I am a Muslim." And he then started *Kalma* [verses from the Quran] and died while doing that.'

By Muhammad Jafar's account Shere Ali acted simply as an instrument of divine vengeance, but had Jafar been privy to any Wahhabi conspiracy to kill Lord Mayo he would certainly not have said so, for fear of incriminating himself. While the British community in India was united in believing that the Wahhabis were behind the assassination, not a shred of evidence was found to support this belief. Yet two possibly unconnected events remain unexplained: a grandson of the late Wahhabi leader Wilayat Ali was found to have visited the Andaman Islands just before Lord Mayo's arrival, and on the night before the murder a person or persons unknown had given a great feast for Shere Ali.

The Wahhabi leaders and brothers Ahmadullah and Yahya Ali both died in exile as convicts on the Andaman Islands. Muhammad Jafar and the remaining Wahhabi convicts were eventually released in 1883 as part of an amnesty announced by the Viceroy, Lord Ripon. Muhammad Jafar returned to his home in Thanesar in December 1883, with a wife he had married during his exile and several children, to be met by his first wife and a twenty-year-old son he had not seen since he was a few months old. Through the good offices of the British magistrate of Amballa he was found a job and resettled in the local community.

By his own admission, Muhammad Jafar returned home a changed man. He had studied English while in the penal colony and it had opened up a new world: 'The English language', he had discovered, 'is a treasure of knowledge and arts. A person not knowing English cannot be well aware of world affairs. Without learning English one cannot become active and business-like.' As well as discovering modern society through his reading, Muhammad Jafar had also mixed with other communities and had learned religious tolerance, even coming to admire some of the British officers he met. Yet, in the end, he was forced to conclude that all this new learning had endangered his soul: 'Under the influence of Western knowledge I stopped offering prayers in the early hours of morning . . . I was not inclined to read Quran or listen to Hadith. I was involved with English language and English books all the time . . . I still remember how in those days Satan used to teach me not to believe in God and I sometimes used to do that. Sometimes when I used to read the arguments given by atheists I felt like believing them.'

Muhammad Jafar's remarkable autobiography ends with a passionate defence of religious conservatism:

This [English] language is so closely connected with materialistic life that it is not only harmful but dangerous for the spiritual life. If a young man, before learning Quran and traditions of the holy Prophet in detail, learns English and reads English books of various types and different disciplines as I used to do, he will become an unreligious, uncultured person with excessively free ideas to such an extent that it would not only be difficult but impossible to reform him . . . Such knowledge will certainly make a person unreligious and atheist if he is not well acquainted with Islam. It will create doubts in his mind which will remain there throughout his life.

It was better therefore to remain in blessed ignorance. His own life history, Muhammad Jafar finally advises the reader, should be read as a moral tale, for 'about a similar story, God in his book Holy Quran says, "In these stories there is a lesson to be drawn."'

The Wahhabi trials and the two assassinations caused great disquiet among both the small British community and India's much larger Muslim population. Since the traumatic events of the Indian Mutiny a view had developed among the British that Muslims were not to be trusted – a view that hardened when a report produced in 1875 found that, for all the round-ups and arrests, Wahhabi mullahs were still actively preaching as far afield as Madras and Rangoon, and that sedition was still being plotted.

At a public gathering a year before his assassination Lord Mayo had posed the rhetorical question: 'Are the Indian Mussalmans bound by their Religion to rebel against the Queen?' It was fiercely debated in the newspapers and a number of leading figures went into print on the subject, most notably the eminent civil servant, statistician and historian Sir William Hunter, who followed Lord Mayo with a polemic entitled *The Indian Musulmans* in which he inveighed against the Wahhabis, but also argued that by doing away with Muslim laws and imposing their own the British Government in India had turned India into the very domain of enmity that the Wahhabis had declared it to be, thus making it incumbent on every Muslim in India to fight against the British as a religious duty.

Where the authorities led, public opinion followed. British India's first unofficial poet laureate was Alfred Lyall, Commissioner of Berar in the late 1860s and early 1870s, and later Foreign Secretary. A number of Lyall's published verses take as their subject Muslims who hark back nostalgically to the years of Muslim glory and who conceal their hatred of the British. One of the earliest is 'A Sermon in Lower Bengal', written in 1864 in the wake of the first Wahhabi trial. It tells of a mullah from Swat named 'Hajee Mahomed Ghazee oorf Moojahid-ood-deen Wahabee' who addresses a secret assembly in the Bengal countryside and calls for volunteers to reclaim the empire they have lost. His audience is moved, but no one steps forward to answer his call and he leaves in disgust:

> Nay, though your spirits be willing, your flesh is but weak for crusading,
> When I face Englishmen's cannon I want better stuff at my back.

Two decades later Lyall yielded his laurels to a younger poet whose collection of *Departmental Ditties*, published in 1887, gave notice that a new laureate had appeared on the Indian scene. Rudyard Kipling's three years as assistant editor of the *Civil and Military Gazette* in Lahore taught him to regard Muslims as strong men worthy of respect but never to be trusted. In his early short story *On the City Wall* the narrator is tricked into aiding the escape of a political prisoner held in Lahore Fort. When he asks who this elderly prisoner might be he is told: '"He fought you in 1836, when he was a warrior youth, refought you in '57, and he tried to fight you in '71 but you had learned the trick of blowing men from guns too well. Now he is old; but he would fight you if he could." "Is he a Wahhabi, then?"' asks the narrator. More intriguingly, Kipling also wrote a strangely ambivalent scrap of verse, entitled 'From the Masjid-Al-Aqsa of Sayyid Ahmed (Wahhabi)', published many years after he left India in his collection of short stories *Traffics and Discoveries*. The narrator of the poem observes a Wahhabi convict in a chain-gang and is so impressed by his demeanour that he questions him about his 'red Yesterday'. But as he listens to the convict's tale the narrator finds himself transfixed by his 'miraculous weaving'. The poem closes with the lines:

> So I submitted myself to the limits of rapture –
> Bound by this man we had bound, amid captives his capture –
> Till he returned me to earth and the visions departed;
> But on him be the Peace and the Blessing: for he was great-hearted.

Much heart-searching about loyalties also took place in the Muslim community. The question of where a Muslim's first duty lay was hotly debated in the vernacular newspapers and in the mosques. Convocations of Sunni muftis and other jurists met in Calcutta and Delhi, and after much agonising produced fatwas pronouncing on whether India under the British was a dar ul-harb or a dar ul-Islam. In Calcutta they declared British India to be a domain of Faith, wherein religious rebellion was unlawful, whereas in Delhi they found the country to be a domain of enmity – but went on to state that rebellion against the British Government was nevertheless uncalled-for. At the same time there remained many ordinary Sunni and Shia Muslims who, for all their misgivings about Wahhabi dogma, saw the Wahhabi trials as victimisation of fellow-Muslims and part of a general pattern of increasing discrimination against Muslims. A number of historians from the Indian sub-continent have subsequently taken this line, citing as evidence the decline in the numbers of Muslims in government employment from this time onwards. The sad reality is that this decline was part of a pattern of withdrawal from public life, as the greater part of India's Sunni Muslim community began a slow retreat into the past.

Prior to British rule the Muslim community in India had always looked for political leadership to a Muslim aristocracy, headed by the Mughal emperor in Delhi who had ruled India through a number of regional viceroys. As Mughal power waned these governors had established themselves as local rulers, as either Muslim nawabs or Hindu or Sikh maharajas, each supported by a land-owning nobility. By degrees the British Government in India replaced or weakened these several tiers of political leadership with a modern administration which had little room for feudal or religious loyalties. The events of 1857 speeded up this transfer of power. The old emperor of Delhi was sent into exile in Burma, the Nawab of Tonk was similarly exiled to Benares, while many of the landowning nobles of Oude and Bihar had their great estates confiscated. At the same time the British set up a number of schools, such as Edwardes College in Peshawar and Aitchison College in Lahore, where sons of the former governing aristocracy could be educated along British lines, effectively isolating them from those whom they traditionally represented.

This restructuring further divided the Muslim community in India. A significant minority took the view that Muslims should embrace modern learning on the Western template and work for the advancement of their religion and community within the power structure of the British Raj until such time as they were ready to stand alone. Remarkably, their standard-bearer was one of the Naqshbandi radicals who had studied in Delhi under Shah Muhammad Ishaq in the 1840s and Sayyid Nazir Husain in the 1850s: the Mughal aristocrat SYAD AHMAD KHAN, founder of the Alighar movement and of the university of that name. Although he was at the same time a fierce critic of many aspects of British rule, he and his supporters found themselves increasingly isolated and abused as the greater part of their co-religionists turned their backs on progress.

Heading this great leap backward – and directing the attack on Syad Ahmad Khan and his progressives – were two groups of mullahs who shared exactly the same background as Syad Ahmad Khan: they too were Naqshbandis educated in the tradition of Shah Waliullah by Shah Muhammad Ishaq and Sayyid Nazir Husain in Delhi in the years leading up to the 1857 Mutiny.

The more overtly extreme of these two groups of mullahs was led by Sayyid Nazir Husain himself, the same man who had led the Wahhabi 'Delhi-ites' in 1857 and who in 1868 had been arrested by the British authorities on suspicion of being the Wahhabis' chief in Delhi. Together with two influential fellow alumni of the Madrassah-i-Rahimiya – Nawab Siddiq Hasan Khan of Bhopal and Maulvi Muhammad Husain Batalvi – he founded within a year or two of his release a politico-religious organisation known as *Jamaat Ahl-i-Hadith*, The Party of the People of the Hadith. Its leaders made no secret of their ambition to 'convert India into an abode of Islam through jihad'. Yet they also made it plain to their followers that this was not the time for jihad. 'Bretheren,' wrote Muhammad Husain Batalvi, 'the age of the sword is no more. Now instead of the sword it is necessary to wield the pen. How can the sword come into the hands of the Muslims when they have no hands? They have no national identity.'

Although determined to avoid direct conflict with the Government of India, the leaders of the Party of the People of the Hadith lost no opportunity to vent their religious spleen on co-religionists and infidels alike in as close an approximation to the ways of Al-Wahhab and his followers as they could manage within the law, even to the extent of employing physical violence against mosques and shrines. As a result, Ahl-i-Hadith preachers were banned from most mosques and denounced as Wahhabis. Fatwas were issued condemning all who followed them as 'disbelievers and apostates'. Eventually, in 1885, the Ahl-i-Hadith leadership published a book denying any links with Wahhabism and calling for the Government of India to cease employing that term in relation to themselves. Not wishing to give religious offence, the Government complied and ordered the terms 'Wahhabi' and 'Wahhabism' to be avoided henceforward in all its official correspondence. However, the Islamic community in India knew no such qualms, and to this day Ahl-i-Hadith continues to be described – with good reason – as Wahhabi in its origins and teachings. Its unremitting anti-polytheist, anti-innovation, anti-Shia and anti-Christian message continues to attract a hard core of fundamentalist Sunnis.

The second group of Delhi alumni adopted a less confrontational approach and benefited accordingly. Their leaders were Muhammad Qasim and Rashid Ahmed, two of the four-man group of jihadis that had left Delhi in the summer of 1857 to create their own dar ul-Islam at Thana Bhawan: Muhammad Qasim had acted as the group's military commander and may well have had a hand in the massacre in Shamlee mosque; Rashid Ahmed had presided over the imposition of sharia as the group's judge.

In May 1866, one year after the ending of the Patna Trial, these two mullahs set up their own madrassah at Deoband, a small town seventy-five miles north of Delhi and within a day's march of their earlier stamping-ground at Thana Bhawan. Initially the school had one teacher, Mullah Mahmood Deobandi, and one student, fifteen-year-old MAHMOOD UL-HASAN, and its premises consisted of nothing more than the courtyard beside an ancient mosque.

The main guiding force behind what became the Deobandi movement was Muhammad Qasim, who made no bones about his reason for setting up Deoband Madrassah – to preserve Islam in the face of British oppression. 'The English', he wrote, 'have perpetrated boundless acts of tyranny against the Muslims for their fault, if at all it was a fault, of the uprising of 1857 and their relentless endeavour for the independence of this country thereafter. They have left no stone unturned to plunder and obliterate the Islamic arts and science, Muslim culture and civilization.'

Initially known as the 'Arab Madrassah', Deoband Madrassah was organised on very different lines from the usual madrassahs in India, which up to this time were run fairly informally, depending very much on the authority of the school's senior mullah. Muhammad Qasim had learned at first hand how the British-backed Delhi College had been set up and he organised Deoband on a British model, with a rector, a vice-chancellor, a dean of studies and instructors, a set curriculum and a time-table. Yet the ethos was entirely that of the seminary: a strict discipline was maintained, the students lived simply and frugally, English was prohibited, Urdu provided the lingua franca, and all students began their studies by learning the Quran by heart in the original Arabic. All classes thereafter were focused on Quranic studies, taught by mullahs who were specialists in the Hadith and who placed great emphasis on the doctrine of oneness, in accordance with the teachings of Shah Waliullah of Delhi as passed down through his descendants Shah Abdul Aziz and Shah Muhammad Ishaq. Elements of Naqshbandi Sufism were maintained, especially those which elevated the authority of the teacher and allowed favoured students to be initiated into the intense master–disciple relationship felt to be in imitation of the close bonds that had existed between the Prophet and his Companions.

At the same time, the school promoted an uncompromising, puritanical and exclusive fundamentalism no less restrictive than Wahhabism. Deobandism denounced the worship of saints, the adorning of tombs, and such activities as music and dancing; it waged a ceaseless war of words against Shias, Hindus and Christian missionaries; it distanced itself from much that was progressive in Indian society, shunning the British law-courts as far as possible without breaking the law; it retained militant jihad as a central pillar of faith, but focused this jihad on the promotion of Islamic revival and identity through the principle of the immutability of sharia, the oneness of God and the overarching, guiding authority of the ulema.

When denounced as Wahhabis, as happened frequently, the Deobandis declared themselves to be pillars of Hanafi orthodoxy. Their official line on Wahhabism was probably best represented by a statement contained in a fatwa put out by Rashid Ahmed which stated that Al-Wahhab 'held excellent beliefs but his creed was Hanbali. Although he was of rather harsh temperament he and his followers are good people.' This did not prevent three hundred mainstream ulema putting out a fatwa forbidding Sunnis to have any dealings with Deoband Madrassah. 'The Deobandis,' read part of this fatwa, 'because of their contempt and insult in their acts of worship towards the saints, prophets and even the Holy Prophet Muhammad and the very Person of God himself, are very definitely apostates and infidels. Their apostasy and heresy is of the worst kind, so that anyone who doubts their apostasy and heresy even slightly is an apostate and infidel. Muslims should be very cautious of them and stay away from them, let alone pray behind them.'

Fundamentalist to the core in its theology, Muhammad Qasim Nanautawi's Deoband was also boldly innovative, particularly in making Islamic studies accessible to the masses. The school very deliberately set out to draw its students from the peasantry, the dispossessed and the uneducated, and refused to accept funding from Government or from wealthy benefactors, insisting that it would accept only religious donations. Students as young as five were accepted and often remained there until adulthood, so that many came to identify with the madrassah as their main home and with their teacher as a surrogate parent. This was in striking contrast to earlier models, where taliban often moved from one mullah to another picking up learning wherever they could, often on a haphazard basis. The consequence was a closed, introverted, tight-knit society of young males approaching or in the throes of puberty, taught to regard their sexuality as innately sinful and women as weak creatures incapable of self-control and easily tempted, therefore best kept in subjection. Homosexuality was recognised to be as great a sin as adultery, yet at the same time intense friendships were accepted as the norm, with all that pent-up sexuality and feeling being channelled into mystical experience and fervid devotion towards God – and towards his regents on earth.

While always proclaiming itself a bastion of conservatism, Deoband nevertheless exploited modern technology, making good use of the print medium to put out its message, especially in the dissemination of fatwas on every issue brought before its muftis. Officially the Deoband muftis rejected *ijtihad*, the use of independent reasoning in interpreting a matter of sharia. But they also took the line that on every issue there was an outer injunction to be taken literally and an inner meaning open to informed interpretation: this was nothing less than ijtihad by the back door. So proficient did Deoband become in its provision of religious judgements on request that it more or less cornered the market, issuing so many thousands of highly conservative fatwas every year that it came to be seen in India as the last word on all matters pertaining to sharia and how a good Muslim should behave. One of the earliest of these fatwas declared the activities of the moderniser Syad Ahmad Khan of Alighar to be un-Islamic, and banned all Muslims from joining his Patriotic Association.

By such populist means Deoband Madrassah gained the support of the masses, leading the way among the several revivalist schools that came into being at this time in providing young Muslims with a new sense of identity and an alternative to the British model. Deoband became known throughout India as the place where boys could safely be initiated into the old religion of their forefathers. In 1879 the institution assumed the additional name of *Dar ul-Ulum*, the Abode of Islamic Learning. By then it was already well on the way to becoming renowned throughout the Islamic world as a centre of religious study second only to the university attached to the great mosque of Al-Aqsa in Cairo.

By the end of the nineteenth century Dar ul-Ulum Deoband had founded more than two dozen allied madrassahs in northern India. At the same time the school produced an ever-expanding cadre of graduates who formed a new class of reformist ulema not unlike the Jesuits of the Catholic Counter-Reformation in their impact: a distinctive, politicised leadership of religious teachers with professional qualifications in the form of degrees who could compete to advantage against all others, outshine critics in public debates, take the lead in public prayers and, above all, disseminate the teachings of the Dar ul-Ulum Deoband school in their own madrassahs.

Towards the end of the nineteenth century these teachings were dignified with the term *salafi*, or 'following the forefathers', based on the ideal of emulating the early fathers as a basis for Islamic renewal first developed by the medieval Hanbali jurist of Damascus, Ibn Taymiyya, and those who followed them became known as *salafiyya* – 'followers of the forefathers'. Both words were associated with the Prophet's Companions and the early scholars of Islam.

The impact of Dar ul-Ulum Deoband and its missionaries on central and south Asian Islam was immense. They gave new authority to the ulema and undermined the traditional authority of secular leaders. They gave new impetus to the old ideals: that a true Muslim's first duty was to his religion; that his only country was the world community of Islam; and that he had an obligation to defend Islam wherever it was under attack. The end result was a seismic shift in the Sunni Islam of South Asia, which became increasingly conservative and introverted, less tolerant, and far more inclined to look for political leadership to the madrassah and the madrassah-trained political leader committed to the cause of leading the umma back to the true path. The consequences were profound.

9

The Frontier Ablaze

One is inclined to sum up the causes of the outbreak under three heads, the first of which is fanaticism, the second, fanaticism, and the third, fanaticism... Wherever Islam is the creed there will be found disciples prepared to preach its cause and to fire the undercurrent of feeling which forms part of this weird belief. All that such preachers ask is that a crisis may arrive which shall stir the popular feeling out of the narrow channels of trade, commerce and homeside agriculture. And in 1897, this crisis came ... the whole business may be claimed to be the successful attempt of the Mullahs to seize a moment of unrest and work upon the fanaticism of the tribesmen.

Lionel James of Reuters, *The Indian Frontier War*, 1898

'Who or why, or which or what, is the Akond of Swat?' wrote the poet Edward Lear in his *Nonsense Songs* in 1871, reflecting the Western world's general ignorance of Indian affairs at this time. To Madame Blavatsky, founding mistress of the Theosophical Society, the Akhund was nothing less than an evil genius. In 1878 she declared Abdul Ghaffur to be 'the founder and chief of nearly every secret society worth speaking of among the Mussulmans, and the dominant spirit in all the rest. His apparent antagonism to the Wahabees was but a mask, and the murderous hand that struck Lord Mayo was certainly guided by the old Abdul.' But Madame Blavatsky was, as usual, wide of the mark.

Despite the Akhund's decisive intervention against them at Ambeyla in 1863, the British authorities in Peshawar recognised him as a positive influence. 'His life', wrote a British official of the Akhund,

> seems to have been one of devotion, humility, abstinence and chastity; the doctrines he taught were as tolerant and liberal as those of his Wahhabi opponents were intolerant and puritanical. Judged by the standard applied to other religious leaders, he used his influence, according to his lights, for good, supporting peace and morality, discouraging feuds, restraining the people from raiding and offences against their neighbours.

But with Abdul Ghaffur's death in 1877 the cohesion he had brought to Swat, Buner and beyond began to unravel. His death coincided with what a distinguished historian of Anglo-Afghan relations, Sir Kerr Fraser-Tytler, has called 'the high water mark of British forward policy' – the theory that India was best served by extending British influence deep into Afghanistan in order to prevent the Russians from doing the same. After two decades of 'masterly inactivity' on the part of Lawrence, Mayo and other viceroys, the pendulum swung the other way with the arrival in India of the new Viceroy, the mercurial Lord Lytton.

In September 1878, in response to the reception of Russian envoys in Kabul by Sher Ali, the Amir of Kabul, Lytton despatched a mission up the Khyber to bring the Amir to his political senses. It was led by that old frontier war-horse Neville

Chamberlain, now a major-general and a KCB, and included in his party as interpreter was another frontier veteran, Surgeon-Major Henry Bellew. Half-way up the pass, beneath the hill fort of Ali Masjid, the party was met by the Afghans and told that if they proceeded any further their lives would be forfeit. This snub was all Lord Lytton required to order the invasion of Afghanistan, an action that received the reluctant backing of the British Prime Minister.

Three armies duly entered Afghanistan by three different routes (one fighting its way through the same mountain region, the Tora Bora, where in December 2001 slipshod planning allowed Osama bin Laden and many of his 'Arabs' to slip through the US Special Forces net into Pakistan). The Amir was forced to flee into exile and a rival, Yakub Khan, was set on the throne of Kabul in his place. The usual pattern of catastrophe, retreat and retribution followed: the killing of the British Resident along with his Guides escort at Kabul; a military disaster at Maiwand, followed by a triumphant march and victory at Kandahar; the collapse of Lytton's forward policy and the installation of a much less pliable amir in Kabul. The hero of the hour was the commander of the Kabul Field Force, Fred 'Bobs' Roberts, now a major-general, who nevertheless left Afghanistan declaring that 'the less the Afghans see of us, the less they will dislike us'.

The real victor of the Second Afghan War was the new Amir of Afghanistan, ABDUR RAHMAN, whose claim to rule with the proverbial rod of iron was no boast. Within the space of twenty years he forged a nation out of a land of semi-autonomous provinces and warring fiefdoms, crushing local rebellions with ruthless cruelty, indulging in mass executions and deportations. To strengthen his authority over the Afghans still further Amir Abdur Rahman declared himself imam, just as Emir Abd al-Aziz ibn Saud had in Nejd a century earlier. Indeed, so confident was Abdur Rahman of his own religious authority that he further claimed for himself the right to interpret sharia as a mujtahid.

Taking the view that the existence of kaffirs on his territory was an affront to Islam, he went on to declare jihad on the Shia Hazaras in the provinces of Wardak and Bamian, and on the genuinely heathen Kalash of Kafiristan. To reduce the power of the troublesome Ghilzai Pathans, who occupied a swathe of territory between Kabul and Kandahar, he transported large numbers into Hazara country as part of his campaign to reduce the Shias there. At the same time, Amir Abdur Rahman brooked no nonsense from the ulema: when an influential mullah of Kandahar dared to accuse the Amir of infidelity, he had him dragged from the mosque where he had sought sanctuary under the famous cloak of the Prophet, and killed him with his own hands.

Yet having secured absolute power within his borders the Amir found himself constantly humiliated by the British, particularly in the case of their partition of the Pathan tribal lands as formalised in November 1893 in the creation of the Durand Line. In that same year the Amir complained to the Viceroy that 'in your cutting away from me these frontier tribes, who are people of my nationality and my religion, you are injuring my prestige in the eyes of my subjects, and will make me weak, and my weakness is injurious to your government.' Fearful that the British were planning a new round of forward policy-making, Abdur Rahman then embarked on a propaganda campaign aimed at securing the loyalties of the trans-border Pathans. He declared himself *Zia-ul-Millat wa-ud-Deen* (Light of Union and Faith), and sent out to every mullah on the frontier a document entitled *Taqwim-ud-Deen* (The Rightness of Faith). This purported to be a book of religious doctrine, but was devoted almost entirely to the promotion of jihad as a religious duty.

Abdur Rahman's actions were bound up with his desire to be seen by the wider Muslim world as a religious leader, taking as his model the Ottoman sultan Abdul Hamid. The first stirrings of pan-Islamic revivalism were now beginning to be felt in several quarters of the Muslim world, accompanied by a growing

awareness among Muslim intellectuals that Islam required a
new model if it was to survive the advance of Western imperialism. Among the first to articulate this new thinking was that
mystery man of Islamic modernism, Sayyid Jamal al-Din al-
Afghani, popularly known as 'the Afghan'. Al-Afghani had first
appeared on the Indian scene just before the Sepoy Mutiny, as
a teenage talib. Whether he took up arms against the British is
debatable, but what he saw in India convinced him that Britain
was Islam's greatest enemy and had to be opposed. In 1866 he
was to be found in Afghanistan working as the chief counsellor
of a warlord of Kandahar. Expelled by Abdur Rahman, he reappeared in India to become a vociferous opponent of the
moderniser Syad Ahmad Khan of Alighar and his philosophy of
revival through co-operation. However, 'the Afghan' also
rejected the Deoband philosophy, arguing that true Islamic
revival could only be accomplished by Muslims uniting and
modernising. Although his last years were spent under house
arrest in Turkey, his promotion of pan-Islamism in the last
decades of the nineteenth century inspired radicals throughout
the Muslim world, leading in the 1920s to the formation of two
anti-imperialist political movements: in Egypt the *Ikhwan-ul-
Muslimeen*, the Muslim Brotherhood; and in India *Jamaat-i-Islami*,
the Party of Islam.

This burgeoning pan-Islamic revivalism went hand in hand
with a growing belief among Muslims worldwide that momentous
times were fast approaching as the Christian millennium drew
near: that centuries of Christian advances were at an end and that
Islam was now in the ascendant. In North Africa this millenarianism found expression in the Mahdiyyah movement, led by the
Sudanese mystic Muhammad Ahmad, who in 1881 proclaimed
himself the Mahdi. Like Al-Wahhab and Syed Ahmad before him,
Muhammad Ahmad set out to revive the golden age of Islam by
raising an army of the faithful and declaring jihad on an infidel
regime – in this instance, the Egyptian Government. The death of

General Gordon in Khartoum at the hands of the Mahdi's followers in 1885 provided an enormous fillip to the Mahdi's cause, while the subsequent failure of the British to overthrow the dervish armies of the Mahdi's appointed caliph, Abdullah, was widely interpreted as a sign that Christian power was on the wane.

In India traditional allegiances were further weakened as the increasingly eager faithful turned away from their secular leaders to listen to the mullahs who preached that the appointed time was nigh. And nowhere was this mood of expectation more charged than among the Afghan–Pathan tribes of the North-West Frontier. In the summer of 1895 an engineer named Frank Martin entered Afghanistan to take up a position as chief engineer to Amir Abdur Rahman. Like Herbert Edwardes and others before him, Martin was struck by the influence of the mullahs over the ordinary people – but what was much more disconcerting was their hatred of non-Muslims:

The sight of a *kafar*, and all who are not Mussulman are infidels, is so obnoxious that they spit in the street, and to kill one of them is quite a meritorious action in their eyes . . . They argue that the enemy of their religion is the enemy of God and therefore a loathsome thing, and that the Koran commands them to kill all such, and promises that if they themselves are killed in doing so, they shall go straight to Paradise, and that a man who fails to kill a Kafar, but suffers death himself in the attempt, has only a little less rank in heaven than the one who succeeds.

This hostility he blamed on the mullahs and the new licence given them by their amir and imam, Abdur Rahman: 'Very few, with the exception of the moullahs, can read the Koran, and the latter apparently give very free translations when it suits their purpose; such, for instance, as that of killing unbelievers, on which is built up the principle of Jihad, holy war, and which the

Amir has had printed in pamphlet form and distributed throughout the country of late.'

In the mid-1890s every Pathan tribe on the North-West
Frontier seemed quite suddenly to acquire its own charismatic
religious leader, a human talisman who had it in his power to sway
his flock to his purpose. These charismatics included the Hadda
Mullah of the Mohmands, Mullah Powindah of the Mahsuds,
Said Akbar of the Akakhel Afridis, Indrej of Bazar, the Manki
Mullah, the Palam Mullah – and, above all, the Sadullah Mullah
of Swat.

In the spring of 1897 an envoy of Sultan Abdul Hamid arrived
in Kabul to encourage the Amir to join his pan-Islamic revival.
This led Amir Abdur Rahman to summon all the leading ulema of
the Pathans to a theological conference in Kabul. Whatever the
Amir may have intended, these delegates left Kabul believing
that the British Empire was on the point of collapse and that the
time had come to strike a mighty blow for Islam. They returned to
their constituencies convinced that the sultan had just won a great
victory against the Christians in Greece, that the Turks had captured the Suez Canal and Aden, and that Germany and Russia
had joined them in a war against Britain. The mood among the
frontier tribes at this time was described by Winston Churchill as
'a vast but silent agitation . . . Messengers passed to and fro among
the tribes. Whispers of war, a holy war, were breathed to a race
intensely passionate and fanatical. The tribes were taught to
expect prodigious events. A great day for their race and faith was
at hand.'

The British authorities in Peshawar and Lahore saw this
sudden agitation as Kabul-inspired, and assumed it would blow
over. They entirely underestimated the potency of the banner of
jihad first planted on the Frontier by Syed Ahmad seventy years
earlier.

It is a remarkable testimony to the legacy of Ambeyla that
despite all the information brought to light in the Wahhabi trials,

the Hindustani Fanatics had been suffered to remain on the Frontier. And it is all the more remarkable when one considers that their leader and amir was Maulvi Abdullah Ali, the same man who had taken over command of the Hindustani Fanatics almost forty years earlier and had subsequently led them through the Ambeyla campaign.

After Ambeyla the Hindustanis had been driven from refuge to refuge as pressure from their now implacable enemy, the Akhund of Swat, had forced one reluctant host after another to send them on their way. In 1868, as mentioned earlier, they had been reported on by that shadowy police officer J. H. Reily. That same winter Alfred Wilde, now a lieutenant-general, had led the Hazara Field Force into the Black Mountains, where the Hindustanis had found shelter, but could do little more than drive them from one mountain hideout to another.

In 1873 Abdullah Ali's youngest brother in Patna, Muhammad Hasan, appealed to the Government of India for an official pardon that would allow the Hindustanis to return to their homes. His request was turned down, on the grounds that since the Fanatics' support had withered away they would eventually be forced to give up. But the authorities, as so often before, were wrong. The Hindustanis clung on, kept alive by irregular and grudging hand-outs from the hill tribes, and still strong enough to play supporting roles in three further tribal uprisings into the Black Mountains in 1881, 1888 and 1891.

After the last of these had been suppressed Abdullah Ali appealed to SAYYED FIROZE SHAH, grandson of the Hindustani Fanatics' first patron Sayyed Akbar Shah and now leader of the Sayyeds of Sittana, to be allowed to recross the Indus, together with his brother and his three sons. After much argument the elders of the local Amazai gave permission for the remnants of the Hindustanis to return to their old haunts on the eastern slopes of the Mahabun Mountain in the village of Tilwai, scarcely a stone's throw from their original camp at Sittana. They now found themselves caught up in the ongoing power struggles between their patron Sayyed Firoze Shah and the male heirs of Abdul Ghaffur, late Akhund of Swat.

And yet when a British journalist from Lahore came to write about the North-West Frontier at this time, he noted that the Hindustanis were still widely admired among the tribes for their 'fierce fanaticism'. Their colony was celebrated locally as the *Kila Mujahidin* (Fortress of the Holy Warriors), wherein they 'devoted their time to drill, giving the words of command in Arabic, firing salutes with cannon made of leather, and blustering about the destruction of the infidel power of the British'. It was said that they were still awaiting the return of Syed Ahmad, their Hidden Imam.

It is unlikely that Abdullah Ali or any of his mujahedeen attended Amir Abdur Rahman's theological conference held in Kabul in the spring of 1897. Nor is it likely that the attendees included a sixty-year-old Bunerwal named MULLAH SADULLAH, also known as the *Mastun* Mullah (Ecstasy Mullah), or the *Sartor Fakir* (Bare-headed Saint), but who became best known to the British as the 'Mad Fakir' or the 'Mad Mullah'. After many years' absence from Buner Mullah Sadullah reappeared quite suddenly in his homeland in the midsummer of 1897, proclaiming that he had been visited by a number of saints who included both the late Akhund of Swat and Syed Ahmad, and had been ordered by them to turn the British out of Swat and the Peshawar vale. God had granted the British an allotted term of sixty years as rulers in Peshawar, and that term was now over. Those who joined him in this jihad need have no fears, for the saints had also informed him that the bullets of the British would turn to water and the barrels of their guns would melt. Furthermore, he was reinforced by a heavenly host, massed but hidden from human sight on the summit of the nine-thousand-foot sacred peak of Ilam Ghar, which overlooks the Swat valley. As for supplies, the single pot of rice he had with him was quite sufficient to feed a multitude.

The Mad Fakir's message spread like a bush-fire through the mountains of Swat and Buner. 'As July advanced,' wrote Churchill, 'the bazaar at Malakand became full of tales of the Mad Fakir. A great day for Islam was at hand. A mighty man had arisen to lead them. The English would be swept away.' To cap it all, Mullah Sadullah had with him a thirteen-year-old boy by the name of Shah Sikander (Alexander) who was the rightful heir to the throne of Delhi and would rule over India once it had been restored to a dar ul-Islam. The identity of this young pretender remains a mystery, but it will be remembered that in 1868 the fugitive Mughal prince Firoze Shah, cousin of the last emperor, had joined the Hindustanis briefly in the Mahabun Mountain before moving on by stages to Kabul, Bokhara and Constantinople. This Mughal Bonnie Prince Charlie died in lonely exile in Mecca in 1897, and his widow promptly applied for and was granted a pension by the Government of India. Officially Prince Firoze Shah died without an heir, but it is just conceivable that thirteen-year-old Shah Sikander's father or mother was the fruit of a union contracted during the Mughal prince's sojourn in the Hindustani camp back in 1868.

In mid-July 1897 Mullah Sadullah raised his green banner in the Swat valley and summoned the surrounding tribes to arms, much to the anger of the heirs of the late Akhund of Swat, who tried and failed to have him expelled. Little is known about Sadullah's theological antecedents but he was supported by Sayyed Firoze Shah, head of the Sayyid clan, in pursuit of his bid to have himself proclaimed Padshah of the Swatis like his grand-father before him. The nickname of 'bare-headed' given to Sadullah disqualifies him as a Wahhabi, since the latters' theology required the head to be covered at all times. But the Mad Fakir's association with a pretender to the throne of Delhi does suggest links with the Hindustani Fanatics. That he had the support of a significant faction of the Hindustanis at Sittana is beyond question, even though their leader Abdullah Ali refused initially to join

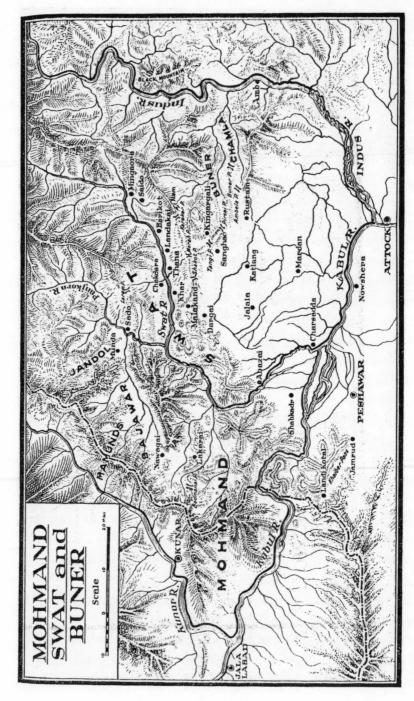

'Mohmand, Swat and Buner': map from 1898

in Sadullah's crusade. Many young mujahedeen from the Hindustani camp, easily identified by their distinctive black waistcoats and dark-blue robes, were spotted among the Fakir's ranks. Their presence prompts the question whence Mullah Sadullah drew his inspiration if not from the legacy of jihad initiated by the first Hindustani Fanatic, Syed Ahmad.

As part of their policy of renewed intervention the British authorities had in 1895 bullied the Swatis into allowing two military forts to be built in their territory, ostensibly to guard the road linking Peshawar with Dir to the north. One outpost stood at a crossing-point of the Swat River at Chakdara, and the second a few miles to the south at Malakand, on the crest of the mountain range overlooking the Vale of Peshawar. The presence of these two forts, manned not by local tribal levies but by regular Indian Army troops with British officers, was regarded by the Swatis as a direct encroachment on their much-vaunted independence – and, no less seriously, as a desecration of Swat as a dar ul-Islam. Consequently, when the Mad Fakir issued his summons thousands of Swatis ignored the advice of their khans and flocked to join his banner. On 21 July 1897 Mullah Sadullah prophesied that by the rising of the new moon in ten days' time the British would have been driven out of Malakand. Five days later two *lashkars* (tribal armies) marched on the forts of Chakdara and Malakand.

At Malakand the last chukka of an afternoon of polo was being played when the grooms attending the officers' ponies were warned by watching Pathans to get off home as there was to be a fight. Shortly afterwards Lieutenant Harry Rattray was riding back from the polo ground to Chakdara, where the regiment raised by his father was on garrison duty, when he met two cavalry troopers galloping the other way. They told him that a tribal army was advancing on Malakand down the left bank of the Swat River with banners flying and drums beating. Rattray put spurs to his horse and rode right through them to reach his post at Chakdara, from where he sent a telegram to Major Harold Deane, the political agent at Malakand, warning him of the danger.

Deane at once advised the local commander to prepare for an attack and to telegraph Hoti Mardan for immediate reinforcements. This prompt action saved both garrisons from annihilation. The message was received in the Guides headquarters at 8.30 p.m. and five hours later, fed, rested and armed, a relief column set off to cover the thirty-two miles to Malakand.

As darkness fell on 26 July both camps at Malakand and Chakdara came under fire. Throughout the night one assault followed another as wave after wave of tribesmen attempted to break through their defences. Just before dawn a squadron of Guides Cavalry came trotting up the road from the plain to the Malakand fort, followed soon afterwards by the 11th Bengal Lancers. They took the pressure off the defenders and a counter-attack reclaimed some of the positions lost in the night. At 5 p.m. that same afternoon the main relief force of Guides Infantry and two battalions of Sikh and Dogra infantry arrived at Malakand, having marched right through the heat of the day at a cost of twenty-one deaths from sunstroke and apoplexy. Despite these reinforcements the defenders continued to be pressed hard for three days and nights, culminating in a massed onslaught on the night of 29 July in which in excess of ten thousand tribesmen took part. 'Bands of Ghazis,' wrote Lieutenant P. C. Elliott-Lockhart of the Guides Infantry, 'worked up by their religious enthusiasm into a frenzy of fanatical excitement, would charge our breastworks again and again, leaving their dead in scores after each repulse, while the standard bearers would encourage their efforts by shouting, with much beating of tom-toms, and other musical instruments.'

In this attack Mullah Sadullah, the Mad Fakir, was slightly wounded and a number of his supporters were killed, including his second-in-command and another leader described as his 'close companion'. Today a well-preserved tomb can be seen beside the

A mullah rallies his mujahedeen at Malakand: a detail from the charge of the 13th (Duke of Connaught's) Bengal Lancers at Shabkadar, August 1897, a watercolour (now lost) painted by Major Edmond Hobday, who fought in the engagement (National Army Museum)

A scene from the great Frontier uprising of 1897–8: Sikh infantry face a charge from Swati tribesmen at Malakand. A watercolour by Major Edmond Hobday (National Army Museum)

British and Indian troops defend Chakdara Fort against Swati tribesmen in a night attack: a watercolour by Major Edmond Hobday, who was present at the engagement (National Army Museum)

The famous charge of the Gordon Highlanders to retake the Dargai Heights on 20 October 1897 during the Tirah Campaign (Mary Evans Picture Library)

A Pathan tribal lashkar come forward under their khan to make their submissions to a British political officer at the conclusion of the shortlived Third Afghan War of 1919 (Charles Allen)

The ruins of Dariyah, first capital of the al-Saud dynasty, photographed by Harry St John Philby in 1917–18 (Royal Geographical Society)

The Emir of Nejd and Imam of the Ikhwan, Abdul Aziz ibn Saud, with his brothers and sons, photographed by Captain Shakespear when he joined his camp near Thaj in 1911

(Royal Geographical Society)

The former British political officer Harry St John Philby shortly after his supposed conversion to Wahhabi Islam in Mecca in September 1930 (Royal Geographical Society)

British diplomats present Ibn Saud with the Grand Cross of the Order of the Bath in Riyadh in 1935. Behind the King stand the heir-apparent, Prince Saud, and Ibn Saud's favourite son, Prince Feisal. Photography was forbidden but the assistant consul, Captain de Gaury, made a sketch of the scene in his notebook. His accompanying note explains that the wearing of Arab dress for foreigners was obligatory (Royal Society of Asian Affairs)

The one-eyed Mullah Muhammad Omar appears on a rooftop in Kandahar draped in the cloak of the Prophet in April 1996 before being acclaimed Amir-ul-Momineen of the Islamic Republic of Afghanistan. A rare photograph taken by the veteran television cameraman Peter Lorimer (Peter Lorimer/Frontline/Getty)

Armed Taliban near Kabul, 1996 (Hurriyet/AP/Empics)

The madrassah of Dar ul-Ulum Deoband in India as it is today. Founded by two Wahhabi survivors of the 1857 uprising, it has become the headquarters of a fundamentalist teaching that now extends to thirty thousand madrassahs worldwide

(David Bathgate/Corbis)

Taliban in a classroom at Dar ul-Ulum Deoband madrassah.
At the core of Deobandi teaching is the Hadith and Tawhid, the oneness of God

(David Bathgate/Corbis)

The emir of Al-Qaeda and his wazir: Osama bin Laden, also known as
'Al-Shaykh', with the man widely viewed as his lieutenant but more
accurately described as his ideologue, Dr Ayman al-Zawahri. Taken
from a video released by Al-Jazeera in October 2001 (AP/Empics)

The Wahhabi–Ahl-i-Hadith–Deobandi axis: leaders of Pakistan's main Islamist political
parties at a rally in Rawalpindi in August 2003. In 2001 they united to form the Muttahida
Majlis-I-Amal (MMA) or United Action Front, which today governs the North-West
Frontier Province, reintroducing Wahhabi sharia and lending tacit support to the Taliban.
In the centre is Shah Ahmed Noorani of JUP, flanked by the burly Maulana Fazal-ur-
Rahman of JUI(F) and the white-bearded Qazi Hussain Ahmad of JI. Beside the Qazi
is Maulana Samiul Haq of JUI(S) (Jewel Samad/AFP/Getty Images)

Malakand road. According to local oral tradition, it covers the grave of Hazrat Sikander Shah Shaheed, Honourable King Alexander the Martyr, who is said to have flown a red and white banner at the battle. This may well be the grave of the young Sikandar Shah, supposed grandson of the Mughal Prince Feroze Shah, of whom nothing more was ever heard.

After this setback the main focus of attack shifted from Malakand to the smaller and more vulnerable garrison guarding the bridge at Chakdara, held by two hundred men of Rattray's Sikhs, many of them sons and grandsons of the men who had served with Thomas Rattray through the Mutiny. For six days they were invested by a force of not less than seven thousand men supported by about two hundred standard-bearers – together presenting, in the opinion of a cavalry officer who saw them, 'a very fine spectacle. The advance was made by their usual rushes and accompanied by their well-known maniacal shouts. Their standard-bearers, leading parties from cover to cover, worked their way up under the walls, where the steady fire of our Sikhs repelled all attacks.'

Although the telegraph line had been cut, communications with Malakand and the outside world were maintained by a signaller named Sepoy Prem Singh, who regularly crawled out under fire to an exposed tower to flash brief messages with his heliograph. On 2 August, by which time the garrison had been without water for three days, he sent his last signal, brief and to the point: 'Help us.' On the following day the Malakand Field Force, consisting of three full brigades under the command of a no-nonsense Anglo-Irish general named Bindon Blood, pushed on through Malakand to Chakdara, and all resistance collapsed.

The refusal of the Mad Fakir's heavenly host to come to their aid turned the Swatis against him and he slipped away as mysteriously as he had appeared. The heads of the tribes duly came in under white flags to make their submissions to Major Deane, explaining that they had been misled and professing their unswerving loyalty to the Government. Once the immediate area had been secured the Malakand Field Force moved on in search of the Mad Fakir and his adherents, the main column under Blood marching eastwards into Buner country to strike at what was believed to be the home of the Mad Fakir, the Sayyeds of Sittana and the last of the Hindustani Fanatics. Yet when General Blood's force reached the heights looking down on the Chumla valley and the scene of the Ambeyla campaign thirty-four years earlier its commander called a halt and, after several days of inaction, turned about.

Lieutenant Winston Churchill, nominally on leave from his regiment but 'embedded' with Blood's field force as a special correspondent representing *The Pioneer* and the *Daily Telegraph*, was furious at this decision, as were many of his fellow officers. 'The Government shrank from the risk,' Churchill fulminated. 'The Malakand Field Force thus remained idle for nearly a fortnight. The news, that the Sirkar [Government] had feared to attack Buner, spread like wildfire along the frontier, and revived the spirits of the tribes. They fancied they detected a sign of weakness. Nor were they altogether wrong ... The opportunity of entering the country without having to force the passes may not recur.' As young Winston feared, no further opportunity to finish the business presented itself and so, once again, the Fanatic Camp survived.

But Churchill was wrong to assume that the authorities had lost their nerve. The Mad Fakir had not fled to Buner country, as was believed, but had travelled westwards, crossing the Swat River to enter the country of the Mohmands. In the village of Jarobi he met an elderly cleric considered so sacred to the Mohmands that no one dared breathe his real name, Najb-ud-din, but knew him simply as the Mullah of Haddah. The Haddah Mullah had long been a thorn in the flesh of the Amir of Afghanistan and a decade earlier had raised the Mohmands against him. However, Abdur Rahman had since recognised the scope of the Haddah Mullah's influence and had gone to great lengths to woo him, even to the extent of acknowledging him as a Light of Islam.

On 7 August the Mohmands rose in revolt under the Haddah Mullah, descended on the Hindu village of Shankargarh on the edge of the Vale of Peshawar and then advanced on the bazaar of Shabkadr, killing and plundering as they went. The smoke from the burning villages was seen from Peshawar, and retribution was swift. Churchill followed General Blood's punitive column as it set about bringing the Mohmands to heel, a task made immensely frustrating by the enemy's tactics of melting away before the advancing column and then attacking from the heights as it withdrew, always striking at a vulnerable point. In one such withdrawal Churchill very nearly lost his life, and afterwards reflected on the difficulties facing a modern army equipped with advanced weaponry when it sought to get to grips with a less well-armed but determined enemy in hostile terrain. 'The actual casualties', he wrote, 'were, in proportion to the numbers engaged, greater than in any action of the British army in India for many years. Out of a force which at no time exceeded 1000 men, nine British officers, four native officers, and 136 soldiers were either killed or wounded.' He attended the hurried burials of several of his brother officers: 'Looking at these shapeless forms, coffined in a regulation blanket, the pride of race, the pomp of empire, the glory of war appeared but the faint and unsubstantial fabric of a dream; and I could not help realising with Burke, "What shadows we are and what shadows we pursue."'

Within a fortnight the Mohmand uprising was over, and the tribal elders had come forward to tender their submissions and to declare that they had fought only because they had been told they faced annexation. But already the revolt had spread. 'The "fiery cross" had roused all to arms,' wrote Woosnam Mills, correspondent of the Lahore newspaper *The Civil and Military Gazette*. 'The first sign of the further spreading of the revolt was the disquieting news from Peshawar that a simultaneous rising had been arranged between the Orakzais and the Afridis, two of the most powerful and warlike of our frontier neighbours.' Whether or not the Mad Fakir was implicated, as was widely believed, three weeks after the start of the Swat uprising and ten days after the beginning of the Mohmand revolt, the third phase of the frontier uprising began with Said Akbar, Akhundzada of the Akakhel Afridis, advancing down the Khyber at the head of fifteen hundred mullahs and ten thousand Afridis.

After the garrison of the first of the chain of forts strung along the Khyber Pass had been massacred to a man the remaining tribal levies declared themselves for Said Akbar. The Afridi lashkars then advanced unopposed to Fort Jamrud, the great fortress which sprawls rather than stands at the mouth of the Khyber – whereupon the entire country of Tirah to the south rose in support, bringing with them another forty to fifty thousand fighting men of the Orakzai and southern Afridi tribes.

The authorities responded with alacrity, and in strength. 'Never had our frontier prestige been so menaced,' wrote Woosnam Mills:

> Never had our authority been so daringly set aside.
> Plunder and rapine ravaged from Ali Masjid to Landi
> Kotal. Insane exultancy prevailed among the
> frontiersmen . . . Can we be surprised if the Pathan, with
> his inordinate vanity and religious fanaticism, imagined
> that the Mussulman millennium was near at hand, that the
> days of the British Raj were numbered, and that the
> 'people of God' were once more to come into their
> inheritance and rule in the land of Hindustan as
> Conquerors.

The Tirah Expeditionary Force was the largest army raised in India since the dark days of the Indian Mutiny, made up of forty thousand fighting men. Commanded by General Sir William Lockhart, who had three decades of frontier campaigning under his Sam Browne belt, it became the first foreign army to break the purdah of Tirah, the wild country abutting the Safed Koh range (today a sanctuary for Osama bin Laden's 'Arabs'). This was hostile territory with a vengeance, 'only to be approached by perilous passes and dark ravines, and only to be traversed via a network of rocky fastnesses, wooded heights, rushing torrents and dangerous defiles – a country, in short, abounding in natural defensive advantages, and full of risks to the invader, hampered as he must be, by an immense transport train, carrying supplies, baggage, hospitals, ammunition, and so forth.'

Lockhart's strategy was straightforward: to enter the Orakzai country from the south and then strike north to reach 'the hub and heart of the Afridi nation . . . in three or four easy marches' before pushing on to reclaim the Khyber Pass. By attacking from the south he hoped to prevent the uprising spreading to Waziristan, where Mullah Powindah of the Mahsuds was already doing his best to foment jihad.

On 18 October Lockhart began his campaign with a frontal assault by the Gordon Highlanders to take the commanding heights of a five-thousand-foot ridge called Dargai. The attack was only lightly opposed and the heights were taken. The position was found to be well-nigh impregnable, consisting as it did of a series of cliffs running along both sides of an extended ridge that could only be approached across open ground offering very little cover. Yet no sooner had the Gordons taken Dargai Heights than they were withdrawn, on the grounds that insufficient supplies had been brought up to allow the position to be held. By the time the delayed supplies had arrived the ridge had been reoccupied by the Afridis, this time in strength. 'There can be little doubt,' commented the correspondent of *The Civil and Military Gazette*, 'that the tribesmen looked upon our abandonment of Dargai – the impregnability of which they fully realised – as, to say the very least of it, a great tactical mistake . . . The tribesmen attributed the abandonment of Dargai by our troops to the prayers of their holy men.' Fifteen standards were counted, suggesting that the ridge was now manned by between two and two and a half thousand men. To make matters worse, many of the enemy bore modern rifled weapons in the form of breech-loading Sniders, muzzle-loading Enfields and a number of the British troops' own Lee-Metfords, captured or stolen.

Dargai Heights had to be retaken before the expedition could advance deeper into the Tirah country, and its retaking became, in the words of Woosnam Mills, the 'high water-mark of British courage before the foe'. It also gave rise to a great deal of bitterness among the troops: 'Not only were grave charges preferred of blundering and causing unnecessary loss of life, but a spirit of ill-feeling, created by invidious comparisons, was aroused in the breasts of the troops who fought that day.'

On the afternoon of 20 October a series of frontal assaults was launched, each preceded by as fierce a barrage as General Lockhart's nineteen mountain guns could muster. 'What appeared to the observer,' wrote Mills, 'was an inaccessible cliff whose top rose five hundred yards away in front . . . The enemy had constructed tiers of stone galleries, some of them four feet thick and proof against the seven-pounder shell from the mountain batteries. Any advance being attempted, the whole side of the cliff for a width of three hundred yards smoked and vomited forth a terrific storm of bullets.' Four assaults were launched, the first two by riflemen of the 1st battalion of the 2nd Gurkha Rifles. Each wave was caught by concentrated fire as it tried to cross the open ground below the cliffs, to be beaten back or broken into small groups of men pinned down behind whatever scant cover they could find. Those who followed could do no better: 'There was an indescribable confusion . . . Two companies of the Dorsets and Derbyshires attempted to cross and were also torn apart, then the 3rd Sikhs, who made more magnificently courageous but perfectly useless attempts to cross the zone of fire . . . Nothing but a wonderful effort could save the situation.'

The Gordon Highlanders, held in reserve, were now called up to repeat their exercise of two days earlier. Once they were in position their commanding officer, Colonel Mathias, stepped forward, ordered his men to charge magazines and fix bayonets, and then addressed them in a 'loud, clear voice: "Men of the Gordon Highlanders, listen to me. The General says this position must be taken at all hazards, and we will take it in front of the whole division."' After a four-minute barrage the field guns stopped firing and there was a moment of silence: '"Are you ready?" again rang the voice of Colonel Mathias, and a mad, wild cheer, bred of the courage which lies deep in the hearts of men, was the response. "Come on," shouted the Colonel. Then the pipers skirled the regimental war song, "and with the lilt of a big parade" the gay Gordons stepped forth.'

The Gordons advanced to the sound of the *Haughs o' Cromdale*, memorably played by Piper Findlater, who earned one of the two Victoria Crosses awarded for this action by playing on with both his legs shot through. Those who survived the first hundred yards of open ground now found themselves crammed behind a low wall of rock with survivors from the earlier charges. Colonel Mathias then waved his cork helmet and again called his men forward:

The effect was magical: as if by resurrection the whole space seemed alive, and a great wave of men – Highlanders, Gurkhas, Dorsets, Sikhs, and Derbyshires – came headlong over the crest. From this moment the fire of the enemy, which had been intense, slackened . . . A mere breathing space under the last cover – just time to brace up the muscles anew – and the mixed band of warriors again moved out to the final assault.

The battle of Dargai Heights occupies a special place in the annals of the scores of North-West Frontier campaigns that took place between 1846, when the Guides were formed, and 1947, when the British finally left India. It reversed the usual norms, by which it was the tribesmen who charged and who took the heaviest casualties. In this instance the Afridi defenders withdrew along the ridge during the last phase of the attack, taking their few dead and wounded with them. By contrast, their attackers suffered more than two hundred casualties, including four British officers, fifteen British NCOs and private soldiers, and twenty Gurkhas killed. Dargai also cemented an 'auld alliance' between the Gurkhas and the Highlanders stretching back to Delhi Ridge and the Second Afghan War: the men of the Gordons helping the Gurkhas bring down their dead and wounded and the Gurkhas reciprocating by putting up the Gordons' tents when they returned late to camp. As Rudyard Kipling's Mulvaney puts it, 'Scotchies and the Gurkys are twins'.

Until recent years, this remained the only occasion on which the tribal lands of Tirah were entered by an outside force. 'The boast of the tribes', declared General Lockhart in his closing despatch, 'was that no foreign army – Moghal, Afghan, Persian or British – had ever penetrated, or could ever penetrate, their country; but after carrying three strong positions, and being for weeks subsequently engaged in daily skirmishes, the troops succeeded in visiting every portion of Tirah.' What his despatch glossed over was that the final submission of the tribes took months to accomplish, accompanied by a bitter campaign of guerrilla warfare in the form of sniping by night and ambushing by day. Only by punitive measures that included the destruction of villages, the burning of crops and the confiscation of livestock did Lockhart's Tirah Field Force finally reduce the Afridi and Orakzai to submission. By the end of the Tirah campaign the casualty figures had risen to 43 British officers killed and 90 wounded; 136 British NCOs and men killed and 415 wounded; 6 Indian Native Officers killed and 36 wounded; and 320 Indian and Gurkha NCOs and men killed and 871 wounded. Most of these casualties were incurred during the 'pacification' phase of the campaign.

This heavy-footed stamping-out of the frontier jihad came at a price. 'Burning houses and destroying crops,' wrote a critical 'Bobs' Roberts, who had left India in 1893 after forty-one years' military service and was now Field Marshal Lord Roberts of Kandahar, 'unless followed up by some sort of authority and jurisdiction, mean . . . for us a rich harvest of hatred and revenge.'

Of the Mad Fakir, Mullah Sadulla, nothing more was ever heard.

10

The Brotherhood

Fortunately they did not succeed. We say fortunately, for
if ever Egypt should cease to be ruled by a vigorous government, the Wahabees would raise their heads: they
would overrun Arabia, being weakened neither in numbers nor in fanaticism, and Turkey would be unable to
protect the holy towns. The consequences of such an
event would produce discontent in the whole East.

T. E. Ravenshaw,
Memorandum on the Sect of the Wahabees, 1864

In the autumn of 1863 two travellers set out from Damascus for the
city of Hail, capital of what had formerly been northern Nejd but
was now the Ottoman province of Jabal Shammar. They gave out
that they were Syrian Christian doctors, and were dressed accordingly. In fact, neither man was a doctor and only one was a Syrian.
The other, then aged thirty-seven, was a Jew by ancestry and a
Christian by upbringing, an Englishman christened William Gifford
Palgrave who also answered at different stages of his life to William
Cohen and Michael Sohail. After distinguishing himself as a scholar

at Oxford, Palgrave had gone out to India with a lieutenant's commission in the 8th Bombay Native Infantry. But he was not cut out for a military career, and after two years he resigned his commission, converted to Roman Catholicism and became a Jesuit missionary. In 1855, drawn to the Arab world by his studies and discovering in himself a remarkable gift for languages, he joined the French Jesuit Mission in Syria. Within a few years he had become so accomplished an Arabic speaker and so at ease with local customs that he could pass himself off as a native of the region. He became a local agent of the French Government and worked to extend French interests in Egypt and the Middle East, and it seems to have been in this capacity that he undertook his remarkable journey to the heart of Arabia, though he afterwards declared that he had been driven by 'a natural curiosity to know the yet unknown; and the restlessness of enterprise not rare in Englishmen'. He travelled as a Syrian doctor, Selim Abu Mahmoud al-Eis, and he took with him several camel-loads of pills, powders and potions bought with French money in Damascus.

When Palgrave and his Syrian companion Barakat reached the city of Hail, lying more or less midway between Basra and Medina, they were warmly welcomed by the Emir and treated as his guests. Indeed, so hospitable were the inhabitants of Hail that Palgrave came to regard it as the ideal state, a place where people of all races and religions mixed freely and as equals. However, Palgrave's ultimate destination was not Hail but Riyadh, a place then considered so dangerous to outsiders that the inhabitants of Hail regarded it as 'a sort of lion's den, in which few venture and yet fewer return'. This was because Riyadh and the country surrounding it were, in Palgrave's words, 'the genuine Wahhabee country . . . the stronghold of fanatics, who consider everyone save themselves an infidel or a heretic, and who regard the slaughter of an infidel or a heretic as a duty, at least a merit . . . Nejd has become for all but her born sons doubly dangerous, and doubly hateful.'

Since the fatal outcome of Ali Pasha's campaign in 1818 the

Wahhabis had regrouped under FAISAL IBN SAUD, great-great-great-grandson of the founder of the dynasty. After establishing himself on the throne of Riyadh in 1842 he had restored something of the vigour and religious zeal that had characterised the first Saudi empire established by Muhammad ibn Saud. However, the Wahhabis had failed to recover Nejd's northern territory, Jabal Shammar, which had become the seat of the Saudis' main rivals, the Ibn Rashid dynasty. This rivalry helps to explain why William Palgrave found the Emir of Hail and his people so hostile towards the Wahhabis, and so concerned when he made it known that Riyadh was his real destination.

With the direst of warnings ringing in their ears, the two 'Syrian doctors' rode out of Hail in early September 1862 as part of a small camel caravan. It took them nine days to reach the borders of Jabal Shammar, the point at which their safe-conducts ran out. They pushed on, reaching the Wahhabi capital of Riyadh on 13 October unmolested and in good shape. To their relief, their supposed Syrian Christian identities aroused no obvious hostility even from the Wahhabi ulema, the explanation offered being that the Wahhabis' real enemies were neither Christians nor Jews but those polytheists who purported to be followers of Islam. The fact that they came as doctors also helped to smooth their presence, for they found themselves in great demand, called upon to treat as many as fifty different maladies.

Palgrave and Barakat spent forty-two days in Riyadh, and between consultations found time to tour every quarter of the city, described by Palgrave as 'large and square, crowned by high towers and strong walls of defence, a mass of roofs and terraces, where overtopping all frowned the huge but irregular pile of Faisal's royal castle, and hard by it rose the scarce less conspicuous palace built and inhabited by his eldest son Abdullah . . . All round for full three miles over the surrounding plain, but more especially to the west and south, waved a sea of palm trees above green fields and well-watered gardens.'

To Palgrave's further surprise, he was allowed into the city's plain and unadorned mosques, where he made the acquaintance of a number of Wahhabi clerics, who left him in no doubt that it was the *aal as-Sheikh*, or the 'Family of the Sheikh', as the descendants of Muhammad ibn Abd al-Wahhab were known, who ran the ulema. 'The whole family', declared Palgrave, 'has constantly held the highest judicial and religious posts in the Wahhabee empire, and has amassed considerable wealth, let us hope by none but honest means. Its members . . . exercise a predominant influence in the state, and, though never decorated with the official titles belonging to purely civil or military authority, do yet, in reality, rule the rulers of the land, and their own masters of the Sa'ood dynasty never venture to contradict them, even on matters of policy or war.'

Although Palgrave never met the ailing Emir, Faisal ibn Saud, he got to know his two eldest sons, who were squaring up to each other in preparation for the struggle for succession that would follow upon the death of their father. The younger son, Saud, Palgrave found to be affable and warm-hearted, but his elder half-brother ABDULLAH IBN SAUD, the heir-apparent, was a more duplicitous figure, who after several consultations asked Palgrave point-blank for a supply of strychnine. This led Palgrave to accuse him to his face of seeking to poison his father the Emir, a charge that so angered Abdullah that he threatened to expose the 'Syrian' as an Englishman and have him killed. Palgrave kept his nerve, but that same night he and his companion slipped out of Riyadh and, after hiding up for several days outside the city, made for the coast. A shipwreck off Bahrain followed in which all Palgrave's notes were lost, and it was not until late in 1863 that he was able to get back to Europe to stake his claim as the first Westerner to visit the Wahhabi capital.

Palgrave's travels have been overshadowed by the Arabian journeys of Burton, Blunt and Doughty – and by the charge of fakery laid against him by the third Westerner to reach Riyadh, Harry St

John Philby. But his description of Wahhabi rule deserves to be remembered. In Nejd he saw much to admire and applaud: 'The Wahhabee empire is a compact and well organised government, where centralisation is well understood and effectually carried out.' And yet, 'how much misdirected zeal; what concentrated though ill-applied courage and perseverance.' Wahhabi rule rested on 'force and fanaticism' and, in his view, it was bound to fail: 'Incapable of true internal progress, hostile to commerce, unfavourable to arts and even to agriculture, and in the highest degree intolerant and aggressive, it can neither better itself nor benefit others; while the order and calm which it sometimes spreads over the lands of its conquest, are described in the oft-cited *ubi solitudinem faciunt pacem appellant* [where they make a desert they call it peace] of the Roman annalist [Tacitus].'

Isolated though Nejd's Wahhabi culture was, to Palgrave it represented 'a new well-head to the bitter wars of Islam' and a threat to the wider world:

> This empire is capable of frontier extension, and hence is dangerous to its neighbours, some of whom it is even now swallowing up, and will certainly swallow more, if not otherwise prevented . . . We may add that its weakest point lies in family rivalries and feuds of succession, which, joined to the anti-Wahhabee reaction existing far and wide throughout Arabia, may one day much disintegrate and shatter the Nejdean empire, yet not destroy it altogether . . . But so long as Wahhabeeism shall prevail in the centre and uplands of Arabia, small indeed are the hopes of civilisation, advancement, and national prosperity for the Arab race.

The second British visitor to Riyadh has, if anything, been even more neglected than Palgrave. Lieutenant-Colonel Lewis Pelly was British Resident in the Gulf for a decade from the mid-

1860s. Concerned and perhaps a little put out by Palgrave's French-sponsored journey, Pelly wrote to Emir Faisal and was invited to call on him in his capital in 1865. He found the Emir blind and enfeebled, but still every inch the ruler. He spoke of himself in the royal plural and considered the entire Arabian peninsula to be rightfully 'ours' – and he used for himself the dual title of emir and imam. 'It is not uncommon to hear the Bedouins speak of the Ameer Fysul as Ben Sood [Ibn Saud],' wrote Pelly in his official report. 'But the title which is current among his own immediate dependants at the capital is that of Imam, implying spiritual leadership . . . The Imam takes precedence of all Moolahs, and is mentioned in public prayers in terms almost equivalent with those that are lavished on the prophet [Prophet Muhammad] himself.' The precedent first established by Faisal's forebear Abd al-Aziz ibn Saud in 1773 was evidently still going strong, and with it the cult status afforded the Wahhabi state's joint emir and imam. The family alliance between the aal as-Sheikh and the Al-Saud was also being maintained through the marriage of Al-Wahhab's granddaughter to the son of the Emir's heir apparent, Abdullah. Nevertheless, it seemed to Pelly that the Saudis rather than the Wahhabis were in charge.

Like Palgrave before him, Pelly left Riyadh troubled by the ideology of Wahhabism: 'I came to the conclusion that while the Imam himself was a sensible and experienced man, yet he was surrounded by the most excitable, unscrupulous, dangerous and fanatical people that one could well come across.' A decade later the traveller Charles Doughty came to the same conclusion after his more famous crossing of the Arabian desert: 'I passed one good day in Arabia: and all the rest were evil because of the people's fanaticism.'

With the passing of Emir Faisal in 1865 the sibling rivalry Palgrave had seen developing in Riyadh in 1863 became open warfare. In his determination to overcome his younger brother

Abdullah ibn Saud turned for help to his father's enemy Muhammad ibn Rashid, Emir of Hail and ruler of Jebel Shammar. In the ensuing struggle Saud was killed and Abdullah imprisoned by his supposed ally, and subsequently exiled. Ibn Rashid then took over southern Nejd in the name of the Ottomans and set about removing all traces of opposition and heresy as far as his tenuous hold over the region would allow. The surviving sons and grandsons of Faisal were driven into exile, the heir presumptive, ABDUL-RAHMAN IBN SAUD, fleeing first to the Empty Quarter and then to Kuwait, taking with him his eldest son Abdul Aziz bin Abdul-Rahman ibn Saud. Accounts differ as to when this exile began or how old the boy was, but it is said that for eleven years he ate 'the bread of adversity'. The upper hierarchy of the Wahhabi ulema, the aal as-Sheikh, accompanied the Ibn Sauds into exile, but the remainder appear to have found shelter among the desert tribes of Nejd.

In 1901 – the same year in which Amir Abdur Rahman, creator of the nation state of Afghanistan, died in Kabul, and Abdullah Ali, amir of the Hindustani Fanatics, died in Buner – Abdul-Rahman ibn Saud stepped down as head of the house of Saud in favour of his eldest son, although he retained the title of Imam of Nejd. Official accounts give the new Emir's age as twenty-one. With the help of his host, Mubarak the Great, Sheikh of Kuwait, the young exile then set about reclaiming his kingdom.

The manner in which IBN SAUD (as he afterwards became known to the outside world) achieved this is the stuff of legend in Arabia: how with a force of eighty – or was it twenty? – camel-men lent him by his protector the young warrior crossed the desert and made his way into Riyadh undetected; how he and fifteen – or perhaps eight – picked men slipped into the Rashidi governor's palace by night and hid in the harem; how, when the governor and his men arrived next morning from the nearby fortress in which they slept at night, they were ambushed and killed; and how the young Emir then took over Riyadh and announced the restoration of the House of Saud. The legend continues with the Bedouin tribes of southern Nejd responding enthusiastically to his call to arms, although rather less is said about the guns and trained marksmen supplied by Kuwait. Within two years Ibn Saud felt strong enough to attempt to reclaim the lost northern territories still held by Emir Abdul Aziz ibn Rashid of Hail. In June 1904 he took on a modern Turkish army sent in response to his rival's appeal for aid, and was soundly defeated. This setback forced him to rethink his tactics.

At this critical juncture Ibn Saud turned for help to the members of two tribes, the Artaiba and Harb, who had isolated themselves from the rest of the Bedouin community in Nejd and had dedicated themselves to Wahhabism in its most austere form. It was here in the desert that the torch of Wahhabism had been kept burning, first during the dark days of Ottoman oppression and later under the Ibn Rashids of Hail – very much as the Hindustani Fanatics kept the message of Syed Ahmad's Wahhabism alive in the Mahabun Mountain.

These Wahhabi zealots had named themselves *Al-Ikhwan* or the Brotherhood. They had abandoned the traditional nomadic life of their forefathers and had retreated into closed settlements which they termed *hujar*. The word – *hijra*, in the singular – had its origins in the term used to describe the Prophet's famous withdrawal from ungodly Mecca to Medina, and it was now used to denote the Ikhwan's intention to live as true *muwahhidun*, or Unitarians, in a domain of Faith, as the Prophet had in Medina. To signal their abandonment of the nomadic way of life they had discarded the traditional Bedouin head-band, said to have come from the rope used to hobble camels, and wore their *kaffiya* (head-cloths) loose. To further distinguish themselves from polytheists and unbelievers, they wore their robes short to leave the ankle exposed and their beards with the moustache trimmed and the beard henna'd and worn long at the front – supposedly in accordance with the Prophet's requirements as set down in the Hadith.

In line with traditional custom reinforced by the founder of their movement, their womenfolk remained out of sight and out of mind.

It was afterwards propagated by Harry St John Philby and others that the Ikhwan phenomenon was the brain-child of Ibn Saud, 'the result not of accident but of a well-considered design, conceived with no less a purpose than that of remedying the shortcomings of the Arab race.' According to Philby, the Emir set out deliberately to build an army that was both fanatical and disciplined 'by laying at Artawiyyaa, an insignificant watering-place on the Kuwait–Qasim track, the foundation stone of a new Freemasonry, which, under the name of *Ikhwan* or the "Brothers" has in the course of a decade transformed the character of Badawin society.' It would be more accurate to say that Ibn Saud recognised in the Ikhwan the most highly motivated element of the population apart from the Wahhabi ulema and then exploited these qualities to their mutual advantage. That Wahhabism was already undergoing a revival before Ibn Saud's intervention can be deduced from the activities of Wahhabi missionaries in Central Asia. In Turkestan in 1871 a group of Wahhabi fighters had attacked a Russian outpost in Khokand, inspired by a Wahhabi preacher named Sudi Badal. Forty years later a Wahhabi named Sayed Shari Mohamed established a mission in Tashkent. Now, in Nejd, Ibn Saud's genius as a nation-builder first revealed itself in his dealings with the Ikhwan zealots.

The Saudi emirs had long claimed for themselves the authority of imamship, but young Ibn Saud's position was unusual in that his father, after abdicating in his favour, had retained the title of Imam of Nejd. To get round this obstacle Ibn Saud presented himself to the Ikhwan specifically as *their* imam – and from this time onwards he was always spoken of among the Ikhwan as *al-Imam* and never as 'the Emir'. By this means Ibn Saud gained the religious authority to declare jihad on their mutual enemy, the non-Wahhabis of Hail.

It is unlikely that the Ikhwan had been mobilised in time to

take part in the first great battle between the forces of the two
emirs of Nejd and Hail fought in 1906, but the death of Abdul
Aziz ibn Rashid of Hail in that encounter gave Ibn Saud the
breathing space he needed to build up the Ikhwan into a force to
be reckoned with. From about 1910 onwards the Imam of the
Ikhwan embarked on an audacious programme to strengthen the
existing Ikhwan communities and establish new ones. By supporting them with funds he induced other Bedouin tribes to
follow the example of the Al-Ikhwan and to settle at desert oases,
each in their own hujar, deliberately relocating families so that the
old tribal loyalties began to break down. Along with agricultural
equipment and training, Ibn Saud provided houses, mosques,
religious schools and, most important of all, religious teachers:
Wahhabi mullahs who were able to instruct the settlers in the
doctrine of God's oneness as enshrined in the teachings of Al-
Wahhab and his descendants. To further reinforce the message,
he required the local chieftain and all the elders in each hujar to
attend courses of religious instruction in the central mosques at
Riyadh and Uyainah. All this cost the Emir and Imam a great
deal of money which he could ill afford, but it secured him an
armed and loyal force that answered to him alone, spread out
strategically in small bases all over the country. 'His new colonies',
wrote St John Philby in 1920,

> are but cantonments of his standing army of 30,000 men or
> more, and every man-child born therein is a recruit to his
> forces from the day of his birth. He found the Badawin
> homeless, poor, without religion, and cursed with a tribal
> organisation which made united action impossible and
> strife inevitable. In the new colonies he has settled them
> on the land with the fear of God and the hope of Paradise
> in their hearts, substituting the brotherhood of a common
> faith for that of a common ancestry, and thus uniting in
> common allegiance to himself as the viceregent of God

elements hitherto incapable of fusion. At the same time he has made war unsparingly on the old tribal practices, the old game of raid and counter-raid is forbidden in his territories, and many a tribe has felt the crushing weight of his wrath for transgression of his laws; peace reigns where peace was known not before.

Within the space of a decade Ibn Saud succeeded in repeating what it had taken his ancestors more than half a century to accomplish: the unification under the conjoined banners of Al-Saud and Al-Wahhab of a number of disparate tribes who now thought and acted almost as one. But the unification of the Nejdi tribes was only the start, for as even Harry St John Philby had to acknowledge, the Wahhabis' 'most remarkable characteristic' was their 'uncompromising hatred of their Muslim neighbours . . . The Shias are frankly condemned as infidels or polytheists, but it is for the orthodox congregation of the four Sunni churches – Turks, Egyptians, Hijazis, Syrians, Mesopotamians, Indians and the like – that the Wahhabis reserve the undiluted venom of their hatred.' The hostility that the tribes had traditionally directed towards each other was now redirected at the outside world.

For the first decade of Ibn Saud's rise to power the British were content to watch from the side-lines, their chief concern being to preserve the status quo as represented by the authority of the Ottomans, reflected in the Anglo-Turkish accord of 1901 by which Britain agreed to remain neutral in the affairs of Arabia. Through their Political Agency in Kuwait, set up by the Government of India in 1904, they maintained good relations with the Emir of Kuwait and viewed the family of Ibn Saud as 'merely notable as hereditary amirs of the Wahhabis'. But by degrees their views changed, a change initiated by the arrival in Kuwait in 1909 of a new Political Agent, a thirty-one-year-old Indian Army captain with the unlikely name of William Shakespear.

Born in the Punjab of a well-known Anglo-Indian military family, fluent in Arabic and a keen traveller, Shakespear first established himself in the region with a number of forays into the desert along Kuwait's western border. Then in April 1910 he had his first opportunity to meet the Emir of Nejd when Ibn Saud and his brothers rode into Kuwait to make a courtesy call on their old patron and ally. 'Abdul Aziz,' reported Shakespear, 'now in his 31st year, is fair, handsome and considerably above average Arab height . . . He has a frank, open face, and after initial reserve, is of genial and courteous manner.' Shakespear was surprised to find the Emir 'broad-minded and straight', even if those about him were 'dour and taciturn'.

A year later a more informal meeting led Shakespear to conclude that here was an Arab leader whose intelligence and strength of character matched his ambition. Ibn Saud told him of his family's struggles and made no bones of his wish to form an alliance with the British against the Ottomans: 'We Wahhabis hate the Turks only less than we hate the Persians for the infidel practices which they have imported into the true and pure faith revealed to us in the Koran.' In his subsequent report Shakespear noted that 'hatred of the Turk seems to be the one idea common to all the tribes and the only one for which they would sink their differences', adding that 'a revolt is not only probable but would be welcomed by every tribe throughout the peninsula'.

Shakespear's enthusiastic promotion of the notion of an 'Arab revolt' against the Ottomans was not well received in Whitehall, in part because the Foreign Office took the view that this was meddling by the Government of India. Nevertheless, Shakespear was given permission to mount a private expedition that took him from Kuwait to Riyadh and then westwards right across the great Arabian desert to the Hijaz. At Riyadh he talked to Ibn Saud in private and at length, and was again told that the future of Arabia rested on an alliance between the Arabs and Great Britain. Towards the end of May 1914 Shakespear and his travel-worn party emerged from the desert at Suez after a journey of some eighteen hundred miles on foot and on camel-back, much of it through regions previously unmapped and unrecorded. He reported to the British Residency in Cairo, where he found Lord Kitchener and others unimpressed by his advocacy of Ibn Saud. In the eyes of the British Government there was only one Arab leader – SHARIF HUSAYN ibn Ali, Emir of the Hijaz, whose Hashimite dynasty was widely (if incorrectly) regarded as hereditary holder of the most sacred office in the Muslim world: guardianship of the holy cities of Mecca and Medina and protectors of the Hajj.

Following the outbreak of war in Europe in August 1914 the Ottoman government made the fateful decision to throw in their lot with Germany and Austria-Hungary and proclaim jihad against Britain, France and Russia in the name of the caliph. For the Triple Entente it now became a matter of urgency to find a Muslim leader who would join with them against the Ottoman Empire, the obvious man being Sharif Husayn. Colonel T. E. Lawrence's masterly report for the British Cabinet, written after the war and entitled *Reconstruction of Arabia*, says it all:

> When war broke out an urgent need to divide Islam was added, and we became reconciled to seek for allies rather than subjects. We therefore took advantage of the dissatisfaction felt by the Arabic-speaking peoples with their alien rulers, and of the tendency, each day more visible, of the subject Eastern peoples to demand a share of the dangers of government. We hoped by the creation of a ring of client states, themselves insisting on our patronage, to turn the present and future flank of any foreign power with designs on the three rivers [Iraq]. The greatest obstacle, from the war standpoint, to any Arab movement, was its greatest virtue in peace-time – the lack of solidarity between the various Arab movements . . . The

Sherif [Husayn] was ultimately chosen because of the rift
he would create in Islam.

Shakespear was ordered to bring Ibn Saud and his Bedouin
tribes in on the side of Britain. After some 'hard trekking' he met
the emir in December 1914 as he rode northwards from Riyadh
with his Ikhwan army to continue his own private war against his
old enemy, the pro-Turkish Emir of Hail. While on the march the
two men worked on a draft treaty of friendship by which Britain
would acknowledge Ibn Saud's independence and guarantee him
against external aggression by his enemies. With his work done
and despite the entreaties of Ibn Saud that he should leave before
the coming battle, Shakespear chose to stay on. According to Ibn
Saud, he refused to leave, declaring that to do so would be 'a
blemish on my honour, and the honour of my country'. On 14
January he wrote to his brother to tell him that Ibn Saud's *ghazu*
(war party), consisting of several thousand horsemen armed with
rifles and an equal number of camel-riders armed with scimitars
and spears, was on the move 'for a biggish battle', and that he was
going with them. He closed his letter with the remark that 'Bin
Saud wants me to clear out but I want to see the show and I don't
think it will be very unsafe really'. All might have been well had
Shakespear but discarded his khaki uniform and eye-catching
cork sun helmet for Arab dress, as he was asked.

On 24 January 1915 the two armies closed on each other in the
desert near an oasis called Jarab. As Shakespear had feared might
happen, one of Ibn Saud's allies changed sides at a critical
moment, turning what would have been a decisive victory for the
Emir of Nejd into a bloody draw. During the mêlée, a party of the
Emir of Hail's horsemen broke away from the main battle to
charge the sand-dunes where Shakespear stood observing the
battle. The Saudi riflemen with him scattered, leaving Captain
Shakespear alone on the summit of a dune armed only with a
revolver. According to his cook, who was briefly taken prisoner

but escaped, he afterwards found Shakespear's naked body lying where it had fallen, with 'the marks of three bullets on him'.

The Foreign Office had now set up the Arab Bureau in Cairo, staffed by such exotics as Miss Gertrude Bell and T. E. Lawrence, its main brief being to bring about the Arab revolt against the Ottomans through the persons of Sharif Husayn and his four sons. After protracted bargaining Husayn agreed to lead the revolt in return for Britain's support for him after the war as ruler of Arabia and Britain's recognition of 'the independence of the Arabs in all the regions lying within the frontiers proposed by the Sharif of Mecca'. In June 1916, as his own tribal forces attacked the Ottoman garrison in Mecca, Sharif Husayn called on all Muslims to join him in liberating their caliph from the atheistic regime in power in Turkey – a call seen in many quarters of the Muslim world as treason against the caliphate. The Emir of Nejd, Ibn Saud, also took offence, but chiefly because Husayn had taken to styling himself 'King of the Arabs'.

It was at this time that Miss Gertrude Bell penned her iconic portrayal of the nation-builder to be: 'Ibn Saud is now barely forty,' she wrote, 'a man of splendid physique, standing well over six feet, and carrying himself with the air of one accustomed to command . . . He has the characteristics of the well-bred Arab: a strongly marked aquiline profile, full-flesh nostrils, prominent lips and a long narrow chin accentuated by a pointed beard.' Miss Bell saw in Ibn Saud the 'weariness of an ancient people, which has made heavy drafts on its vital forces, and borrowed little from beyond its own forbidding frontiers'. Yet she was also conscious of the man's formidable reputation: 'Among men bred in the camel-saddle he is said to have few rivals as a tireless leader. As a leader of irregular forces he is of proved daring, and he combines with his qualities as a soldier that grasp of statecraft which is yet more highly prized by the tribesmen.' He had 'drawn the loose mesh of tribal organisation into a centralised administration and imposed on wandering confederacies an authority which, though fluctuating, is recognised as a political factor'. Given these qualities, it was doubly important that Ibn Saud should be reined in and encouraged to 'come to a full understanding with the Sharif'.

A replacement for Shakespear had now arrived in Kuwait in the colourful person of thirty-year-old Harry St John Philby. Like his predecessor, Philby was colonial-born – Ceylon, in his case – and he had links with India on his mother's side, but in appearance, temperament and intellect he was in a class of his own: a big, bulky man, arrogantly self-assured, with a brilliant record of scholarship at Winchester and Trinity College, Cambridge behind him. He had gone out to the Punjab in December 1908 as a member of the imperial élite, the Indian Civil Service, but had failed to impress. Indeed, he had gained a reputation as a rough diamond and a radical, and he had cocked a snook at convention by marrying too soon and below his class. In 1915 Philby was languishing in the counter-sedition section of the Indian Police's Special Branch when he was selected – purely on the strength of his linguistic skills – to join Sir Percy Cox's Political Mission in Mesopotamia. Here he at last began to show his worth, leading to his instruction in October 1917 to establish a British political agency in Riyadh and to draw Ibn Saud into the fold. Before the end of November Philby was presenting himself to the Emir of Nejd – complete with new-grown beard and Arab dress, down to sandals and kaffiya. After ten days of talks, Philby's two British colleagues departed for the coast, leaving Philby to continue his dealings with Ibn Saud alone. Initially Philby toed the British line, but in the months that followed there grew within him an admiration for the Emir, coupled with a growing affinity for the culture to which he belonged, that developed into a state bordering on infatuation, and eventually led to a transfer of loyalties.

The story of the Arab Revolt, culminating in the occupation of Damascus by Sharif Husayn's eldest son Emir Feisal in October 1918, is well known. The part played by the Saudis can be judged by the fact that the name of Ibn Saud crops up just once in Lawrence's classic *Seven Pillars of Wisdom*, and then only in passing.

But the fact is that Lawrence got it wrong and Philby got it right when these two brilliant, driven, flawed men each picked a champion of the Arabs. For all his fine words, Lawrence's romanticising of Prince Feisal – 'the pure and very brave spirit . . . a prophet who, if veiled, would give cogent form to the idea behind the activity of the Arab revolt' – was always that of the Orientalist and manipulator. St John Philby's relationship with Ibn Saud was altogether more whole-hearted, however heartless he himself appeared in his personal life.

Philby had at first been struck by Ibn Saud's 'consuming jealousy' of Sharif Husayn, whose overriding concern at their early meetings had been to secure British funds and guns so that he could pursue his twin ambitions: to reclaim Hail, and to restore the kingdom won by his ancestor and namesake Abd al-Aziz ibn Saud a century earlier. But the longer Philby lingered in Riyadh the more he became transfixed by the manner in which Ibn Saud was transforming himself into the father of his country, in a literal as well as a figurative sense. He was in his physical prime and already well embarked on the traditional ruler's strategy of alliance- and loyalty-building through marriage, although still short of the 235 wives and 660 concubines he is traditionally credited with. Marriage to the daughter of the then head of the Wahhab clan had recently produced a son, Prince Faisal, who later became a leading proponent of Wahhabism, initially as crown prince and prime minister of Saudi Arabia and subsequently as its king.

For all Ibn Saud's long exposure to the relatively liberal Islam practised in Kuwait and for all the pragmatism of his dealings with the British, he was a committed devotee of Al-Wahhab and determined that his people should follow suit. As Philby witnessed and recorded, Ibn Saud arranged in 1918 for a Wahhabi history and a number of Al-Wahhab's original texts to be printed in Bombay for mass distribution throughout his land. While accepting the title of Imam of Nejd upon the death of his father, he ensured that it was the aal as-Sheikh who filled all the senior posts in the ulema, from that of Grand Mufti downwards. 'Under their general direction,' wrote Philby,

> the instruction and religious administration of the country was entrusted to a body of Ulama or Vicars . . . Besides their administrative functions these Vicars are responsible for the administration of the Sharia law, and their decisions are binding on the provincial Amirs, who merely sign and execute them . . . They are also responsible for the training and direction of the *Mutawwa'in* or Deacons, who enjoy no administrative or judicial functions but are entrusted with the religious instruction of the Badawain, among whom they are distributed apparently in the proportion of one for every fifty men. Beneath these again is a body of *Talamidh* or candidates for orders, who, under the guidance of the Mutawwa'in aspire one day to be enrolled among them, and so to take an active share in God's handiwork among men.

By these and other steps Ibn Saud institutionalised Wahhabism throughout his land, under the absolute religious authority of the aal as-Sheikh.

Harry St John Philby's initial response to the creed promoted so vigorously by these clerics was no less hostile than that of his British predecessors, from Palgrave to Shakespear. The Ikhwan, for their part, treated him with contempt, turning away their faces when he approached and refusing to return his salaams. One even hissed at him that God was the witness of his hatred for him. His response was to treat them with amused disdain. 'Their souls sour with fanaticism', he wrote in a note surviving from this early period. But with time and further exposure his views changed.

In January 1918 Philby followed Palgrave's example by crossing the Arabian desert from Riyadh to Jedda, keeping to the ancient trail of pilgrims' camp-fires. In Jedda he presented himself to Sharif Husayn, whom he found 'old, small, calm, and the pink of courtesy' but also thoroughly put out by Philby's unannounced arrival from the camp of his chief enemy. Like Shakespear before him, Philby went on to argue Ibn Saud's case to the Arab Bureau, only to be told bluntly that, in Lord Curzon's words, 'British policy was a Hashemite policy'. He returned to Riyadh with the news that Britain would continue to provide Ibn Saud with a modest monthly stipend of gold, but would also continue to back Sharif Husayn. Philby then went home on leave, taking with him Ibn Saud's gifts of a ceremonial sword and a white Arab stallion.

Ibn Saud's reponse to this rebuff was to unleash his Ikhwans on Sharif Husayn's British-trained army at the oasis of Kurma, securing an overwhelming victory that drove the Sharif's forces back to the outskirts of Mecca and had his second son Prince Abdullah fleeing in his nightshirt. Philby was asked to mediate, but before he could get back to Jedda a temporary peace had been patched up. From this time onward he became an outspoken critic of British policy in the Middle East and ever more passionate in his advocacy for Ibn Saud as the 'only great and outstanding figure' in Arabia.

In March 1920 Lawrence's man, Prince Feisal, was proclaimed ruler of Syria, only for France to take exception and force him out. In 1921 Feisal's brother Prince Abdullah had better luck when Britain allowed him to set up the emirate of Trans-Jordan. But in that same summer the remnants of the Rashidi emirate of Hail finally fell to the Ikhwan, so restoring the kingdom of Nejd to its former size. Sharif Husayn was now left with only the emirship of Hijaz, but still expected Britain to honour its promise to secure his dynasty as rulers of Arabia.

In 1924 secular rule was established in Turkey by Kemal Atatürk, and a liberal government was formed in Egypt, causing alarm in conservative Muslim circles. Sharif Husayn responded by claiming the title of Caliph of Islam for himself and his Hashemite dynasty, further alienating an Arab community disenchanted by his close links with the British. He then banned the Ikhwan from making the Hajj – a fatal provocation to Ibn Saud's warriors and a perfect excuse to resume their war. The Ikhwan needed only to be given their marching orders. While a diversionary thrust menaced Jordan and Iraq their main army took the holy cities of Mecca and Medina and then closed on Jedda. In the iconoclasm that followed, the tombs of many Muslim saints were torn down, including that of the Prophet's daughter Fatima. But at the gates of Jedda Ibn Saud held back, waiting to see if the British Government would come to the aid of Sharif Husayn. Its response was to oversee his abdication and provide an escort into exile.

Harry St John Philby, still nominally an officer of the Government of India's Foreign and Political Service, was then on extended leave in England. He now resigned and returned to Arabia, meeting Ibn Saud in secret on the Red Sea coast and, by his own admission, providing details of Jedda's weak defences. Three weeks later the Ikhwan took Jedda, and Ibn Saud proclaimed himself Emir of the Hijaz and keeper of the Holy Places. For his services the residence of the former representative of the Turkish Government in Jedda was bestowed on Philby, and became his home.

Well aware of the concerns of both the European powers and the wider Muslim world, Ibn Saud now worked hard to keep the religious enthusiasm of his Ikhwan zealots and his Wahhabi kinsmen within bounds. In spite of occasional alarms – as when a reveille call sounded on a bugle by a group of unsuspecting pilgrims caused the Ikhwan to riot through the streets of Mecca – the holy places were left relatively undisturbed and pilgrims were allowed to make the Hajj, if under the stern gaze of the Wahhabi mutawihin. With Philby's assistance Ibn Saud mounted a diplomatic offensive to persuade the British Government that he was a force for stability in the Middle East and had no ambitions regarding the caliphate, and that Wahhabism was an instrument for 'true democracy' in the region. One expression of this campaign was the remarkable lecture on Wahhabism given to the Central Asian Society in the summer of 1929 with Lord Allenby in the chair.

The speaker was Sheikh HAFIZ WAHBA, described as 'Counsellor to His Majesty the King of the Hedjaz and Minister for Education'. Despite the name, Hafiz Wahba was no Bedouin but an Egyptian intellectual who had concluded early in the 1920s that Arab independence would be best served by supporting Ibn Saud. He had made his way to Riyadh in 1922 and embraced Wahhabism, rising to become Ibn Saud's most articulate spokesman overseas. In his lecture to the Central Asian Society Hafiz Wahba presented the theology of Al-Wahhab as an Arab version of Protestantism, and to show how eminently respectable it now was he assured his listeners that two of the most eminent figures in the ulema – the current Grand Mufti of Egypt and the head Imam of the Al-Aqsa mosque in Cairo – were preaching the teachings of Al-Wahhab and the medieval jurist Ibn Taymiyya. He further declared that 'the enlightened class in every Muslim land is Wahhabi in practice, though not in name and origin, because it is this class, as is duly recognised in all the Muslim world, that preaches the gospel of self-reliance'. Both claims went unchallenged.

Sheikh Wahba's lecture to the Central Asian Society was followed by an article for the Society's *Journal* under the nom de plume 'Phoenix', almost certainly contributed by Philby, giving an outline of the Wahhabi movement and its doctrines. The Wahhabi interpretation of jihad was here defined simply as 'the fostering of a martial and fanatical spirit to keep the law in force'.

To T. E. Lawrence, Ibn Saud's Arab empire was 'a figment, built on sand'. He and most other observers were convinced that Ibn Saud's kingdom must fall apart. The Wahhabi ulema were reacting with hostility to every attempt by Ibn Saud to introduce such modern developments as the telephone and the motor-car, on the grounds that there was no precedent for such innovation in the Quran or the Hadith. At the same time, the Ikhwan were increasingly defying their imam's authority by carrying out unauthorised raids into infidel Iraq and Syria. It soon became clear to Ibn Saud that if the Ikhwan continued their raiding, Britain would intervene. His response was to dismiss three Ikhwan commanders, whose troops reacted by massacring some Nejdi merchants. An offer of reconciliation was made and rejected and in 1929 Saudi loyalists, supported by four British aircraft and some two hundred radio-equipped armoured cars and troop carriers, took on the Ikhwan cavalry with their ancient rifles, lances and swords. After ten months the revolt ended with the surrender of the remaining rebels to British forces on the Kuwait border.

At the end of 1930 the chronic inter-tribal warfare that had bedevilled Arabia since before the days of the Prophet was finally brought to an end, giving way to the Islamic nation-state of Saudi Arabia. By a diplomatic mix of give and take Ibn Saud reconciled his Wahhabi ulema to innovations that posed no challenge to their authority. He ensured that they received the religious taxes that were their due and consulted them on such crucial issues as whether he as Imam had the final authority to order and suspend jihad. In return for their support the ulema, under the guidance of the aal as-Sheikh, was given absolute authority to impose Wahhabi sharia not only in the mosques and law courts but right across the land.

For his efforts on Ibn Saud's behalf Harry St John Philby was branded little short of a traitor by the British Government. 'He has lost no opportunity', minuted a Foreign Office official to the Cabinet, 'of attacking & misrepresenting the Govt. & its policy in the Middle East. His methods have been as unscrupulous as they have been violent. He is a public nuisance & it is largely due to him & his intrigues that Ibn Saud – over whom he unfortunately exercises some influence – has given us so much trouble during the last few years.' But in his new home in Jedda Philby was no less an object of suspicion. To the Dutch consul, Colonel van der Meulen, he cut a forlorn figure, 'apparently determined to outrage English convention in dress, appearance and general social behaviour', but also 'always in conflict: with the Arabs of his caravan, with the government, with its policy, with his own personnel and, I think, most of all with himself.' According to van der Meulen, a time came when the outcast came to him and remarked, '"We are not Christians, why should not we become Muslims?"'

In August 1930 Philby wrote a formal letter to Ibn Saud informing him of his earnest desire 'to become a Muslim and to abandon all other religions'. He went on to make the required public declaration, that 'there is no God but Allah and that Mohammad is His Slave and Messenger'. He declared himself anxious to follow 'all that is written in the books of the good ancestors and more especially the statements of Shaikh Ibn Taimia [Ibn Taymiyya, the medieval jurist], Ibn al Qaiyem aj-Jowziah [al-Qayyim al-Jawziyah, leading student of Ibn Taymiyya], and in the later ages those of Shaikh Mohammed Ibn Abdul Wahhab, may God have mercy on him'.

Philby was soon afterwards summoned to join Ibn Saud in Mecca. At the outskirts of the holy city he stripped in a tent set up for him, performed the required ablutions, dressed in the white garments of the pilgrim, and was escorted into Mecca's great square, where he kissed the black stone of the Kaaba and made the sevenfold circuit before going on to drink at the holy well of Zamzam. After morning prayers next day he was received by the Wahhabi Emir and Imam, kissed on both cheeks and given the name Abdullah, Servant of God.

A British consular officer, Hope Gill, who met Philby that same summer was convinced that Philby's conversion was simply a matter of expediency: 'He made no pretence whatever that his conversion was spiritual.' Yet there can be no doubt Philby believed that he was furthering the cause of Ibn Saud's

Arabia. At the Emir's suggestion he wrote an article for the press explaining, to quote the title, 'Why I turned Wahhabi?' Part of it read: 'I believe that the present Arabian puritan movement harbingers an epoch of future political greatness based on strong moral and political foundations . . . I consider an open declaration of my sympathy with Arabian religion and political ideals as the best methods of assisting the development of Arab greatness.'

When asked by Philby soon after their first meeting to explain the basis of his leadership, Ibn Saud had replied: 'We raise them not above us, nor do we place ourselves above them. We give them what we can . . . And if they go beyond their bounds we make them taste the sweetness of our discipline.' What Philby omitted in his accounts of Ibn Saud's rise to power was that this sweetness of discipline was harsh in the extreme, accounting for several hundred thousand violent deaths and mutilations. In taking over towns and cities the Ikhwan carried out wholesale massacres. The regional governments installed by Ibn Saud were ruthless in the suppression of opposition and the maintenance of Wahhabi sharia. The governors appointed by him were reported to have carried out forty thousand public beheadings and no fewer than three hundred and fifty thousand amputations by the sword, with Ibn Saud's cousin Abdulla taking the lead in his zeal to extinguish every pocket of polytheism disfiguring the land.

Over two long spells of duty as consul in Jedda between 1926 and 1945 the Dutchman van der Meulen became a jaundiced observer of events in Arabia. His reports detailing the ruthless methods employed in the creation of Saudi Arabia were apparently seen by Ibn Saud and approved. The Emir expressed himself content that the Queen of the Netherlands should know the facts: 'We have often acted severely, even mercilessly . . . It is good that you should know the truth about our creed and that of our brothers. We believe that Allah the Exalted One uses us as His instrument. As long as we serve Him we shall succeed, no power can check us and no enemy will be able to kill us.'

The Dutchman was able to follow the civil war between Ibn Saud and his Ikhwan with greater objectivity than Philby. 'The Ikhwan movement demonstrated the extreme to which Wahhabism could lead,' he afterwards wrote. 'If religion is used to encourage self-righteousness and feelings of superiority in primitive souls and if it then teaches the duty of holy war, the result is heroism, cruelty, narrowing of the mind and atrophy of what is humane and what is of true value, in a man and in a people.'

In 1932, with the country of his ancestors consolidated, pacified and secure, Ibn Saud united his dual emirates of Nejd and Hijaz, and proclaimed his country the Kingdom of Saudi Arabia. Hajji Abdullah, formerly Harry St John Philby, played his part by helping to secure an exploration concession for the Standard Oil Company of California over a rival bid from the British Iraq Petroleum Company, thereby laying the foundations of the Aramco concession, of Saudi Arabia's wealth, and of the kingdom's future co-operation with the United States of America.

In 1953 Saudi Arabia's founding father died and the throne and Wahhabi imamship passed to the eldest of his many sons, first Saud and then Faisal. With the establishment of socialist governments in Muslim countries such as that of President Nasser in neighbouring Egypt, the need to counter the spread of irreligious forces now became a priority. The Founding Committee of the Muslim World League, the Supreme Committee for Islamic Propagation, the World Supreme Council for Mosques and other religious bodies were set up specifically to promote Wahhabism. However, the relative poverty of the Kingdom of Saudi Arabia initially prevented the ulema from promoting Wahhabism effectively beyond its borders – until 1973, when the price of crude oil went through the roof following the

Arab–Israeli war and the formation of the OPEC oil cartel. Saudi Arabia was suddenly awash with petrodollars, and at last the Wahhabi authorities were able to commit massive sums to producing Wahhabi literature and funding mosques and madrassahs wherever there were Sunni communities. The Indian sub-continent became the leading beneficiary of this largesse.

11

The Coming Together

To understand the spirit which might be evoked we
must recall the state of feeling – the ignorance, bigotry,
enthusiasm, hardihood, and universal agreement –
amidst which the Crusades took their rise, and to which
a parallel might be found amongst the excitable population beyond the border. There are fully developed 'the
implicit faith and ferocious energy' in which the essence
of original Mahomedanism has been said to consist, and
which the propagation of the Wahabi Puritanism has
done much to inflame.

Extract from *Government of Punjab Report*, 1868

In 1911 two very different outdoor gatherings took place in northern India. The grandest by far was the Imperial Assembly,
popularly known as the Delhi Durbar, held to celebrate the acces-
sion of King George V as King-Emperor. Its site beside Delhi
Ridge had been chosen deliberately, for it was here that the
British had rallied prior to assaulting the rebel city in the summer
of 1857. Across twenty-five square miles of the Delhi plain 233

tented encampments were laid out, linked by a specially built railway. At its heart was an open-sided pavilion, within which on 12 December the King-Emperor sat enthroned to receive the homage of the more important of his Indian subjects. The next day he and Queen Mary proceeded to the ramparts of the Red Fort of the Mughals to be presented to the Indian masses gathered on the open ground below. Here, according to an official Government booklet, 'a vast troubled sea of humanity swept forward with banners waving and bands playing, a great concourse of Moslems, Sikhs and Hindoos to salute the Padshah.' The entire spectacle was designed to evoke the splendours of the Mughals, and to demonstrate that the British, as their natural successors, were there to stay.

Eight months earlier a very different gathering had taken place, a deliberate riposte to the costly propaganda exercise then being prepared outside Delhi. It was staged eighty miles to the north, on the by then extensive campus grounds of the Dar ul-Ulum Deoband Madrassah. Billed as a reunion, it was more in the nature of a conference, attended by some thirty thousand teachers and former students, and presided over by the madrassah's rector, sixty-year-old Maulana MAHMOOD UL-HASAN, widely regarded as the most influential Muslim cleric in India and on whom the title of *Shaikh-ul-Hind* had been bestowed by his admirers.

Mahmood ul-Hasan's rise to religious authority mirrored that of the religious institution to which he had dedicated his life since joining Deoband Madrassah as its first student in 1866. After graduating in 1877 Mahmood ul-Hasan had gone on, with the full support of Deoband's founder Muhammad Qasim, to set up his own organisation which he called *Samaratut Tarbiyat* (Results of the Training). This was a quasi-military body in which volunteers known as *fedayeen*, or 'men of sacrifice', were taught to prepare themselves for armed jihad against the British – although in practice this preparation was limited to marching and drilling in khaki uniforms, for weapons carrying nothing more lethal than staves.

To the British authorities this body was about as menacing as a cadet corps, and Mahmood ul-Hasan's fedayeen were allowed to parade about freely. With the death of Muhammad Qasim in 1880 the leadership of the Deoband organisation passed first to its co-founder Rashid Ahmad and then, after his death in 1905, to Deoband's first graduate.

As rector of Dar ul-Ulum Deoband, Mahmood ul-Hasan presided over its continuing expansion as the leading Muslim university in Asia, ensuring that it and the scores of branch Deobandi seminaries now in existence adhered to the original curriculum and continued to propagate the strict pro-tawhid, pro-ulema, anti-innovation, anti-polytheist, fundamentalist revivalism first initiated in Syria by Ibn Taymiyya, in Arabia by Al-Wahhab and in India by Shah Waliullah. Yet even as Deobandi theology reshaped mainstream Sunni thinking in India along more conservative lines, so its political philosophy of jihad through withdrawal and separatism lost ground. The formation of the Indian National Congress, attracting support from both Hindu and Muslim intellectuals, led to growing fears among many Muslims that representative government on the British model would lead to Hindu majority rule. One response was the formation in 1906 of the All-India Muslim League, dedicated to the protection of Muslim interests. But Mahmood ul-Hasan and other radicals saw even the Muslim League as playing into the hands of the British authorities by helping them 'divide and rule'.

It was against this background that Mahmood ul-Hasan stood up before the assembled delegates at the April 1911 Dar ul-Ulum Deoband reunion to announce that the time had come to resume the armed struggle against the British colonial government in India. 'Did Maulana Nanautawi [Deoband's founder, Muhammad Qasim Nanautawi] found this madrassah only for teaching and learning?' he is said to have demanded. 'It was founded in 1866 to teach and prepare Muslims to make up for the losses of 1857.'

This announcement appears to have been received by the

assembled alumni with considerable disquiet, and led eventually to a split in the Deobandi movement and the appointment of a new rector at Dar ul-Ulum Deoband. However, Mahmood ul-Hasan pressed on. The quasi-military organisation that he had nurtured with little success for so many years was reconstituted as *Jamiat-ul-Ansaar*, the Party of Volunteers. Its exact purpose was kept from the British authorities: it was to be the nucleus of an army of resistance. Deobandi graduates would provide the Party of Volunteers with its officers and religious commissars, while its rank-and-file would be drawn from the Pathan tribes of what was now the North-West Frontier Province (NWFP).

Under Mahmood ul-Hasan's direction the Party of Volunteers held a number of anti-British rallies, provoking the authorities into banning it as an organisation. Mahmood ul-Hasan's response was to set up a new body, *Nazzaarat ul-Maarif* (Offering of Good Actions), with its headquarters and recruiting base in Delhi. Then in the spring of 1914 he put into execution plans for hijra and jihad remarkably similar to those first drawn up by Syed Ahmad almost a century earlier, even to the extent of seeking to replicate his model of a supply base in the plains and a fighting base in the mountains. A group of fifteen volunteers, made up of Deoband old boys under the joint command of two of Mahmood ul-Hasan's lieutenants, Maulana OBAIDULLAH Sindhi and Maulvi Fazal Ilahi, set out for the NWFP with the intention of linking up with other students from Peshawar and Kohat and then proceeding through Mohmand country to join the remnants of Syed Ahmad's Hindustani Fanatics in the mountains.

Old Abdullah Ali, having commanded the Hindustanis for over four decades, had finally expired in 1901. A year later his son Amanullah and the remaining faithful had been expelled from Swat and Buner for the last time. They had then migrated north-westwards to the village of Chamarkand in Dir, close to the Afghan border and far beyond the reach of the British authorities. Government intelligence reports suggested that they no longer

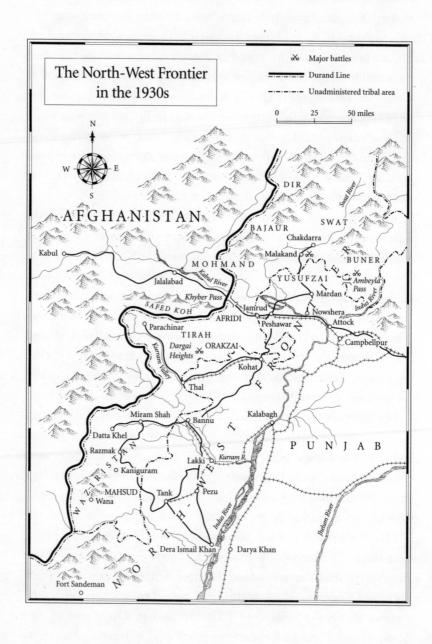

The North-West Frontier in the 1930s

⚔ Major battles
— Durand Line
—··—··— Unadministered tribal area

0   25   50 miles

N
W   E
S

AFGHANISTAN

DIR

BAJAUR   SWAT
        Chakdarra
    Malakand   ⚔
Kabul   MOHMAND   BUNER
                                   Ambeyla
            Jalalabad   Kabul River   YUSUFZAI   Pass
                    Khyber Pass   Mardan
            SAFED KOH   Jamrud   Nowshera
                    AFRIDI   Peshawar   Attock
        Parachinar   Campbellpur
            TIRAH
        Dargai   ORAKZAI
        Heights ⚔
                Kohat
            Thal
                        Kalabagh
        Miram Shah   Bannu
    Datta Khel   PUNJAB
    Razmak
    WAZIRISTAN   Lakki   Kurram R.
        Kaniguram
    MAHSUD   Tank   Pezu
    Wana
                N
                O
                R   Dera Ismail Khan   Darya Khan
                T
    Fort Sandeman
            H

Swat River
FRONTIER
Indus River
Kurram Valley
Jhelum River
Indus River
NORTH-WEST FRONTIER

represented a military threat, even though they were putting out 'intensive propaganda' through a news sheet called the *Al-Mujaheed* (the Holy Warrior). According to the *Peshawar Gazetteer*, they were reduced to a mere handful, but still preaching jihad. 'Politically,' noted the writer of the *Gazetteer*, 'their most dangerous doctrine is that it is a religious duty for all Muslims to wage the holy war against infidels.'

Obaidullah and his volunteers succeeded in reaching the Fanatic Camp only to find the Hindustani Fanatics reluctant to practise what they so fervently preached. At this point the Great War of 1914–1918 intervened, and with it came the Sultan of Turkey's call for Muslims to unite in jihad against Britain.

In plains India the call went largely unheeded, despite the serious efforts made to persuade Muslims serving with the Indian Army to desert. 'Raise your fellow caste-man against the English and join the army of Islam,' reads a letter sent anonymously to the Risaldar-Major of the 6th Bengal Cavalry. 'All the Muslims who have died in this war fighting for the British will spend an eternity in hell. Kill the English whenever you get the chance and join the enemy ... Be watchful, join the enemy, and you will expel the Kaffir from your native land. The flag of Islam is ready and will shortly be seen waving.'

However, the Sultan's call for jihad now led Mahmood ul-Hasan to change his plans. Obaidullah was ordered to proceed with his student volunteers to Kabul, while he himself sailed to Jedda. What followed has never been satisfactorily explained, for the very good reason that Mahmood ul-Hasan's bid to replicate Syed Ahmad's holy war was such a fiasco that he and his supporters preferred to keep silent about it. But enough details survive to give the lie to those who claim that the Dar ul-Ulum Deoband was never in the business of promoting armed jihad.

Early in 1915 Mahmood ul-Hasan, now calling himself *Al-Qayed*, The Leader, turned up in Mecca. There he presented himself to Ghalib Bey, the Turkish Governor of the Hijaz, to solicit the Ottoman Caliphate's support for his cause in the form of funds and guns. To his dismay, he and his party were given the cold shoulder, although one of their number, Muhammad Mian, was permitted to return to his home in Peshawar with a letter from Ghalib Bey inviting the tribesmen of the Frontier to invade the Punjab. Muhammad Mian took this letter into Mohmand country, where it was acted upon by two mullahs, the Hajji of Turangzai and the Babrhai Mullah, with predictable consequences for those who followed their banner. An account of this swiftly suppressed minor uprising of 1915, set down by one of those who took part, Qasoori Sahib, perfectly illustrates the degree to which the Frontier tribes had been 'jihadised' by the example of Syed Ahmad the Martyr. 'As soon as the fighting was over,' wrote Qasoori Sahib in a memoir,

> local women came out singing Pashto battle songs with their *daf* and *dhols* [pipes and drums] . . . A mother would kiss the forehead of her *shaheed* [martyr] son. A sister would cry out of happiness for her shaheed brother and the wives would hug their shaheed husbands. They would sing to their beloved, 'Go, we have handed you over to Allah. Because you are a shaheed, go and enjoy *Jannah* [Paradise]. But do not forget us for Allah's sake. Ask Allah that he give the ability to your brothers as well, that they might follow in your footsteps.'

In the meantime, Obaidullah and his Deobandi volunteers had made their way over the mountains into Afghanistan and, after a period in detention, were given permission by Amir Habibullah to join with a number of Indian nationalists in establishing a government-in-exile in Kabul. In the late summer of 1915 Obaidullah and his colleague Maulvi Fazal Ilahi formed the *Junood ul-Rabbaniyah*, or Army of God. Under the leadership of the still absent Mahmood ul-Hasan it would spearhead an invasion of

India on the Syed Ahmad model. Obaidullah then wrote a self-congratulatory letter, in Persian on yellow silk cloth, giving his leader a full account of his activities. Enclosed with this first letter were two further letters on silk from another member of the group, the grandson of Dar ul-Ulum Deoband's founder, containing details of the Army of God's organisation and battle plans and listing the names of its leading players and supporters in India. These three silk letters were entrusted to a senior student, Abdul Haq, with instructions to deliver them by hand to a sheikh of Hyderabad in Sind, who would then send them on to Mahmood ul-Hasan in Mecca.

Most unwisely, Abdul Haq went out of his way to call on the father of two students who had skipped college in Lahore to join Obaidullah's army of volunteers. This man – named in reports simply as 'the Khan Bahadur' – happened to be a highly respected figure in Multan and a great supporter of the British. When he learned from Abdul Haq what his two sons were doing in Kabul he had him beaten until he revealed the full story, including the fact that he was the bearer of an important letter sewn inside a coat. The coat was produced and cut open to reveal the three silk letters. Being unable to read Persian, the Khan Bahadur took the letters to the Commissioner of Peshawar – who after one look immediately passed them on to the Government of India's Criminal Intelligence Department.

The inevitable outcome was the arrest in August 1915 of no fewer than 222 clerics from all over northern India, in what came to be known as the Silk Letter Conspiracy Case. A large proportion of these arrestees were Deobandi alumni. To further compound the disaster, Sheykh Huseyn of the Hijaz was then leaned on by the British Government to detain Mahmood ul-Hasan and five senior members of his entourage. They were duly brought to trial in Cairo in 1917, found guilty of sedition, and each sentenced to several years' imprisonment in Malta. Although Obaidullah and other members of his organisation in Kabul remained free, they now found themselves high on the Indian Police Special Branch's 'most wanted' list and unable to return to their homeland.

The traitorous activities of Mahmood ul-Hasan and his associates were publicly repudiated by the Dar ul-Ulum Deoband authorities, who were able to show the British Government in India that they had severed all links with his organisation long before the war. From this time onwards the Deoband movement's political ambitions were concentrated on a new politico-religious party known as *Jamiat-i-Ulema-i-Hind* (JUH), the Party of Clerics of Hindustan, formed in October 1920. Mahmood ul-Hasan was freed in time to attend the JUH's inauguration. 'I gave a lot of thought to the causes of the sorry state of this ummah [the world community of Islam] while in prison in Malta,' he declared. 'Our problems are caused by two factors: abandoning the Quran and our in-fighting.' He died a year later, aged seventy, his health broken by his three and a half years' imprisonment.

India's contribution to the British war effort between 1914 and 1918 was unstinting. More than eight hundred thousand Indian troops fought as volunteers, and expectations were high that India would be rewarded with dominion status. Instead, the British Government in India responded by bringing in the repressive Rowlatt Acts, introduced to deal with subversion of the sort exemplified by the Silk Letter Conspiracy. For many loyal subjects of the British Raj this was a turning point. Large numbers of middle-class Indians now gave their support to the Congress Party, as did the JUH. Calls for civil disobedience led to violent disturbances in the Punjab, to which the authorities reacted with greater violence, culminating in the Amritsar Massacre. Meanwhile, in Europe the Paris Conference of January 1919 had begun the dismemberment of the Ottoman Empire, embodiment of all the past achievements of Islam. A month later Afghanistan's cautious neutrality ended with the murder of Amir Habibullah while out hunting. Misreading the mood in India, his more combative son AMIR AMANULLAH launched a half-hearted invasion down the Khyber. The outcome was the short, sharp Third Afghan War, lasting no more than twenty-nine days and leaving the new Amir badly bruised.

But there were some Sunni Muslims in India who saw Amir Amanullah as the new champion of Islam. What became known as the Hijrat Movement swept like a summer whirlwind through the Punjab, leading thousands of Muslims to abandon jobs and homes and decamp with little more than what they stood up in to the dar ul-Islam of Afghanistan. Among them was an earnest young man in his twenties named Sayyid Abulala MAWDUDI, whose ancestors had entered India as Sufi scholars and had thereafter served first the Mughals and then the Nizams of Hyderabad. Forced to abandon his education by the death of his father, as an adolescent Mawdudi had moved to Delhi where he became an activist for the Khalifat Movement, which sought to restore the Turkish sultanate. Caught up in the fervour of the moment, he joined the Hijratis and travelled with them up the Khyber Pass into Afghanistan. Here they very quickly discovered they were not wanted. The Amir of Afghanistan had lost his enthusiasm for armed conflict, and was not prepared to support them. After some months the civil authorities in Peshawar found themselves in the curious position of having to repatriate several thousand destitute and disillusioned ex-mujahedeen.

With the collapse of the Khalifat Movement in the early 1920s many Muslim intellectuals began to look for new Muslim identities through the development of their own Islamic nation states, among them the young Mawdudi, who returned to Delhi and there became a student at the Dar ul-Ulum Deoband's Fatihpuri Madrassah, something he never acknowledged in later years. For a time he was closely involved with the Deobandi JUH political movement, now led by Maulana Hussain Ahmad Madani,

Mahmood ul-Hasan's successor as rector of Dar-ul-Ulum
Deoband. Under Madani's leadership the JUH continued to support Congress and resisted the calls of the Muslim League for a
separate Muslim state in the Indian sub-continent. The JUH also
established links with Wahhabi Arabia. In 1921 it sent a delegation of mullahs to Nejd and thereafter continued to maintain ties
with Ibn Saud and the aal as-Sheikh.

The JUH's alliance with Congress led to two splinter groups
breaking away to form new politico-religious parties. The first to
do so was led by the Naqshbandi Sufi Maulana Muhammad Ilyar,
whose party, *Tablighi Jamiat* (Preaching Party), followed the teachings of Shah Waliullah but sought to apply them in largely
apolitical terms. The second was led by Mawdudi, who began to
promote a new political agenda based on his belief that, to survive
in the modern world, Islam had to present itself as a viable political and social alternative to both Western capitalism and
socialism. Islam, he believed, had to confront non-Islam head on,
and out of that 'Islamic revolution' would emerge the modern
Islamic state purged of all accretions, a 'democratic caliphate'
whose citizens would embrace sharia willingly, even those aspects
of sharia that were undemocratic. He put together an entirely
new political platform based on Islamic revival and separatism,
taking on board Deoband's interpretative reading of Islam but
setting aside its sectarian theology in favour of salvation through
political action and jihad. These views became hugely influential
among Muslim intellectuals in setting a new agenda for Islamic
revival. In 1939 Mawdudi moved to Lahore, where two years later
he and a number of like-minded individuals founded the *Jamiat-
i-Islami* (JI), the Party of Islamists, in direct opposition to the then
pro-Congress JUH.

Throughout the period leading up to Independence in 1947, as
India became increasingly secularised and while Muhammad Ali
Jinnah, the modernising leader of the Muslim League, urged
Muslims to resist what he termed the 'reactionary' calls of 'the

undesirable element of Moulvis and Maulanas', the JI, JUH, Tablighi Jamiat and other political parties led by clerics kept the banner of Islamic revival flying in the Sunni community. As demands grew for a separate Muslim nation-state, a number of younger Deobandis in the JUH broke with their leader to reconstitute themselves as the *Jamiat-i-Ulema-i-Islam* (JUI), Party of Scholars of Islam, formed in 1945 under the leadership of two Deobandi mullahs, Maulana Shabbar Ahmad Othmani and Maulana MUFTI MAHMUD. The JUI's declared aim was shape the new nation of Pakistan into a truly Muslim state, with an Islamic constitution in conformity with the Quran and sharia – a vision it shared with the JI, Tablighi Jamiat, and a number of smaller ulema-led political parties.

After independence and the creation of Pakistan, these overtly Islamist parties competed for a minority constituency inside Pakistan, consistently failing to win popular support at the polling booths. Although they attracted leaders of high calibre they were riven by internal rivalries and religious disputes. Only in one region did they have any success, the JUI under the leadership of Mufti Mahmud establishing such a firm foothold in the NWFP and the tribal areas that it came to be viewed as a largely Pathan politico-religious party. It is no coincidence that the only other ulema-led party to gain a following in the Pathan tribal belt was the smaller Jamiat Ahl-i-Hadith. This was the sub-continent's only overtly Wahhabi party, with its origins in the organisation formed by Sayyid Nazir Husain, the cleric who had led the Wahhabi 'Delhi-ites' in 1857 and was later arrested by the British authorities on suspicion of being the Wahhabis' leader in Delhi. In relocating to the northern Punjab, the Ahl-i-Hadith party had, in a very real sense, returned to its jihadi roots.

With the ending of the British Raj in August 1947, the Pathans in the tribal areas lost their traditional enemy. Some supported the chimera of Pakhtunistan, a separate Pathan nation, others committed themselves to integration with the emerging state of

Pakistan. Only a seemingly insignificant minority turned to the new Islamist religious parties.

Everything changed for Pakistan with the coming to power of the military dictator General Muhammad Zia-ul-Haq in July 1977. His military calling notwithstanding, General Zia came from a traditionalist clerical background and was determined to Islamicise his country. He turned to Mawdudi's JI party, and for the eleven years of his rule the JI and the other Islamist parties enjoyed unprecedented influence, providing the ideological driving force that enabled the General to create an authoritarian Islamic state which had little support from the people of Pakistan. By now there were more than nine thousand Deobandi madrassahs in the sub-continent, the majority in Pakistan. Many Deoband-trained idealists joined the Pakistan Army and the civil service, where General Zia's patronage ensured their rapid promotion. A significant number were subsequently recruited into Pakistan's greatly expanded Inter-Services Intelligence agency, the ISI.

In 1979, two years after General Zia's coming to power, the Soviet Union sent troops into Afghanistan to support a Marxist regime that had seized power in a bloody coup four years earlier. This provoked the ulema of Afghanistan into declaring an anti-government jihad. Despite the overwhelming support of the tribal chiefs, this jihad would have had little chance of success but for the intervention of Pakistan, Saudi Arabia and the United States of America. For quite different reasons these three nations (along with Iran, China, Egypt, and even Britain, in a more limited capacity) stepped in to support the Afghan mujahedeen with military and financial aid. As a direct result of this support so many rival anti-Soviet groupings came into being that General Zia eventually put his foot down and announced that he would recognise only seven. Six of the seven were Pathan-dominated and four avowedly Islamist. These four were:

the *Ittihad-i-Islami*, formed by a Kabuli theologian named Abdul Rab Rasoul Sayyaf with strong links to Saudi Arabia, describing itself as *Salafi* and to all intents a Wahhabi warparty;

the far bigger *Harakat-i-Inqilab-i-Islami*, headed by Maulana Mohammed Nabi Mohammedi, which had a strong following among village ulema and the Ahmadzai Pathans of Northern Waziristan;

Hizb-i-Islami (Hekmatyar), led by the Pathan Gulbuddin Hekmatyar, with a strong base among the Mohmand, Shinwari and other Pathan tribes in Nangahar province, stretching east of Kabul to the Khyber; and

Hizb-i-Islami (Khalis), led by Younis Khalis, a Deobandi graduate with a following in the Kandahar and Pakhtia provinces close to the Pakistan border, in whose ranks marched the mujaheed mullah Muhammad Omar.

The last two parties had their origins in a branch of the JI set up in Kabul in the 1960s. The two rival leaders split in 1979 to form their own parties, but subsequently Gulbuddin Hekmatyar's *Hizb-i-Islami (Hekmatyar)* gained the backing of the main JI party in Pakistan and of the ISI to become the most effective mujahedeen fighting force in south-east Afghanistan.

For more than a decade the governments of Pakistan, Saudi Arabia and the United States worked through their respective intelligence agencies to direct the mujahedeen in their war against the Soviet-backed regime in Afghanistan. Over this same period thousands of Muslim idealists from outside the region volunteered to join the jihad, and did so with the active support of the three main supporting nations. Agents of the United States and Saudi Arabia worked together to set up a bureau in Peshawar, the *Maktab al-Khidamat* (Services Offices), which became the single most important cell in the prosecution of the war in Afghanistan.

Over this same period – or, at least, until his death in an air-crash in 1988 – General Zia sought to bring the Pathans on-side by encouraging the establishment of madrassahs in the tribal border areas, subsequently extended throughout the NWFP, Baluchistan, the Punjab and Sindh. This was part and parcel of his programme of Islamicisation. However, it was only made possible by the support of Pakistan's Islamist parties, who provided the teachers and the teachings, and of Saudi Arabia, which provided the greater part of the funding for the building and maintenance of the madrassahs.

There was now a coming-together of two ideologies; or, more precisely, a reuniting of two strands of a common ideology, long separated.

At the time of Partition in 1947 there had been approximately two hundred madrassahs on Pakistan's soil. Many were still of the old model: ramshackle institutions with ill-educated mullahs of the sort that Edwardes, Bellew and other British observers had mocked. All that changed with the proliferation of the Dar ul-Ulum Deoband madrassahs and those of their rivals. With the arrival in Peshawar, Nowshera and elsewhere along the NWFP of these modern madrassahs and their better-educated and more motivated teachers, increasing numbers of young Pathans and Afghans became radicalised and politicised. The support given to the JI, JUI and other Islamist parties by President Zia greatly enlarged the process, which then received a further boost with the stepping-up of funding from Saudi Arabia. Understandably enough, the Saudis channelled their financial support through and to those religious organisations with which they felt most comfortable, and who shared their vision of jihad: those that were overtly Wahhabi or had Wahhabi associations.

In 1972, of Pakistan's 893 madrassahs, 354 or 40 percent were Deobandi, 144 Ahl-i-Hadith and 267 Barelvi, representing the more moderate school of Sunni Islam. By the end of the 1980s an estimated 65 per cent of Pakistan's madrassahs were directly or indirectly Deobandi. In April 2002 (the first time accurate figures became available) Pakistan's Minister of Religious affairs put the total number of madrassahs in Pakistan at ten thousand, of which approximately four hundred were Shia, four hundred Ahl-i-Hadith, five hundred JI – and no fewer than seven thousand Deobandi. Of the 1.7 million students these ten thousand madrassahs accommodated, 1.25 million were receiving a Deoband-based or Ahl-i-Hadith religious education.

As the jihad against Soviet Afghanistan wore on in the 1980s, increasing numbers of these madrassahs became indoctrination and training schools for jihad, with those in and close to the tribal areas filled almost entirely by Pathans. Many of the most hard-line of these madrassahs were linked to the JUI, and it was chiefly in their spartan classrooms and prayer halls that the boys who later filled the ranks of the Taliban received their education. The Jaamiah Dar ul-Ulum Haqqania madrassah at Akora Khattack, beside the Islamabad Highway out of Peshawar, has its origins in a religious school opened in 1937 by Dar ul-Ulum Deoband's rector Madani and his fellow-Deobandi Maulana Abdul Haq (father of the present principal Samiul Haq). Many of the Taliban's Pathan leaders received their schooling either here or at the JUI madrassah founded by Deobandi Maulvi Mohammad Yusaf Binnori in the suburbs of Karachi. The JUI also spawned a number of extremist organisations such as the *Sipahi-e-Sahaba* (Soldiers of the Companions), and *Lashkar-e-Jhangvi* (Army of Jhangvi), both violently anti-Shia, anti-Hindu and anti-Christian terrorist groups.

Nor should the role of the smaller fundamentalist parties be overlooked, most notably that of the *Markaz ad-Dawa wal Irshad* (Centre for Invitation and Instruction), and the *Tehreek-i-Nafaz-i-Shariat-i-Mohammadi* (Movement for the Enforcement of Islamic Law), both Wahhabi organisations derived from the Ahl-i-Hadith party. As might be expected, Ahl-i-Hadith developed a particularly strong membership in Swat and Dir, where descendants of Wilayat Ali and his son Abdullah Ali are said to be living to this day.

One of the very few Wahhabi prelates whose names have become well known outside Saudi Arabia in recent times is Sheikh Abdul Aziz bin Abdullah BIN BAZ, who died in Mecca in May 1999 at the age of eighty-nine. At the time of the first Gulf War Bin Baz acquired some notoriety by issuing fatwas against women drivers, Saudi and American, but he had earlier attracted notice with a fatwa denouncing as atheists those who held the earth to be round – a position he was forced to change after a minor Saudi prince went into space in a US space shuttle. Born in Riyadh in 1910, Bin Baz witnessed the rise to power of Ibn Saud, but lost his eyesight at the age of fourteen. He was then receiving his religious education from three members of the aal-as-Sheikh, an education that included ten years at the feet of Ibn Saud's leading prelate, Sheikh Muhammad bin Ibrahim Aal-Shaikh, Grand Mufti of Saudi Arabia.

Despite his blindness Sheikh Bin Baz became an outstanding scholar. He served as a judge for fifteen years before teaching jurisprudence and Hadith at the faculty of Sharia at Riyadh's Institute of Religious Studies during the 1950s. After fifteen years as Vice-Chancellor and then Chancellor of the Islamic University of Medina he became President of the General Presidency of Islamic Research, and finally Grand Mufti of Saudi Arabia. For a quarter of a century he was the most powerful religious figure in Saudi Arabia, and Wahhabism's most active champion. Among the many committees he chaired were the Founding Committee of the Muslim World League, the Supreme Committee for Islamic Propagation and the World Supreme Council for Mosques, all bodies set up to export Wahhabi teachings in response to such secular challenges as President Nasser's socialist government in Egypt. The Wahhabi ulema was already well funded, both from the Saudi national budget and from the *zakat*, the religious levy of one-fortieth of income required by the Quran of all believers. However, as stated earlier, the huge rise of oil prices in the wake of the 1973 Arab–Israeli war enabled Bin Baz to make this funding count. From 1979 onwards the main beneficiaries of this largesse were the madrassahs of Afghanistan and Pakistan, where the Wahhabi ulema were as much troubled by the growing influence of the Shia ayatollahs in neighbouring Iran as by the Russians in Afghanistan. It is said that since 1979 the Wahhabi Establishment has committed an estimated seventy billion dollars to Islamist missionary work, 'ranging from the funding of some 10,000 madrassas in Pakistan to the construction of thousands of mosques and seminaries and community centers all over the Muslim and Western worlds'.

However, inside the Kingdom of Saudi Arabia both pro- and anti-Wahhabi elements were becoming disenchanted with the way the five-thousand-strong royal House of Saud was conducting itself. A first sign of trouble came in 1975 when King Faisal was assassinated by his nephew, who harboured a grudge against the head of his family after the death of his brother while leading a Wahhabi demonstration against the introduction of television. Then in November 1979, as crowds gathered in Mecca to celebrate Islam's fourteen-hundredth anniversary – and just weeks before the Soviets sent their tanks and troop-carriers into Afghanistan – several hundred armed men burst into the Grand Mosque and took it over in the name of the Mahdi. Their leader was a Nejdi named Juhaiman al-Utaibi, raised in an Ikhwan settlement and a member of the Saudi National Guard originally composed of loyalist elements of the Ikhwan half a century earlier. He claimed to be the disciple of an imam, Muhammad Abdullah al-Qahtani, who was the long-awaited Mahdi come to overthrow the houses of Saud and aal-as-Sheikh. The revolt was violently suppressed, the supposed Mahdi dying in the fighting and Juhaiman among those subsequently beheaded, but the episode gave notice to the Saudi Government that idealists inside the country were joining forces with non-Wahhabi Islamists from outside.

Many of these Islamists received their religious education directly or indirectly from Sheikh Bin Baz, among them the Palestinian Sheikh ABDULLAH AZZAM.

Born in Jenin in 1941, Abdullah Azzam studied sharia at Damascus University and Al-Aqsa University in Cairo. Following the catastrophe of the 1967 Six-Day War he fled to Jordan and worked in a Palestinian refugee camp funded by Saudi Arabia's aal-as-Sheikh. Disillusioned by the secularism of the Palestinian resistance under Yasser Arafat he moved to Egypt to continue his religious studies at Al-Aqsa. Here he met supporters of Sayyid Qutb, the recently executed co-founder of the Muslim Brotherhood. The role of Sayyid Qutb and groups such as the Muslim Brotherhood and Islamic Jihad in promoting Islamist jihad falls outside the scope of this book. What is relevant in the present context is that Sayyid Qutb had espoused the centrality of tawhid and the absolute necessity for Islam to combat un-Islamic ignorance (*jahiliyya*), as represented by the pagan West and Muslim countries like Egypt whose governments tried to follow the Western model. Despite the pleas of Sheikh Bin Baz and other leading Muslims, in 1966 Sayyid Qutb was executed, after ten years' incarceration.

In 1974 or 1975 Abdulla Azzam was given sanctuary from Egyptian persecution by the government of Saudi Arabia and offered a lecturing post at the King Abdul Aziz University of Jedda, where he was joined by Sayyid Qutb's brother, Muhammad Qutb. It is claimed that during this period Abdullah Azzam came under the direct influence of Bin Baz and became a Wahhabi. It is probably closer to the truth to describe Abdullah Azzam as a supporter of the Muslim Brotherhood who, during his time in Saudi Arabia, gained a greater understanding of Wahhabism and of Ibn Taymiyya's philosophy of militant jihad.

Abdullah Azzam first came to international prominence with a fatwa entitled *Defence of the Muslim Land*, issued in the wake of the Soviet invasion of Afghanistan in December 1979. In it he declared it obligatory on all Muslims to make jihad against the Russians in Afghanistan and the Israelis in Palestine. This fatwa was supported by Bin Baz and the Wahhabi ulema. Abdullah Azzam then moved with his family to Pakistan, taking as his inspiration the declaration of the Prophet that 'a few moments spent in jihad in the path of Allah is worth more than seventy years spent praying at home'. Initially he taught at the International Islamic University in Islamabad, but then moved to Peshawar to set up an organisation he named the *Bait al-Ansar*, the House of Ansar, after the man who first gave the Prophet refuge when he and his Companions fled from Mecca to Medina. Its purpose was to assist Arab volunteers arriving on the Frontier to engage in jihad in Afghanistan. His political philosophy was now summed up in his terse declaration 'Jihad and the rifle alone; no negotiations, no conferences, and no dialogue.'

Abdullah Azzam's many admirers claim that he took an active part in the fighting in Afghanistan, but his real contribution was as an organiser and inspirational firebrand who preached locally and published internationally on the duty of every Muslim to make jihad, not just in Afghanistan but wherever Muslims were oppressed. 'Jihad', he wrote, 'continues until Allah's Word is raised high; jihad until all the oppressed peoples are freed; jihad to protect our dignity and restore our occupied lands. Jihad is the way of everlasting glory.' From 1980 to 1989 he worked unceasingly but largely unavailingly to persuade the many mujahedeen commanders waging war in Afghanistan to set aside their rivalries and unite – ideally, under one leader.

Abdullah Azzam has been called the 'Emir of Islamic jihad', but it would be more accurate to describe him as its godfather. Which leads on, at last, to the present (2005) amir of world jihad, Osama bin Muhammad bin Awad BIN LADEN.

Born in Saudi Arabia in 1957, Osama bin Laden was the seventeenth of 52 children of a Yemeni immigrant contractor,

Muhammad bin Laden, his mother a Syrian whom his father subsequently divorced. Bin Laden senior accumulated prodigious
wealth through his work as a construction contractor for the Saudi
royal family and Osama bin Laden was raised in privileged circumstances, although he himself was never part of the Saudi inner
circle. His father kept his children together in one household,
usually the family's main mansion in Jedda, to ensure they
received a strict religious education on Wahhabi lines. However,
as one of several fourth wives married and then divorced, the
status of Osama's mother was lowly and not enhanced by her
being a follower of the Syrian Alawite sect, considered heretical
by the Wahhabis. The death of his father in a helicopter crash
when he was eleven may well have added to his sense of being an
outsider. After this tragedy Prince Faisal, the pro-Wahhabi half-
brother of King Saud, stepped in to protect and support the
children, but Osama seems to have rejected the opportunity
afforded his step-brothers and step-sisters to be educated abroad,
in favour of local schooling in Jedda. In 1977 his eldest brother led
a family party on the Hajj, during which the twenty-year-old
underwent a religious experience that led him to abandon his
Western links, grow a beard and commit himself seriously to
Islamic studies. At this time he was enrolled as an undergraduate
at King Abdul Aziz University at Jedda to study either economics
or engineering, a degree course probably never completed. Here
he came under the direct influence of the Palestinian and
Egyptian radicals Abdullah Azzam and Muhammad Qutb, whose
recorded sermons were widely circulated among students at this
time. Osama bin Laden may thus be described as a Saudi-born
Yemeni raised as a Wahhabi who was politicised by Abdullah
Azzam and the revolutionary anti-imperialist ideology of the
Muslim Brotherhood.

In 1979, when he was twenty-two, three disparate but profoundly unsettling events caused Bin Laden to abandon his
studies for direct action: the revolution of the ayatollahs in Iran;

the violent seizure of the Great Mosque at Mecca; and the Russian intervention in Afghanistan. If the reports are correct, he was one of the first Saudis to fly to Afghanistan, almost certainly with the encouragement of Abdullah Azzam, whom he preceded. The Bin Laden family's close links with the Saudi royal family now became extremely valuable. The Government of Saudi Arabia was most anxious to show its commitment to the Afghan cause, as were the Wahhabi aid and propaganda organisations overseen by Sheikh Bin Baz. So Bin Laden became an unofficial ambassador and bag-man for Saudi Arabia in Pakistan and Afghanistan. He also committed his own considerable private wealth to the cause, supported by family members and friends. He spent time on the front line, although gilded accounts of him as a battle-hardened jihadi fighting alongside such groups as the Hizb-i-Islami can be dismissed as wish-fulfilment on the part of his supporters. His real talent lay in ensuring that jihadis went where military commanders most needed them, and that the supplies kept coming. In the process Osama made direct, personal contact with many thousands of volunteers drawn from all corners of the Muslim umma. He is known to have performed many individual acts of kindness towards wounded mujahedeen and the families of martyrs who were suffering hardship – and it may well have been in this connection that he met Mullah Omar, who had recently lost an eye to an exploding rocket. This first encounter is said to have taken place in 1989 in a Deobandi mosque in the Banuri suburb of Karachi. By that time the conspicuously tall and well-dressed Arab known as 'al-Shaykh' had become a familiar and greatly admired figure throughout the Frontier region, an unassuming and, at this time, far from charismatic young man who was nevertheless recognised as the personification of Saudi Arabia's commitment to the Afghanistan jihad.

Yet Bin Laden's efforts would have counted for little had it not been for his mentor and patron Abdullah Azzam, whose rudimentary set-up for the recruitment, training and support of foreign fighters grew, with Saudi funding, into a highly sophisti-cated organisation. It became the *Maktab al-Khidamat an-Mujahedeen*, the Office of Services to the Mujahedeen, with an international network of overseas branches linked by mobile tele-phones, personal computers and lap-tops. It also became, in effect, a parallel bureau to that established earlier in Peshawar by Pakistan's ISI. Abdullah Azzam's control of the Office of Services to the Mujahedeen allowed him to channel financial support to those mujahedeen groups whose agendas came closest to his own: principally, Gulbuddin Hekmatyar's Hizb-i-Islami (Hekmatyar) and Ittihad-i-Islami (Unity of Islam). Both these mujahedeen fighting forces came increasingly to be seen as Wahhabi lashkars (war parties) with Saudi-led agendas.

In excess of twenty-five thousand foreign jihadis are said to have passed through the portals of the Office of Services to the Mujahedeen, set in a leafy, middle-class extension of Peshawar's Civil Lines, north-west of the old city. Many of them came from the most militant organisations in the Islamic world, including Islamic Jihad and Hamas. To the local population these volunteer fighters were known collectively as 'the Arabs', and they were welcomed and honoured for their courage and sacrifices.

It is no exaggeration to say that from this office the seed of international jihad was planted in the now fertile and receptive soil of the North-West Frontier, to be fertilised by all the resent-ments real and perceived of fundamentalist, revivalist Islam, watered by Osama bin Laden's pipeline to Saudi Arabia – and, finally, to take root as *Al-Qaeda*, the [Military] Base.

Among those who came knocking on the doors of the Maktab al-Khidamat an-Mujahedeen was the bespectacled Egyptian physician and revolutionary Ayman AL-ZAWAHRI, known famil-iarly as 'The Doctor'. He was from one of the most respectable middle-class families in Cairo, Arabic in origin, many of whose male members had distinguished themselves as diplomats, academics, doctors and theologians. One of his grandfathers had served as Egypt's ambassador to Saudi Arabia and Pakistan and had founded King al-Saud University in Riyadh in the 1950s. One of his great-uncles had fought against the British in Egypt and after many years' service as a diplomat had helped found the Arab League, being credited as the man who persuaded Ibn Saud to join that organisation in 1945. Yet another great-uncle had served as the Grand Imam of Cairo's Al-Aqsa mosque from 1929 to 1933 – and was the man whom Sheikh Hafiz Wahba, in his lecture to the Central Asian Society in 1929, had identified as being linked, together with the then Grand Mufti of Egypt, as a disciple of Muhammad Ibn Abd al-Wahhab.

A close connection had thus existed between Al-Zawahri's family and the Sauds for two generations – until Ayman al-Zawahri broke with family tradition by joining the Egyptian Islamic Jihad revolutionary party. He was among the several hundred suspects rounded up and jailed following President Sadat's assassination in 1981, and emerged three years later an embittered man. He moved to Saudi Arabia and then on to Pakistan and Afghanistan, which he twice visited in the early 1980s as a volunteer doctor working for the Kuwait Red Crescent Society.

In 1986 Bin Laden flew his several wives and children from Jedda to Peshawar and set up home in a rented house outside the city. That same summer he established a training camp for a group of his Arab volunteers at Khost, on the lower slopes of the Spin Ghar mountain range close to the Pakistan border. Copying Abdullah Azzam, he named this camp Bait al-Ansar, the House of Ansar, and used his family construction equipment to turn long-abandoned Buddhist caves above his camp into fortified bunkers. His plans suffered a setback when Russian Special Forces attacked the camp in the following year, forcing its Arab defenders to retreat across the border. However, the Khost complex survived to became the Afghan equivalent of the Fanatic Camp of the Hindustanis at Sittana, where thousands of international jihadis received the military training and political indoctrination they later applied in domains of war as far afield as Algeria, Chechnya and Xinjiang.

One of these 'Arabs' was the man who currently (September 2005) masterminds the bombing campaign in Iraq, as well as presiding over some of the worst terrorist beheadings and atrocities: the Jordanian Abu Musab AL-ZARQAWI. Al-Zarqawi arrived in Peshawar as a twenty-year-old in the summer of 1986, bringing with him an unenviable reputation as a street thug and bully. He had missed the boat as far as taking up arms against the Russians was concerned, so he began working for a radical Islamist newsletter, where he came under the influence of a fundamentalist cleric named Sheikh Muhammad al-Maqdisi, a fellow Jordanian whose Salafi beliefs made him a natural ally of the Deobandis. These beliefs appear to have caused Al-Maqdisi and his new student to hold back from joining either Abdullah Azzam or Bin Laden. Instead, they formed their own group, naming it *Bait al-Imam*, the House of the Imam, before returning to Jordan with the intention of overthrowing the Hashemite monarchy. Both men were arrested for plotting against the state and given long prison sentences.

In the meantime, the Egyptian doctor Al-Zawahri had followed Bin Laden's example by also moving his family from Arabia to Peshawar, where he and other Egyptian revolutionaries set up a local faction of the Egyptian Islamic Jihad. Inevitably, a rivalry developed between the Egyptians led by Al-Zawahri and the Arabs led by Abdullah Azzam from the Office of Services to the Mujahedeen. These differences became acute when in 1988 Soviet Russia decided to cut its losses in Afghanistan and began to pull out its troops. A decade of warfare against the Russian infidels had created a battle-hardened and highly politicised international brigade. Abdullah Azzam wished these foreign jihadis to remain in Afghanistan and secure it for the Islamist cause, after which they would join forces with the Deobandi politico-religious parties and other Islamist groups to liberate Pakistan and Kashmir. Al-Zawahri, however, argued that the pan-Islamist armed movement created in the course of the anti-Soviet jihad in Afghanistan should now be employed in liberating the entire umma, beginning with Egypt.

In the late summer of 1989 a plot by persons unknown to assassinate Sheikh Abdullah Azzam was foiled when a large cache of primed explosive was found under the pulpit of a mosque where he was about to preach. A face-to-face confrontation followed at which Al-Zawahri accused Abdullah Azzam of indulging in 'cat's-piss politics'. It ended with the Doctor winning over to his camp the idealistic and impressionable man whom he was then treating for a kidney complaint: Osama bin Laden, aged thirty-one to Al-Zawahri's thirty-eight. On Friday 24 November of that same year Abdullah Azzam, now increasingly isolated, was targeted once again as he and his teenage sons made the journey from their home to the local mosque for evening prayers. In a narrow lane just short of the mosque they got out of their vehicle to walk the rest of the way – at which point three mines were detonated. 'A great thundering was heard over the city,' relates a website dedicated to Abdullah Azzam:

> People emerged from the mosque and beheld a terrible sight. The younger son Ibrahim flew 100 metres into the air; the other two youths were thrown a similar distance away, and their remains were scattered among the trees and power lines. As for Sheikh Abdullah Azzam himself, his body was found resting against a wall, totally intact and not at all disfigured, except that some blood was seen issuing from his mouth. That fateful blast indeed ended the worldly journey of Sheikh Abdullah, which had been spent well in struggling, striving and fighting in the Path of Allah.

Although the CIA was blamed, the most obvious beneficiary of the Sheikh's death was the man who spoke the eulogy at his funeral: Dr Ayman al-Zawahri, who now became world jihad's leading ideologue.

Although the withdrawal of Soviet troops was completed in February 1989 it was not until 1992 that a coalition of muja-hedeen forces finally overthrew the Soviet-backed Afghan Government. To the dismay of their foreign patrons, the seven mujahedeen armies then turned their guns on each other, leading to a catastrophic breakdown of law and order. Ever since 1980 Afghan refugees had been crossing into the border areas of Pakistan and Iran to escape the fighting, but as con-ditions worsened in the early 1990s their numbers swelled to a point where the Government of Pakistan found itself having to absorb and shelter well over three million refugees, mostly Pathans.

The emergence of the Taliban in the winter of 1994–5, seem-ingly from nowhere, and its rapid rise to power, culminating in the capture of Kabul in September 1997, has been meticulously chronicled by the Pakistani journalist Ahmed Rashid. The rise of Bin Laden and Al-Qaeda over this same period has been no less meticulously researched and graphically told by Malise Ruthven, Bernard Lewis, Giles Keppel, Jason Burke and other respected authorities. It remains only for a few last gaps in the convergence of these two movements to be filled in.

After the withdrawal of Soviet troops many of the foreign jihadis left Afghanistan and Pakistan to take the struggle to their homelands. But before the final departure of the bulk of the 'Arabs' a meeting took place in Bin Laden's camp at Khost in the spring of 1988. Here Al-Zawahri and perhaps a dozen like-minded individuals representing Islamic Jihad and other organisations agreed to form a loose-knit organisation that would take jihad to wherever Islam was under threat – and to whoever threatened it.

The name given to this organisation, Al-Qaeda, with its connotations of a military base, may be seen as an indirect homage to the *burra godown*, the 'big storehouse' in the Mahabun Mountain first established by Syed Ahmad in 1827 and known thereafter to the British as the Hindustani or Fanatic Camp. Directly after this meeting at Khost Abdul Rab Rasoul Sayyaf, leader of the Wahhabi Ittihad-i-Islami group, left Peshawar with a large party of his followers for the Philippines where, as the 'Abu Sayyaf gang', they introduced Wahhabi terror to the Western Pacific. Others fanned out to take the Islamist revolution as far north as Chechnya and Kyrgyzstan and as far west as Algeria, Morocco – and the United States.

Bin Laden himself was not present at the Khost gathering, having gone home with his family to Jedda to establish a welfare organisation for returned Arab fighters. In Jedda he might well have stayed but for Iraq's invasion of Kuwait in August 1990, which prompted him to contact the Saudi Defence Minister, Prince Sultan, with a proposal to defend Saudi Arabia by calling on his global network of ex-Afghanistan jihadis, beginning with the several thousand Wahhabi veterans now back in Arabia. According to one account, he left the meeting believing his offer had been accepted, so that when he learned subsequently that the Saudi Government had turned instead to the United States of America, it seemed a double betrayal. His strong Wahhabi convictions could not countenance the affront of infidel desert boots on the sacred soil of Arabia, which he saw as a direct defiance of the Prophet's injunction that there should not be two religions in Arabia. Within months Bin Laden was set on the course that was to send him into permanent exile as a bitter enemy of the House of Saud and of the Wahhabi Establishment that had betrayed its founding fathers. Although his assets in Saudi Arabia were frozen he still had sufficient funds and contacts to became the banker of Al-Zawahri's Islamic Jihad and the Al-Qaeda confederacy.

In September 1993 New York's World Trade Center was bombed and six persons killed. This was Al-Qaeda's first serious act of aggression against the United States of America, and it was followed by further operations in Somalia and Egypt.

12

The Unholy Alliance

A spring at its source can be turned with a twig,
But when grown into a river, not even an elephant can
cross it.

Sheikh Muslihu-ud-Din, better known as Saadi,
thirteenth-century poet of Shiraz

In early April 2001 a vast encampment of canvas tents and brightly coloured cotton shamianas sprang up on the plains beside the village of Taro Jaba on the eastern limits of the Vale of Peshawar. Over the course of three days what was reported as the largest gathering ever seen in Pakistan celebrated the achievements of the Dar ul-Ulum Deoband madrassah movement. According to its organisers, the JUI, well over one million delegates attended, representing madrassahs in countries as far afield as the United States and South Africa. More than a score of countries sent official delegations, and messages of congratulation were read from such luminaries as Libya's Colonel Gadhafi. However, the two speeches that received the greatest acclaim were both taped messages. The first was from Mullah Omar, Amir ul-Momineen of the Islamic Emirate of Afghanistan. The second, for all that the conference organisers blandly denied it, was from 'al-Shaykh': Osama bin Laden.

Presiding over the conference was Maulana Fazal-ur-Rahman, a burly, genial, white-turbaned and, of course, bearded figure in his early fifties, widely known in Pakistan as the 'Diesel Maulana' following allegaions – not proven – concerning his part in a fuel permit scandal. He had inherited his position as head of a militant faction of JUI from his Dar ul-Ulum Deoband-educated father Maulana Mufti Mahmood, who had guided the JUI party through the turbulent 1960s and 1970s. He now chaired a coalition of five Deobandi political groups and was spoken of as the 'mentor' of the Taliban. In his concluding address he called on Muslims to unite behind their brothers wherever they were in trouble. 'No one', he ended, 'can bar us from supporting the Taliban or other Muslims fighting for their independence and identity in any part of the world.' This was five months before the coordinated attacks on the twin towers of the World Trade Center and the Pentagon of 11 September 2001.

In September 1994, so the popular version goes, a thirty-five-year-old mullah from the Maiwand region outside Kandahar happened upon the scene of a murder: a family driving from Herat to Kandahar had been held up by a local warlord who had raped and killed all the girls and boys in the family. With the help of some local taliban the mullah washed the bodies and gave them a proper burial. This was Mullah Omar, a landless and barely literate Ghilzai Pathan and veteran jihadi who had lost his right eye fighting the Russians but had afterwards become so disillusioned by the corruption of the mujahedeen warlords that he had exchanged his AK-47 for the Quran. He had then resumed his religious studies at the Sang-i-Hisar madrassah in Singesar, a hamlet to the north-west of Kandahar not far from the scene of a famous Afghan victory over the invading British in 1880. So sickened was Mullah Omar by this latest atrocity that he gathered a group of mujahedeen veterans together and swore with them to rid Afghanistan of the devils who were destroying it – and to restore true sharia. This little group then went from mosque to mosque calling for volunteers, and out of this local reaction there developed – with more than a little military assistance from the Hizb-e-Islami and Pakistan's ISI – the Taliban.

The man who almost by accident founded the Taliban was no ideologue, but the men who joined him and who became his closest lieutenants were very much of a type, for nearly every one of them was the product of a madrassah in one form or another. As Ahmed Rashid says in his book *Taliban: The Story of the Warlords*, 'the Taliban represented nobody but themselves and they recognised no Islam but their own'. They described themselves as Sunnis who followed the Hanafi form of Islamic jurisprudence and insisted they were neither Deobandis nor Wahhabis nor followers of any other religious party. But they did have an ideological base, which was linked to 'an extreme form of Deobandism'. As Rashid explains, 'The links between the Taliban and some of the extreme Deobandi groups are solid because of the common ground they share . . . The Deobandi tradition is opposed to tribal and feudal structures, from which stems the Taliban's mistrust of the tribal structure and the clan chiefs.'

In April 1996, nineteen months after Mullah Omar's intervention, an unprecedented gathering of Pathan leaders took place in Kandahar. This was not the usual loya jirga but a gathering of ulema on the Arab model, a *shura* or religious council that bypassed the usual tribal leaders. It was at this shura that Mullah Omar was elected *Amir-ul-Momineen* (Commander of the Faithful) before cloaking himself in the Prophet's mantle and receiving the oath of allegiance (*baiat*) from all those present. A Pathan-dominated council of ten was then formed with Mullah Omar at its head, and a jihad proclaimed against those Muslims who refused to acknowledge its authority. These actions won widespread support among Afghanistan's Pathan population but were not welcome to the Tajiks, Uzbeks and other groups who together made up the other half of the country. Nevertheless, with the continuing support of Pakistan and a Saudi-backed switch of sides by Gulbuddin Hekmatyar and his Hizb-i-Islami (Hekmatyar) armed force, the ever-growing Taliban army was strong enough to lay siege to Kabul throughout the summer of 1996, culminating in an August offensive which saw thousands of armed but raw taliban from the frontier madrassahs hurrying to join its ranks. Kabul fell to the Taliban in September 1996 and within twenty-four hours the strictest form of sharia ever seen outside Saudi Arabia was imposed on the country. Indeed, it took Saudi Arabia as its model and was in conformity with the theology of Muhammad ibn Abd al-Wahhab of Nejd, founder of Wahhabism. Only two governments recognised the Taliban Government: Saudi Arabia and Pakistan.

In May 1996, while the Kabul offensive was still being fought, Bin Laden and his ideologue Dr Al-Zawahri were forced by US diplomatic pressure to leave Sudan, where Bin Laden had sought to establish a dar ul-Islam on the Wahhabi model. The Egyptian moved from country to country, cementing ties with local militants, before arriving in Chechnya in December 1996. Meanwhile his Yemeni partner had flown to Jellalabad in a chartered jet crammed with Afghanistan veterans and their families, its hold reportedly filled with US dollars. Pathan xenophobia was by now beginning to reassert itself and 'Arabs' were no longer welcomed, but memories of the unstinting support and generosity of 'Al-Shaykh' ensured that he was given sanctuary at Hadda outside Jellalabad. In October of that same year Bin Laden flew to Kandahar and there met Afghanistan's newly appointed but strangely reclusive Amir ul-Momineem. He offered Mullah Omar his unconditional support and financial backing, and was given the Taliban Government's protection in return, so initiating the unholy alliance that eventually led to the destruction of the Taliban Government.

Having secured the regime's support, Bin Laden returned to his original Bait al-Ansar camp complex near Khost and there set about building up what has been described by Jason Burke as 'the most efficient terrorist organisation the world has ever seen'. In February 1997 Bin Laden felt confident enough to put out his first fatwa, issued without any claims to religious authority. He declared it to be a duty of all Muslims to 'kill the Americans and their allies, civilians and military . . . in any country in which it is possible'.

In April 1997, after being warned from Peshawar that the CIA were preparing to mount a military operation against his Bait al-Ansar camp, Bin Laden moved at the invitation of Mullah Omar to an abandoned Russian air base outside Kandahar. In that same month Al-Zawahri was arrested in Dagestan. Unaware of his guiding hand in a string of spectacular acts of violence, the Russian authorities sentenced him to six months' detention for illegal entry. Bin Laden paid his bail and the two duly met in Afghanistan, where Bin Laden reoccupied his Bait al-Ansar camp at Khost.

A triple alliance was now joined as these three entered into a symbiotic relationship with each other. Logically, the traditional role of imam should have been filled by the cleric Mullah Omar. But while Mullah Omar enjoyed the unconditional support of Afghanistan's Pathan majority as their Amir ul-Momineen, he remained irredeemably provincial, clinging to a medieval world view in which even Kabul was a foreign land. Bin Laden was a purely secular leader without any sort of religious qualification but with a deep faith based on his early Wahhabism. As for Al-Zawahri, here was a man whose education, sophistication and intelligence far surpassed that of the other two and who alone of the three had a clear vision of the way forward, a vision he combined with an almost pathological desire to seek revenge on the non-Islamic world for all the perceived humiliations heaped on Islam and on himself. Logically, the Egyptian was the man to take on the role of amir/emir – except that he lacked precisely the qualities that Mullah Omar and Bin Laden had in full measure: charisma and a capacity for leadership. So Al-Zawahri, the organiser and ideas man, remained in the shadows in the role of wazir (counsellor), content to stand at the shoulder of the man to whom the world community of Islam could rally as *both* amir and imam of world jihad: Osama bin Laden, idealist and romantic, dreamer of past and future glories and perhaps even then harbouring apocalyptic visions of martyrdom, a Wahhabi Arab at heart but fully conscious of Islam's ache for a Mahdi, the 'expected one' who would set matters to rights – and well aware that already as 'Al-Shaykh' he was adored by his 'Arabs' and by many Afghans and Pathans as the personification of Islamic resistance to Western imperialism.

At Khost in February 1998 Bin Laden and Al-Zawahri issued a joint fatwa entitled *World Islamic Front Against Jews and Crusaders*. The US Embassy bombings in East Africa followed on 7 August 1998, the suicide attack on the USS *Cole* on 12 October.

Early in 1999 the Jordanian Al-Zarqawi was inadvertently released from prison in Jordan as part of a general amnesty. In jail his views had further hardened and after a brush with the local authorities he moved to Peshawar and then on to Kandahar to meet up with Bin Laden. However, Al-Zawahri's political agenda – the liberation of Jordan and Syria – did not fit in with Al-Qaeda's and he subsequently struck out on his own, setting up his own dar ul-Islam outside Herat, in eastern Afghanistan, and his own organisation, *Tawhid wal Jihad* (Monotheism and Holy War). Following the overthrow of the Taliban Government he and his band slipped across the border into Iran and then on to the mountains of northern Iraq, where he joined forces with the Kurdish Islamist group Ansar-i-Islam. The US-led invasion of Iraq has since provided him with a heaven-sent opportunity both to lead his own jihad against unbelievers and apostates and to act as a rallying-point for a new generation of jihadis, to whom he presents himself as both ally and natural successor to the Shaykh, Osama bin Laden.

The Muslim umma is made up overwhelmingly of pious, law-abiding men and women with strong moral values who wish nothing more than to live in harmony with their Muslim and non-Muslim neighbours. They want to see others embrace their faith, but are no more and no less bent on world domination than Christian Evangelicals who wish to see humankind 'saved'. Islamist fundamentalism, as characterised by men like Osama bin Laden and bodies like the Taliban, is as much a threat to this Muslim majority as to the·West. It believes that inclusiveness and tolerance of other values stand in the way of Islam's destiny as a universal religion, and is prepared to use violence, oppression and fear to achieve its goal.

History teaches that fundamentalist theocracy does not work, because people simply will not put up with it. It may secure a foothold in societies that are isolated and ignorant, but rarely does it outlast its main propagator. Its usual course is to fragment into splinter groups, each accusing the others of heresy. Saudi Arabia became the exception to the rule, initially because of the unique pact between a clerical and a ruling dynasty that greatly benefited both parties, and subsequently because of a unique chain of events involving oil and global politics that made petrodollar multimillionaires of a few thousand male members of one family whose paternal grandfather or great-grandfather (Abul-Rahman ibn Saud) had quite literally measured his means in camels, goats and sheep. Thereafter it was in the interests of the House of Saud to support the religious status quo in Saudia Arabia, and in the interests of the US Government to support the House of Saud. So long as the world buys oil from the Saudis, Wahhabism will prosper in Arabia.

History also demonstrates that fundamentalists will always be listened to whenever and wherever people believe themselves or their religion or their co-religionists to be threatened. That does not mean the fundamentalists will be followed, but it does mean that they will find popular support. This was why Syed Ahmad's brand of Wahhabi anti-imperialist revivalism took root on Indian soil; why Deobandism, for all its intolerance and sectarianism, came to be seen as a shield of Islam; and why Osama bin Laden is today by far and away the most popular figure in Pakistan – and a cult figure among many young Muslims in much of the umma. At the same time, it has to be remembered that the explosion of fundamentalist madrassahs that began in the 1970s was no expression of popular religious zeal but a direct consequence of political intervention only made possible by Saudi funding.

Deobandism has been the main repository of 'Wahhabi' fundamentalism outside Arabia since the mid-nineteenth century, but it is not as monolithic as this short history may have made it appear. Since its inception it has produced many outstanding Asian leaders, very few of whom have chosen the path of violence. General Pervez Musharraf, President of Pakistan at the time of writing (2005), is the product of a Deoband education, and anyone who is familiar with the sub-continent will know Deobandis who are pillars of both Indian and Pakistani society. The same is true of Deobandis and Deoband institutions overseas. Yet it cannot be denied that Deobandis and their more overtly Wahhabi rivals, the Ahl-i-Hadiths, have in their zeal to revitalise Islam in their own image, played the principal role in promoting Islamist extremism in South Asia and beyond.

The Christian and secular West is often blamed by Muslims for shortcomings in their own societies. Writing in his book *Orientalism*, first published in 1978 and since reprinted many times over, the Palestinian intellectual Edward Said was courageous enough to speak of the Arab world as being 'disfigured by a whole series of outmoded and discredited ideas' and shortcomings which included 'its political failures, its human rights abuses . . . the fact that alone of all modern peoples, we have receded in democratic and technological and scientific development'. However, Said's Orientalism, with its central charge that Western scholarship was a weapon of imperialism, became *the* key text in Arab and Middle Eastern studies in the 1980s and 1990s, and has itself contributed mightily to the revisionism and myth-making which have given many Muslims a highly distorted understanding of their own history; in particular, giving further credence to the widespread Muslim self-image of the umma as innocent victim of Western oppression. A central pillar of this myth of innocence is the belief that before the rise of Zionism the umma of the Ottomans was tolerant in a way that Western Christendom was not, particularly in its treatment of non-Muslim *dhimmi* – Christians and Jews. This is pure fantasy, as any reading of the reports of ambassadors, envoys and travellers in the eighteenth and nineteenth centuries will demonstrate.

And yet . . . set these shortcomings to one side and there remain political injustices that Western governments and pro-Western regimes in Muslim countries could and should have put right. First among those wrongs is the failure to support the creation of a viable state of Palestine. The ill-conceived invasion of Iraq – the Ambeyla Campaign multiplied by a factor of twenty – is another case in point, for all its good intentions. By allowing such grievances to continue, the West has done Islamist fundamentalism a huge and continuing favour. It has allowed the extremists to turn to the Muslim umma and say, 'We told you so! Only we can help you. Together we can turn back the secular, Western tide and return to a glorious past.' Remove the grievances, and the extremists and terrorists must wither away for lack of popular support.

On the Afghanistan–Pakistan border, Osama bin Laden's Fanatic Camp survives, in part because he and his remaining 'Arabs' and Taliban allies have been offered sanctuary, but also because of the active connivance of the jihadised Pathans of the North-West Frontier Province – supported to a significant degree by the greater Pakistani populace. In October 2001 a pro-Taliban and anti-American coalition made up of five politico-religious parties was voted into power in the North-West Frontier Province. Dominated by the JI, JUI and Ahl-i-Hadith, its leaders have since sought to reintroduce Wahhabi sharia, issued fatwas proclaiming death to Americans and offered tacit support to Osama bin Laden. So widespread is the support for this coalition that the Pakistan Government has, to date, been powerless to act against it. Nevertheless, the same lesson applies: remove the grievances and mainstream, moderate Islam stands a better chance of reasserting itself.

Leading Muslim personalities

Names are listed in alphabetical order by the first letter of the abbreviated name

Abd al-Aziz ibn Saud	Son of **Muhammad ibn Saud**, first titular imam of Wahhabi Arabia (not to be confused with **Ibn Saud**, below).
Abdul Aziz bin Abdul-Rahman ibn Saud	see **Ibn Saud**.
Abdullah Ali	Eldest son of **Wilayat Ali**, assumed leadership of Hindustani Fanatics in 1858 after the death of his uncle **Inayat Ali**, remained leader until his death in 1901.
Abdullah ibn Saud	Succeeded **Faisal ibn Saud** as Emir of Nejd in 1865 but driven into exile by Emir of Hail.
Abdullah Azzam	Palestinian ideologue, follower of Syed Qutb, called the 'Emir of Islamic jihad', spearheaded Muslim support for mujahedeen in Afghanistan, radical Islamist, assassinated in Peshawar 1989.
Abdul Ghaffur	Sufi saint, first known as 'Saidu Baba', but later to achieve great eminence as the **Akhund** of Swat.
Abdul-Rahman ibn Saud	Exiled father of Abdul Aziz bin Abdur-Rahman ibn Saud (see **Ibn Saud**).
Abdur Rahman	Amir and Imam of Afghanistan 1880–1901.
Ahmadullah	Maulvi Ahmadullah, eldest son of **Elahi Bux** and brother of **Yahya Ali**, led Wahhabis in 1860s until his arrest.
Ahmad Sirhindi	Sheikh Ahmad Sirhindi, 16th-century hard-line Naqshbandi Sufi.
Akhund	see **Abdul Ghaffur**.

Al-Wahhab	Muhammad ibn Abd al-Wahhab of Nejd, founder of Wahhabism, father of *aal as-Shaikh* clerical dynasty.
Al-Zarqawi	Abu Musab al-Zarqawi, Jordanian follower of radical cleric Abu Muhammad al-Maqdisi, founded terrorist group Tawhid wal Jihad in Herat in 1999, joined Ansar-i-Islam in Iraq to lead Al-Qaeda in Iraq.
Al-Zawahri	Ayman al-Zawahri, Egyptian doctor and radical Islamist, founding ideologue of Al-Qaeda.
Amir Amanullah	Succeeded his father **Amir Habibullah** as Amir of Afghanistan in 1919, launched Third Afghan War.
Amir Habibullah	Succeeded his father **Abdur Rahman** as Amir of Afghanistan in 1901.
Amir Khan	Nawab Amir Khan of Tonk, Pathan Pindari mercenary recognised as ruler of Tonk in 1818.
Bin Baz	Sheikh Abdul Aziz bin Abdullah bin Baz, leading Wahhabi authority in Saudi Arabia until his death in 1989.
Bin Laden	Osama bin Muhammad bin Awad bin Laden, Saudi-born Yemeni radical Islamist, revered as 'Al- Shaykh', nominal leader of Al-Qaeda.
Elahi Bux	Head of one of the three Patna families, father of **Ahmadullah** and **Yahya Ali**.
Faisal ibn Saud	Emir of Nejd, 1842-65, great-grandson of **Muhammad ibn Saud**.
Farhat Husain	Married daughter of **Muhammad Husain**, Wahhabi leader in 1830s and 1840s.
Fatah Ali	Head of one of the three Patna families, father of **Wilayat Ali** and **Inayat Ali**.
Firoze Shah	Nephew of the last Mughal emperor Bahadur Shah, fought against British in 1857, then in exile for many years.

Ghazan Khan	Pathan Daffadar of Mounted Police at Panipat who with his son uncovered evidence of Wahhabi supply route in 1863.
Ghulam Rasul	Also known as Hajji Abdul Haq, first known Wahhabi in India, teacher of **Wilayat Ali** in Benares before he met **Syed Ahmad**.
Hafiz Wahba	Sheikh Hafiz Wahba, Egyptian convert to Wahhabism who became **Ibn Saud**'s envoy in 1920s.
Hedayut Ali	Rissaldar Sheikh Hedayut Ali, senior Indian officer in Rattray's Sikhs.
Ibn Saud	Abdul Aziz bin Abdul-Rahman ibn Saud, son of **Abdul-Rahman ibn Saud**, Emir of Nejd, founded Kingdom of Saudi Arabia, succeeded 1953 by his eldest son Saud.
Ibn Taymiyya	Sheikh Ibn Taymiyya of Damascus, 14th-century hard-line Hanbali jurist, godfather of Islamist extremism through his reinterpretations of *sharia*.
Imdadullah	Hajji Imdadullah, disciple of **Sayyid Nazir Husain**, teacher of **Muhammad Qasim**, **Rashid Ahmad** and **Rahmatullah** in 1857.
Inayat Ali	Son of **Fatah Ali**, younger brother of and successor to **Wilayat Ali** as leader of Hindustani Fanatics.
Mawdudi	Sayyid Abulala Mawdudi, radical Islamist, founded Jamiat-i-Islami (JI) in 1939.
Mowla Baksh	Dewan Mowla Baksh, deputy magistrate in Patna under Commissioner Tayler.
Mahmood ul-Hasan	First student of Deoband Madrassah, subsequently its rector, in 1915 made abortive attempt to lead a jihad against British India.
Mufti Mahmud	Co-founder of Jamiat-i-Ulema-i-Islam (JUI) in 1945, Deobandi party with strong following in NWFP, father of Fazal-ur-Rahman, present leader.

Muhammad Hayat	Muhammad Hayat of Sind, admirer of **Ibn Taymiyya** and **Ahmad Sirhindi**, with his father in Medina taught **Al-Wahhab** and **Shah Waliullah**.
Muhammad ibn Saud	Bedouin chieftan of Dariya, formed an alliance with **Al-Wahhab** to become first emir of the Wahhabis and founder of Al-Saud dynasty.
Muhammad Hussain	Syed Muhammad Hussain, head of one of the three Patna families, whose house in Sadiqpore Lane became the movement's headquarters.
Muhammad Jafar	Petition-writer of Thanesar whose incriminating letter provided first hard evidence of Wahhabi conspiracy in 1863, wrote autobiography after release.
Muhammad Qasim	Muhammad Qasim Nanautawi, student of **Sayyid Nazir Husain** and **Imdadullah**, co-founder with **Rashid Ahmad** of Deoband Madrassah.
Mullah Omar	Mullah Muhammad Omar of Kandahar, Amir of the Taliban.
Mullah Sadullah	Mullah Sadullah of Buner, also known as the 'Mad Fakir', Mastun Mullah, or Sartor Fakir, initiated the Malakand uprising of 1897.
Nasiruddin	Maulvi Nasiruddin, Wahhabi caliph, led war party of Hindustanis to Sind and later to Ghazni.
Obaidullah Sindhi	Deputy of **Mahmood ul-Hasan**, set up government in exile in Kabul in 1915.
Panipati	Maulvi Qasim Panipati, led Hindustanis at Sittana after death of **Syed Ahmad** and initiated cult of Hidden Imam.
Pir Ali	Pir Ali Khan, bookseller of Patna, executed for conspiracy in 1857.
Rahmatullah	Rahmatullah Kairanawi, student of **Sayyid Nazir Husain** and **Imdadullah**, fled to Arabia after 1857.

Rashid Ahmad	Rashid Ahmad Gangohi, student of **Sayyid Nazir Husain** and **Imdadullah**, co-founder with **Muhammad Qasim** of Deoband Madrassah.
Sayyed Akbar Shah	Head of Saiyyed clan at Sittana, gave **Syed Ahmad**'s Hindustanis land, was later made Padshah of Swat.
Sayyed Firoze Shah	Grandson of **Sayyed Akbar Shah**, son of **Sayyed Mubarik Shah**.
Sayyed Mubarik Shah	Son of **Sayyed Akbar Shah**, succeeded his uncle **Sayyed Umar Shah** as leader of the Sayyeds of Sittana, patron of Hindustani Fanatics.
Sayyed Umar Shah	Brother of **Sayyed Akbar Shah**, failed to secure recognition as Padshah of Swat, patron of Hindustani Fanatics.
Sayyid Nazir Husain	Sayyid Nazir Husain Muhaddith of Delhi, leading successor to **Shah Muhammad Ismail**, suspected leader of Wahhabis in Delhi in 1857, co-founder of Jamiat Ahl-i-Hadith.
Shah Abdul Aziz	Shah Abdul Aziz Delhavi, eldest son of **Shah Waliullah**, succeeded him as principal of Madrassah-i-Rahimiya.
Shah Abdul Hai	Son-in-law of **Shah Abdul Aziz**, **Syed Ahmad**'s second disciple.
Shah Muhammad Ishaq	Son of **Shah Abdul Aziz** of Delhi and his successor, devoted to **Syed Ahmad**, if not a follower.
Shah Muhammad Ismail	Nephew of **Shah Abdul Aziz**, **Syed Ahmad**'s first disciple.
Shah Waliullah	Shah Waliullah Delhavi, Naqshbandi Sufi student of **Muhammad Hayat**, influenced by **Ibn Taymiyya**, founded Madrassah-i-Rahimiya, father of **Shah Abdul Aziz**.
Shariatullah	Hajji Shariatullah of Bengal, returned from Mecca in 1818 to found Faraizi movement.

Sharif Husayn	Sharif Husayn ibn Ali, Hashemite Emir of the Hijaz, guardian of Mecca and Medina, sought to become ruler of Arabia but deposed in 1924.
Shere Ali	Afridi mounted orderly, found guilty of murder and transported, in 1872 assassinated Viceroy Lord Mayo.
Syad Ahmad Khan	Student of **Shah Muhammad Ishaq** and **Sayyid Nazir Husain**, modernising founder of Alighar university.
Syed Ahmad	Shah Syed Ahmad of Rae Bareli, born Syed Ghullam Muhammad in Rae Bareli, revivalist and revolutionary, founder of Wahhabi movement in India and first of the Hindustani Fanatics.
Titu Mir	Born Mir Nasir Ali of Bengal, became follower of **Syed Ahmad** in Arabia, led Wahhabi rebellion in 1831 and killed in battle.
Turki ibn Saud	Grandson of **Muhammad ibn Saud**, Emir of Nejd 1842–63, sought to restore Wahhabi empire.
Wilayat Ali	Maulvi Wilayat Ali, son of **Fatah Ali** and elder brother of **Inayat Ali**, early convert to Wahhabism, revived Indian Wahhabis after death of **Syed Ahmad**.
Yahya Ali	Son of **Elahi Bux**, younger brother of Ahmadullah, leading Wahhabi in 1850s and 1860s.
Zaidulla Khan	Zaidulla Khan of Daggar, Buner chief who briefly gave British forces at Ambeyla his protection in 1863.

Appendix 1: The roots of the Al-Saud–Al-Wahhab family alliance

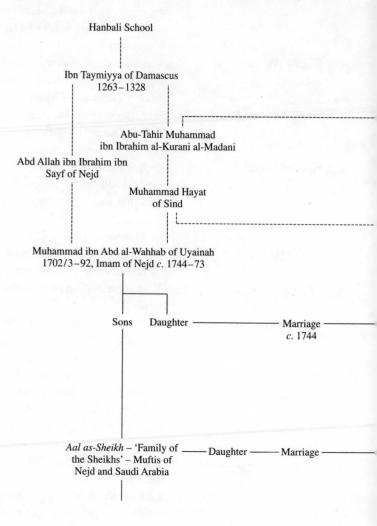

Hanbali School

Ibn Taymiyya of Damascus
1263–1328

Abu-Tahir Muhammad
ibn Ibrahim al-Kurani al-Madani

Abd Allah ibn Ibrahim ibn
Sayf of Nejd

Muhammad Hayat
of Sind

Muhammad ibn Abd al-Wahhab of Uyainah
1702/3–92, Imam of Nejd c. 1744–73

Sons   Daughter ——————— Marriage ——————
                                 c. 1744

Aal as-Sheikh – 'Family of ——— Daughter ——— Marriage ——
the Sheikhs' – Muftis of
Nejd and Saudi Arabia

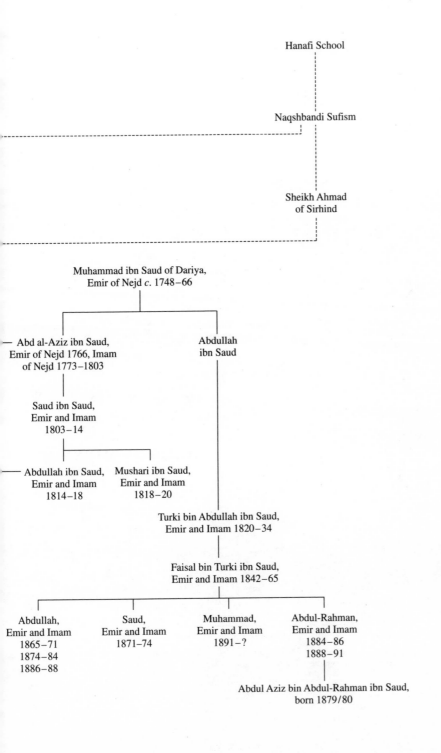

Hanafi School

Naqshbandi Sufism

Sheikh Ahmad
of Sirhind

Muhammad ibn Saud of Dariya,
Emir of Nejd *c.* 1748–66

Abd al-Aziz ibn Saud,
Emir of Nejd 1766, Imam
of Nejd 1773–1803

Abdullah
ibn Saud

Saud ibn Saud,
Emir and Imam
1803–14

Abdullah ibn Saud,
Emir and Imam
1814–18

Mushari ibn Saud,
Emir and Imam
1818–20

Turki bin Abdullah ibn Saud,
Emir and Imam 1820–34

Faisal bin Turki ibn Saud,
Emir and Imam 1842–65

Abdullah,
Emir and Imam
1865–71
1874–84
1886–88

Saud,
Emir and Imam
1871–74

Muhammad,
Emir and Imam
1891–?

Abdul-Rahman,
Emir and Imam
1884–86
1888–91

Abdul Aziz bin Abdul-Rahman ibn Saud,
born 1879/80

Appendix 2: The 'Wahhabi' family tree in India

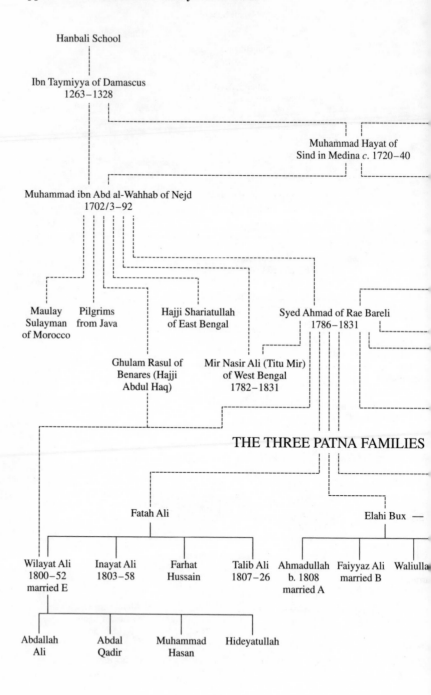

Hanbali School

Ibn Taymiyya of Damascus
1263–1328

Muhammad Hayat of
Sind in Medina *c.* 1720–40

Muhammad ibn Abd al-Wahhab of Nejd
1702/3–92

Maulay
Sulayman
of Morocco

Pilgrims
from Java

Hajji Shariatullah
of East Bengal

Syed Ahmad of Rae Bareli
1786–1831

Ghulam Rasul of
Benares (Hajji
Abdul Haq)

Mir Nasir Ali (Titu Mir)
of West Bengal
1782–1831

THE THREE PATNA FAMILIES

Fatah Ali

Elahi Bux —

Wilayat Ali
1800–52
married E

Inayat Ali
1803–58

Farhat
Hussain

Talib Ali
1807–26

Ahmadullah
b. 1808
married A

Faiyyaz Ali
married B

Waliulla

Abdallah
Ali

Abdal
Qadir

Muhammad
Hasan

Hideyatullah

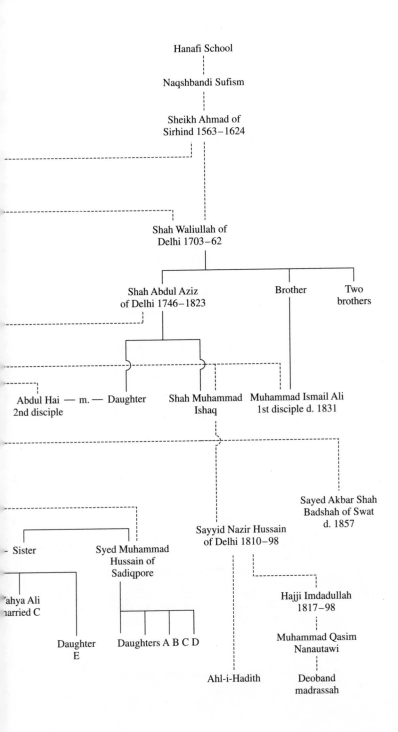

Hanafi School
┊
Naqshbandi Sufism
┊
Sheikh Ahmad of
Sirhind 1563–1624

Shah Waliullah of
Delhi 1703–62

Shah Abdul Aziz   Brother   Two
of Delhi 1746–1823   brothers

Abdul Hai — m. — Daughter   Shah Muhammad   Muhammad Ismail Ali
2nd disciple   Ishaq   1st disciple d. 1831

                                          Sayed Akbar Shah
                                          Badshah of Swat
                                              d. 1857

                              Sayyid Nazir Hussain
─ Sister   Syed Muhammad   of Delhi 1810–98
                Hussain of
                Sadiqpore   Hajji Imdadullah
ahya Ali   1817–98
narried C
                                          Muhammad Qasim
         Daughter   Daughters A B C D   Nanautawi
            E
                                          Deoband
                        Ahl-i-Hadith   madrassah

Glossary

For ease of reading Arabic, Persian and Pushtu words are shown without stress guides. Archaic spellings are included.

Aal as-Sheikh	the Family of the Sheikhs, descendants of Muhammad ibn Abd al-Wahhab.
Ad Dawa lil Tawhid	'the Call to Unity', the name given to his doctrines by Muhammad ibn Abd al-Wahhab, founder of *Wahhabism*.
ahl	people, thus *Ahl al-Kitab* – 'People of the Book', those who share a revealed book with Islam, thus Christians and Jews; *Ahl-i-Hadith* – 'People of the Hadith'; see *Jamiat Ahl-i-Hadith*.
Akhund	teacher, used to describe Abdul Ghaffur, the Akhund of Swat.
Al-muwahhidun	unitarian or monotheist, the name by which the *Wahhabis* call themselves.
Al-Qaeda	'the [military] Base', the formal title of a loose network of global terrorism headed by Osama bin Laden, drawing on *Wahhabi*, *Salafi*, and *Ikhwan-ul-Muslimeen* politico-religious philosophy by way of the *Jamaat al-Takfir wa al-Hijra*.
Ali	son-in-law and cousin of the *Prophet*, whose followers broke away to form the *Shia* community.
alim	one learned in the ways of Islam; plural *ulema*.
amir	commander, governor, local ruler; thus *Amir-ul-Momineen* – Commander of the Faithful, official title of the Caliphs, and *Amir-e-Sharia* – Leader of the Law.
badal	blood feud among Pathans.
Badawin	camel-owners, Bedouin, as distinct from Arab – sheep-owners.

badmash	bad character.
badshah	see *padshah*.
baiat	oath of religious allegiance.
Barelvi	a Hanafi Sunni religious school established in India in 1870s that incorporated traditional *Sufi* beliefs and practices and regards the *Deobandis* as *kaffir*.
bidat	innovation, a great sin in the eyes of *Wahhabis*.
Bunerwals	men of Buner, made up of several Yusufzai tribes.
burqa	coverall worn by Muslim women.
Caliph	see *khalifa*.
cantonment	standing camp or military quarter of the *station* in British India.
Chamlawals	men of Chamla.
daffadar	sergeant in Indian cavalry.
daftar, dufter	office or register.
dak	post, system of post-relays established in India by the Mughals; thus *dak*-bungalows for travellers.
dar	domain, thus *dar ul-Islam* – 'domain of Faith', a land under Islamic *sharia*; *dar ul-harb* – 'domain of war or enmity', a land opposed to the cause of Islam; *dar ul-jahiliya* – land of ignorance; *dar ul-kufr* – land of unbelief; *dar ul-ulum* – domain of Islamic learning, the honorific title accorded to the Deoband Madrassah in 1879.
darb	path; see also *tariq*.
darrah	mountain pass.
dawa	call, invitation.
Deen	the Way (of *Islam*).
Deoband	the religious school established at Deoband in northern India in 1866 by a group of quasi-*Wahhabis*. It condemns aspects of *Sufism* and other practices as *bidat* and promotes a strictly fundamentalist form of *Sunni Islam* derived from Shah Waliullah and Syed Ahmad; thus Deobandi; see *Salafi*.

emir	see *amir*, local ruler in Arabia and north Africa.
Eid	Muslim festival marking the end of *Ramadan*.
fakir	holy man.
faraiz	obligatory duty.
fatwa	legal ruling of a *mujtahid* or *mufti* on a matter of Islamic *sharia*.
fedayeen	men of sacrifice.
fiqh	Islamic jurisprudence.
firman	written order.
fitna	discordance within the Muslim community due to such activities as polytheism.
ghar	mountain, thus Spin Ghar, the White Mountain.
ghazu	war party in the cause of religion; thus *ghazi* – 'champion of the Faith', in British eyes a 'religious fanatic'.
Hadith	'Tradition', the established statements and examples of conduct of the *Prophet* as remembered by his Companions, gathered together into a corpus to become, together with the *Quran*, the basis of *sharia*; see also *Sunnah*.
Hajj	pilgrimage to Mecca; one of the five Pillars of Islam; thus *Hajji* – one who has made the pilgrimage.
hakim	judge or doctor.
Hanbali	the Sunni school of law established by Ahmad bin Hanbal (d. AD 855), the last of the four schools of law accepted in Sunni Islam and regarded by many as the most intolerant and reactionary.
haram	forbidden.
hegira	see *hijra*.
Hijaz	Arabian province beside the Red Sea containing the holy places of Mecca and Medina and the sea port of Jedda, traditionally ruled over by the *Sharifs* of Mecca.
hijra, hijrat	retreat, withdrawal, thus the name given to the migration of the Prophet from Mecca to

Medina in the year 622 of the Christian calendar, later chosen to mark the beginning of Islamic history, which starts with the first year of the Islamic calendar, usually written AH.

Hindustan   the land of the Hindus east of the Indus, thus *Hindustani* – an inhabitant of that India, and the lingua franca spoken there.

hizb   party or group, thus *Hizb ut-Tahrir al-Islami* – Party of Islamic Liberation, formed to restore the caliphate and establish *sharia* throughout the world.

ibn/bin   son of.

ijma   doctrine of community consensus, the mainstay of *Sunni Islam*.

ijtihad   the use of independent reasoning in interpreting a matter of *sharia*, it being agreed that by about AD 900 all issues had been agreed by *ijma*, thus 'the gates of ijtihad were closed'; see *mujtahid*.

Ikhwan   'Brotherhood'; name given to themselves by *Wahhabi* revivalists of Nejd in about 1912, whose conquest of Arabia under the tribal chief Abdul Aziz ibn Saud led to the formation of Saudi Arabia. In the 1930s the name was taken up in Egypt by the *Ikhwan-ul-Muslimeen* – Muslim Brotherhood, a politico-religious revolutionary party formed to liberate Islamic states.

imam   leader of public prayers but also a title denoting a spiritual leader; among *Shias* the spiritual and temporal head of their community by virtue of his direct descent from the *Prophet*, *Shias* and some *Sunnis* also believe that a last or 'Hidden' Imam is still to come, heralding the final victory of *Islam* and the end of the world; see *Mahdi*.

irtidad   apostasy, under *sharia* a capital offence.

ISI   Inter-Services Intelligence Directorate, Pakistan's equivalent of the CIA, which played a major role in the training and arming

	of the *mujahedeen* in the 1980s and the *Taliban* in the mid-1990s.
Islam	'submission', thus submission to the will of God as set out in the *Shahada*, one of the Five Pillars of Islam.
jahiliyah	'state of ignorance', thus the time before the *Prophet* received God's revelations, but also used by fundamentalists to describe governments they regard as un-Islamic.
jamaat/jamiat	assembly, political party, thus *Jamiat Ahl-i-Hadith* – Party of the People of Tradition, politico-religious group, founded by Sayyid Nazir Husain in India *c.* 1870; *Jamaat-i-Islami* (JI), Islamic Party, Pakistani political party with *Deobandi* roots; *Jamiat-e-Ulema-e-Islam* (JUI), Assembly of Islamic Scholars, extremist Pakistani political party with *Deobandi* roots linked to *Al-Qaeda* and *Taliban*; *Jamaat-ul-Dawa*, Party for Invitation (to Islam), political party with *Wahhabi* roots; *Tablighi Jamaat* – Preaching Society, Pakistani political party with *Deobandi* roots; *Jamaat al-Takfir wa al-Hijra* – Party of Excommunication and Emigration, Egyptian revolutionary group set up in Egypt in the 1980s that drew on both *Wahhabi* and *Ikhwan-ul-Muslimeen* politico-religious philosophy and called for the overthrow of rulers in the Muslim world it regarded as betrayers of Islam; etc.
jemadar	camel keeper, in Indian Army a junior Indian officer.
jezail	long-barrelled flintlock, the standard weapon of the Afghans and Pathans until the First World War.
jihad	'striving', thus 'striving in the path of God', often interpreted as holy war against non-Muslims but, more accurately, a striving to the utmost in the cause of Allah; made up of two main elements: *Jihad Akbar* or the Great

Jihad – to strive against self (an inner struggle against the forces of Satan); and *Jihad Kabeer* or *Jihad Asghar*, also known as the Lesser Jihad – to strive physically against the forces of Satan and all who oppose the spread of Islam, sometimes referred to as 'Jihad of the Sword'; thus *jihadi* – one who strives, commonly referred to as a 'holy warrior'. Many Muslims incorrectly regard *jihad* as the sixth Pillar of Islam.

jirga   tribal assembly or deputation among the Pathans; thus *loya jirga* – inter-tribal assembly.

jiziyah   poll tax paid by non-Muslims in an Islamic state.

kaffiya   Arab head-cloth.

kafila   caravan, usually of camels.

kafr, kufr   paganism; thus *kaffir, kuffir* – pagans, heathens.

khalifa   deputy, thus successor to the *Prophet*, ruler of the Islamic world community as caliph; thus *khalifat* – the caliphate or Islamic state ruled over by successors to the *Prophet*.

khan   lord, head of the clan or tribe among the Pathans.

khassadar   paramilitary police in tribal areas.

khatib   preacher.

Koran   see *Quran*.

kotal   summit of a pass.

kutcherry   district officer's office or court house.

lashkar   Afghan/Pathan tribal army or war party.

lathi   staff, thus *lathial* – a stick-carrier or 'enforcer'.

madrassah   college for the teaching of *Islam* and *sharia*, plural *madaris* (but here written *madrassahs*); in Pakistan known as *deeni madaris* – schools of the Faith.

Mahabun   'great forest', a mountain massif in Buner.

Mahdi   'expected one', the divinely-appointed saviour of Islam, the Twelfth or Hidden Imam who will reappear in the last days to establish the rule of Islam on earth, a belief popular among Shias, thus Mahdism; a title taken by Muhammad Ahmad ibn Abdullah, who declared himself al-Mahdi al-Muntazar, successor of God's Messenger, in the Sudan in June 1881; rejected by many orthodox Sunnis because the *Quran* makes no mention of a Mahdi, the concept still finds popular acceptance; see also *imam*.

majlis	assembly, council (Arabia).
malik	king, but headman among the *Pathans*.
masjid	mosque, the place of Friday prayers.
maulana	Muslim teacher more learned than the *mullah*.
maulvi	Muslim cleric more learned than the *mullah*.
melmastia	code of hospitality among *Pathans*.
mian	saint who abstains from politics and violence.
mufti	jurist, senior judge in Arabia who issues *fatwa*.
muhajir	one who emigrates.
mujahedeen	those who strive or undertake militant *jihad* for the Faith; singular *mujaheed*; sometimes interpreted as a 'holy warrior'. Those who fought the Russians in Afghanistan were deemed *mujahedeen* but when they turned on each other the term was felt to have become corrupted.
mujtahid	scholar competent to exercise *ijtihad*.
mullah, maula	'one who shows', thus religious teacher, leader of prayers at a mosque; see also *maulana, maulvi*.
Mumineen	'the faithful', thus *Muslims*.
munshi	scribe, translator or language teacher.
murid	follower.
mushriq	one who commits *shirk*, worshipper of false gods, thus polytheist.
Muslim	'one who submits' (to the will of God); more correctly *muslimun*; thus *Musulmans*.
mutawihin	'those who obey', thus enforcers of public morality; an order of religious commissars instituted by Muhammad ibn Abd al-Wahhab in Nejd.
nanawati	code of sanctuary among *Pathans*.
nang	code of honour among *Pathans*.

Naqshbandi	strict *Sufi* order originating in Bokhara that gained popularity in India among followers of Shah Waliullah.
Naqshbari	*Sufi* order seeking esoteric knowledge through contemplation while upholding *Sunni* values, tracing its heritage back to Abu Bakr, the first Caliph.
Nasrani	Nazarenes, thus Christians.
nawab	'deputy', thus ruler of a province or state under *Muslim* law.
padshah	supreme shah or king of kings.
pagri	turban or headcloth.
Pakhtun, Pashtun	see *Pathans*.
Pakhtunwali	'the way of the Pakhtuns', the social code of the *Pathans*.
Pathans	a large group of tribes predominant in the Afghanistan/Pakistan border regions with shared origins, language and culture.
pindaris	bands of marauders of mainly *Pathan*/Afghan origin who ravaged central India through the 18th and early 19th centuries.
pir	a saint, head of a *Sufi* order.
pirzada	descendant of a *pir*.
powinda	nomad, the name given to the Mullah Powindah.
Prophet	the respectful term used to describe Muhammad, 'seal of the Prophets', born in Mecca in about the year 570 of the Christian era. In Islamic terms Moses and Jesus are *rassul* – messengers of God – whereas Muhammad is a *nabi* – universal prophet. After his teachings led to his persecution he fled to Medina in the year 622, later returned to conquer Mecca and establish the first Islamic state. His dictated revelations from God were set down as the *Quran*, while his sayings and actions as remembered by his Companions were set down as *Hadith*. Muhammad died in Medina in 632.

purdah	curtain, the state of concealment required of women in some Islamic cultures.
qadi, kadi, qazi	magistrate.
Quran	'recitation'; the holy scripture of *Islam* containing the authentic words and revelations of God as dictated by the angel Gabril to the *Prophet*.
Qutbee	follower of the political philosophy of the Egyptian Islamist revolutionary Sayyid Qutb.
Ramadan	month of fasting, one of the Five Pillars of Islam.
Rashidun	'rightly guided ones'; title given to the first four *Caliphs* who followed the *Prophet* as religious and political leaders of the Islamic world, seen by reformers as exemplary rulers of Islam's golden age.
rawaj	*Pathan* customary law, which traditionally took precedence over *sharia*.
rissaldar	see *subedar*.
sahib, saheb	'master', Arabic title applied to man of rank, in British India came to be applied to Europeans.
salaam	'peace', thus *salaam alaikum* – 'peace be upon you', the traditional *Muslim* greeting.
salaf	'forefathers', from *al-Salaf al-Salih* – 'the Righteous Forefathers', the *Prophet*'s Companions and the scholars of the two generations who came after them; thus *salafi* – 'following the forefathers', and *salafiyya* – 'followers of the forefathers'. The ideal of emulating the forefathers of early Islam was first proposed by Ibn Taymiyya. In modern Islam the term has wider connotations although is still associated with fundamentalists who seek to emulate the early Muslims and reject *bidat* and *shirk*.
salat	obligatory five daily prayers; one of the Five Pillars of Islam.
sangar	stone breastwork in mountain warfare.
sarai	traveller's rest house, thus caravanserai; palace (in Arabia).

sawm	fasting during the month of Ramadan; one of the Five Pillars of Islam.
saiyyed, sayyed, syed	descendant of the Prophet; see also *Sayyeds*.
Sayyeds	a tribe of questionable origin occupying the Khagan valley in northern Hazara who claim descent from the Prophet.
sepoy	infantry soldier in Indian Army.
shah	king, title of respect accorded to *saiyyeds*.
shahadah	profession of faith in God and his *Prophet*: 'There is no god but Allah and Muhammad is his Apostle'; one of the Five Pillars of Islam.
shaheed	martyr.
shaykh, sheikh	leader of Arabic stock, learned man.
sharia	'the path'; the divinely ordained laws of *Islam* governing all aspects of *Muslim* behaviour. By about AD 900 it became accepted among Sunnis that all issues had been resolved by the four schools of the understanding of *sharia* – Hanafi, Shafii, Maliki and Hanbali – leaving no further room for the exercise of *ijtihad*.
sharif, sherif	one who has direct descent from the *Prophet*; member of Arab tribal aristocracy; ruler of holy places.
Shia	'the party'; the largest minority sect of *Muslims*, which regards *Imam Ali* and his descendants as the legitimate descendants of the *Prophet* and thus leaders of the *umma*; itself divided into a number of lesser sects, and regarded as heretical by the *Sunnis* because it rejects the doctrine of *ijma* and turns instead to the authority of *imams* from the line of *Ali*.
shirk	the act of associating anything with God, a sin in the eyes of *Wahhabis*.
shura	religious council.
Sikh	'disciple', thus follower of the Sikh religion originating from the teachings of Guru Nanak.
sowar	Indian cavalry trooper.

station	in British India, the area where British officials lived and worked.
subedar	most senior officer rank held by Indian in Indian Army infantry; the cavalry equivalent is *rissaldar*.
Sufi	form of Islamic mysticism seen by many Sunni reformers as heretical.
sunnah	'custom'; precedents provided by the practices of the Prophet and his immediate successors as laid down in the *Hadith*, regarded by strict Muslims as no less binding than the Quran; see *Sunni*.
Sunni	'of the sunnah', the mainstream group of *Islam*, which accepts the authority of the *sunnah* and of the line of *caliphs* who came after the *Prophet*.
talib-ul-ulm	'seeker of knowledge', thus religious student; plural *taliban*; thus *Taliban*, a fighting move-ment formed originally from religious students by Mullah Muhammad Omar of Kandahar in 1996 to bring *sharia* to Afghanistan.
talwar	curved fighting sword.
taqlid	following past interpretations of *sharia* as interpreted by the four schools of *Islamic* jurisprudence.
tariq	path, thus *Tariqa-i-Muhammadia*, 'Path of Muhammad', the name given by Syed Ahmad to his revivalist movement.
tawhid	the doctrine of God's oneness, absolute monotheism or unitarianism, the central pillar of *Wahhabism*.
thana	police post.
tserai	land granted to a holy man or his followers in perpetuity.
ulema, ulama	those learned in the ways of Islam, thus the collective body of Islamic scholars and others recognised as part of the Islamic religious hier-archy, including judges, teachers and religious administrators; singular *alim*.

ulm, ulum	Islamic learning.
umma	world community of Islam.
wadi	dry water-course (Arabia).
Wahhabi	follower of the Arab reformer and revolution-ary Muhammad ibn Abd al-Wahhab (*c.* 1700–92), who called for a return to the pure Islam of the *Salafi* and waged violent *jihad* against those he and his followers regarded as idolaters, polytheists and apostates; thus *Wahhabism*, the form of Islamic fundamental-ism now dominant in Saudi Arabia; see *Al-muwahhidun.*
wali	friend of God, honorific title usually used by *Sufis*, thus Wali of Swat.
wazir	vizier, chief minister, counsellor; also name of member of Waziri Pathan tribe.
zai	son, thus *Yusufzai* – sons of Joseph, a major *Pathan* tribe.
zakat	tithe all Muslims pay as religious tax; one of the Five Pillars of Islam.
zamin	land; thus *zamindar* – landowner.
zan	women, thus *zanana* – women's quarters.
zar	gold.

Bibliography

Key sources in English include the reports of various British political officers such as Francis Warden of the East India Company
based at Bushire and elsewhere in the Persian Gulf, and the later
compilations of a number of government officials in India including J. H. Reily, John Colvin, Dr H. W. Bellew, T. E. Ravenshaw,
James O'Kinealy, Edward Rehatsek and Sir William Hunter. As
might be expected, their writings show pronounced anti-Wahhabi
and pro-British bias.

Exactly the same in reverse applies to the writings of
Qeyamuddin Ahmad, Balkhi Fasihuddin, Burhanuddin Qasmi,
Taufiq Ahmad Nizami and other historians in post-Independence
India and Pakistan writing in English, who have portrayed the
Wahhabis in India either as nationalist freedom fighters or as
jihadis and martyrs. Of the above, the research work of Professor
Qeyamuddin Ahmad, late Professor of History at Patna University
and author of *The Wahhabi Movement in India*, stands in a class of its
own and I have drawn heavily on the material he has uncovered,
particularly relating to letters and reports contained in Government
files in Patna and Allahabad. An important source for the early life
and teachings of Syed Ahmad is Shah Ismail Shaheed's *Taqwiyat-
ul-Iman* (Strengthening of the Faith), recently published by
Dar-us-Salaam Publications with a preface by Ghulam Rasool Mehr.

Among more modern and more objective authorities consulted
were Francis Robinson and John Voll, writing on Muslim history
in South Asia; Barbara Metcalf, on the Deobandi movement in
India; Natana J. DeLong-Bas, on the origins of Wahhabi theology;
and Yoginder Sikand, Aziz Ahmad, Akbar S. Ahmed and Tariq
Rahman, on Islam in South Asia. I have also drawn on the essayists

edited by Ali Rahnema and published under the title *Pioneers of Islamic Revival.*

As to recent history, I have listed only a handful of titles which I have found especially useful, most particularly Ahmed Rashid's authoritative study of the Taliban movement. The world wide web has also provided a rich source of ideas, if often of dubious provenance. Even the most cursory surf will show how widespread and fierce is the debate within the Muslim *umma* over such issues as Wahhabism, jihad, and the responsibilities of the good Muslim. Faced with a multiplicity of conflicting interpretations, the best a modern historian can do is to be aware of where his sources are coming from, and of his own prejudices and preconceptions. The reader should be aware that my deficiencies in Arabic, Persian and Urdu have meant that a number of important original sources remain unexamined.

Arabia and the Middle East: primary and historical sources (pre-1947)

H. J. Brydges, *An Account of the Transactions of His Majesty's Mission to the Court of Persia in the Years 1807–11, to which is Appended a Brief History of the Wahauby*, Vol. II, 1834

J. L. Burckhardt, *Travels in Arabia*, 1829

—— *Notes on the Bedouins and Wahabys*, 1830

Sir Richard Burton, *A Pilgrimage to Al Medina and Mecca*, 1893

Louis Alexandre Olivier de Corancez, *Histoire des Wahabis depuis leur origine jusqu'à la fin de 1809*, 1810, republished as *History of the Wahabis*, trans. R. M. Burrell, 1994

Giovanni Finati, *Narrative of the Life and Adventures of Giovanni Finati who under the assumed name of Mahomet made the campaigns against the Wahabees for the recovery of Mecca and Medina*, edited by W. J. Bankes, 1830

A. B. Kemball, *Observations on the Past Policy of the British Government towards Arab Tribes of the Persian Gulf*, Punjab Index 687, 1845

—— *Chronological table of events connected with . . . the Wahabee tribe 1795–1844*, Punjab Index 689, c. 1854

R. H. Kiernan, *The Unveiling of Arabia*, 1937

T. E. Lawrence, *Reconstruction of Arabia*, Report to the British Cabinet, 1919

—— *Seven Pillars of Wisdom*, 1927

—— *Revolt in the Desert*, 1927

—— *The Letters of T. E. Lawrence*, 1938

J. G. Lorimer, *Gazetteer of the Persian Gulf*, 1913

W. W. Loring, *A Confederate Soldier in Egypt*, 1884

V. van den Meulen, *The Wells of Ibn Saud*, 1957

C. C. R. Murphy, *Soldiers of the Prophet*, 1921

William G. Palgrave, *Central and Eastern Arabia*, 1865

Lewis Pelly, *Report on a Journey to the Wahabee Capital of Riyadh in Central Arabia*, 1865, reprinted 1978

Harry St John Philby, *Operations of the Nejd Mission Oct.–Nov. 1917*, 1918

—— *Report of a Trip to Southern Nejd and Dawasir*, 1918

—— *The Heart of Arabia*, 1922

—— 'The Triumph of the Wahhabis', in *Journal of the Royal Society for Asian Affairs*, Vol. XIII (iv), 1926

—— *Arabia of the Wahhabis*, 1928

—— *Arabian Days*, 1948

—— *Letters 1908–1961*, St Anthony's College, Oxford

'Phoenix' (probably H. St J. Philby), 'A Brief Outline of the Wahhabi Movement', in *Journal of the Royal Society for Asian Affairs*, Vol. XVII (iv), 1930

Sheikh Hafiz Wahba, 'Wahhabism in Arabia, Present and Past', in *Journal of the Royal Society for Asian Affairs*, Vol. XVI (iv), 1929

Francis Warden, *Historical Sketch of the Wahabee tribe of Arabs 1795 to 1818*, with continuation [1819–1853] by Lieutenants S. Hennell, A. B. Kemball and H. F. Disbrowe, Punjab Index 699, *c.* 1853

Arabia and the Middle East: secondary and modern sources (post-1940)

Ishrat Ansari, 'Muslim Religious Leaders in India's Freedom Struggle', *AIM Journal*, August 1997.

Hamid Algar, *Wahhabism: a Critical Essay*, 2002

N. N. E. Bray, *A Paladin of Arabia*, 1936

Anthony Cave-Brown, *Treason in the Blood: St John Philby, Kim Philby and the Spy Case of the Century*, 1994

Natana J. Delong-Bas, *Wahhabi Islam: from Revival and Reform to Global Jihad*, 2004

Dore Gold, *Saudi Support for International Terrorism*, testimony presented to the US Senate Committee on Governmental Affairs, 31 July 2003

Philip Graves, *The Life of Sir Percy Cox*, 1941

E. and I. Karsh, *Empires in the Sand: the Struggle for Mastery in the Middle East 1789–1923*, 2001

Elie Kedouri, *In the Anglo-Arab Labyrinth*, 1976

Bernard Lewis, *The Middle East*, 1995

Middle East Media Research Institute, *Special Despatch Series No. 526: Saudi Arabia*, 20 June 2003

Elizabeth Monroe, *Philby of Arabia*, 1978, reprinted 1998

Fergus Nicoll, *The Sword of the Prophet: the Mahdi of Sudan and the death of General Gordon*, 2004

John Sabini, *Armies in the Sand: the Struggle for Mecca and Medina*, 1981

U. M. Salih, *The Political Thought of Ibn Taymiyya*, 1990

Robert Spencer, 'The People of Saudi Arabia: Allies against Terrorism?', in *FrontPageMagazine.com*, 15/7/03

Ted Thornton, *History of the Middle East Database*, www.nmhschool.org/thornton/mehistory/database

Charles Tripp, 'Sayyid Qutb: The Political Vision', in Ali Rehnema, *Pioneers of Islamic Revival*, 1994

John Voll, 'Muhammad Hayya Al-Sindi and Muhammad ibn Abd al-Wahhab: an Analysis of an Intellectual Group in Eighteenth Century Madina', in *Bulletin of the School of Oriental and African Studies*, 38, No. 1, 1975

H. V. F. Winstone, *Captain Shakespear: a Portrait*, 1976

—— *The Illicit Adventure: the Story of Political and Military Intelligence in the Middle East from 1898 to 1926*, 1982

India, Afghanistan and Central Asia: primary and historical sources (pre-1947)

James Abbott, 'First Expedition against Black Mountain, Huzara in 1853', OIOC Eur. Mss. C.210

—— 'The Chiefs of Huzara', 1850, OIOC Eur. Mss. C.120

John Adye, *Sitana: A Mountain Campaign on the Borders of Afghanistan in 1863*, 1867

Sayyid Ahmad of Barelli [Syed Ahmad], 'Khutbehs and correspondence, some in Arabic, compiled for James O'Kinealy', undated, OIOC Mss. Or. 6635

Shaik Hedayut Ali, *A Few Words relative to the Late Mutiny of the Bengal Army, and the Rebellion in the Bengal Presidency,*1858

Mir Shahmat Ali, 'Translation of the *Taqwiyat ul-Iman* [Strengthening of the Faith], preceded by a Notice of the Author, Maulavi Ismail Ali', in *Journal of the Royal Asiatic Society*, XIII, 1852

Muhamad Ali, 'Makkhzan-I-Ahmadi, a biography of Sayyid Ahmad Shahid', undated, OIOC Mss. Or. 6650

Anon, *Arrah: the Siege, Defence and Victory of, in July 1857, by One of the Garrison,* 1897

John F. Baddeley, *The Russian Conquest of the Caucasus,* 1908

J. R. Becher, *Memorandum on the Hazara District during the Mutiny in India,* 1858

H. W. Bellew, *A General Report on the Yusufzais,* 1864

—— *An Enquiry into the Ethnography of Afghanistan,* 1891

—— (as 'A Punjab Official'), *Our Punjab Frontier, with a Concise Account of the Various Tribes by which the North-West Frontier of British India is Inhabited,* 1868

Govt of Bengal, *Correspondence connected with the removal of Mr W. Tayler from the Commissionership of Patna and the arrest and trial of Lootf Ali Khan, a Banker in Patna,* 1858

H. P. Blavatsky, 'The Akhood of Swat, the founder of many mystical societies,'in *The New York Echo,* 1878

R. V. Boyle, *Brief Narrative of the Defence of the Arrah Garrison,* 1858

Sir Owen Tudor Burne Collection, 'Papers relating to assassination of Lord Mayo', OIOC Mss. Eur. D.951/15–16

Neville Chamberlain Papers, OIOC Mss. Eur. C203

Hugh Chichester Letters, OIOC Mss. Eur. Photo 271

Winston Churchill, *The Story of the Malakand Field Force: an Episode of Frontier War,* 1898

—— *Young Winston's Wars: the original despatches of Winston S. Churchill,* ed. F. Woods, 1972

John Russell Colvin, *Report to The Government of Bengal on the Disturbances at Bararasat,* 1831

—— (as 'J. R. C.'), 'Notice of the Peculiar Tenets Held by the Followers of Syed Ahmad, taken chiefly from the Sirat-ul-Mustaqim, written by

Moulavi Mohammaed Ismail', in *Journal of the Asiatic Society of Bengal*, I, 1832

Sydney Cotton, *Nine Years in the North-West Frontier of India*, 1868

Lord Dalhousie, *Minutes on Wahabees*, 1852

—— 'Correspondence', BL Mss. Add. 48590, 57411–12

Algernon Durand, *The Making of a Frontier*, 1899

Lady Edwardes, *Memorials of the Life and Letters of Sir H. B. Edwardes*, 1886

Sir Herbert Edwardes, *A Year on the Punjab Frontier*, 1851

—— *The Life of Sir Henry Lawrence*, 1872

R. M. Edwards, 'Mutiny Diary', OIOC Mss. Eur. C148/1–2

P. C. Elliot-Lockhart and A. E. Murray, *A Narrative of the Operations of the Malakand and Buner Field Forces, 1897–98*, 1898

Mountstuart Elphinstone, *An Account of the Kingdom of Kabul*, 1815

George Elsmie, *Notes on some of the Characteristics of Crime and Criminals in the Peshawar Division of the Punjab, 1872 to 1877*, 1884

G. W. Forrest, *Life of Field-Marshal Sir Neville Chamberlain*, 1909

Alexander Gardner, *Soldier and Traveller: Memoirs of Alexander Gardner, Colonel of Artillery in the Service of Maharaja Ranjit Singh*, ed. H. Pearse, 1898

Govt of India, *Frontier and Overseas Expeditions from India*, *c.* 1900

Sir Frederick James Halliday, *Minute: The Mutinies as they affected the Lower Provinces under the Government of Bengal*, 1858

W. W. Hunter, *Our Indian Mussulmans: are they Bound in Conscience to Rebel against the Queen?* 1876

—— *A Life of the Earl of Mayo*, 1875

H. D. Hutchinson, *The Campaign in Tirah 1897–98*, 1898

Hugh R. James, *Report on the Settlement of the Peshawur District*, 1864

Lionel James (Reuters), *The Indian Frontier War, being an account of the Mohmund and Tiral Expeditions 1897*, 1898

Sir Charles Patton Keyes Collection, 'Letters 1860–63', OIOC Mss. Eur/D1048/7; 'Military papers 1860–69', OIOC, Mss. Eur/D1048/3

Amir Khan, *The Great Wahabee Case, being a full report of the proceedings in the matters of Ameer Khan and Hashmadad Khan before the Honourable Mr Justice Norman in the High Court Calcutta*, 1870

M. A. Khan, *Selections from British Government Records relating to Wahabee trials*, 1961

Sir Syed Ahmed Khan, *The Causes of the Indian Revolt, Written by Syed*

Ahmed Khan Bahadur, CSI, in Urdoo in the Year 1858 and Translated into English by his Two European Friends, 1873

Syud Emdad Ali Khan, *Translation of an epitome of the history of the Wahabees, edited by Moulvee Syud Emdad Ali Khan, Bahadur, Judge of Small Causes Court, Tirhoot*, 1871

James O'Kinealy, 'The Wahhabis in India', in *The Calcutta Review*, Vols C and CI, 1895

Edward Lockwood, *The Early Days of Marlborough College, with a Chapter on Patna during the Mutiny*, 1893

H. B. Lumsden, 'Report on the Yoozoofzaee District', in *Punjab Papers*, 1953

G. B. Malleson, *History of the Indian Mutiny*, 1878

Frank Martin, *Under the Absolute Amir*, 1907

H. Mason, *Report on the Black Mountains*, 1888

—— 'The Hindustani Fanatics', in *Journal of the United Services Institution of India*, 1890

L. A. Mendes, *Report of Proceedings in the Matters of Amir Khan and Heshmetdad Khan*, 1870

C. T. Metcalfe, *Two Native Narratives of the Mutiny in Delhi*, 1898

H. W. Mills, 'The Pathan Revolt in North-West India, 1897', 1898

—— *The Tirah Campaign*, 1898

H. L. Nevill, *Campaigns on the North-West Frontier*, 1912

Sir Michael O'Dwyer, *India as I Knew it*, 1925

Edward A. Oliver, *Across the Border: or Pathan and Biloch*, 1890

W. H. Paget, *Records of Expeditions Against Tribes of the North West Frontier since the Annexation of the Punjab*, 1874, revised and updated 1884.

Pakistan Government Secretariat, *Selections from Bengal Government Records on Wahhabi Trials, 1863–1870*, 1961

E. Gambier Parry, *Reynell Taylor*, 1888

Pearse Collection, 'Concerning the suppression of the revolt in 1852 in Kagan',1852, OIOC Mss. Eur. E. 417/10

Theodore L. Pennell, *Among the Wild Tribes of the Afghan Frontier*, 1912

Pioneer Press, *The Risings on the North-West Frontier, 1897–98*, 1898

Govt of the Punjab, *Report on Hindustani Fanatics of Sittana*, 1864

—— *Report showing the Relations of the British Government with the Tribes on the North-West Frontier of the Punjab*, 1865

—— *Mutiny Records: Correspondence and Records*, Part II, 1911

—— *Gazetteer of the Delhi District*, 1883–84

—— *Gazetteer of the Hazara District*, 1907

—— *Gazetteer of the North-West Frontier Province*, 1931

—— *Gazetteers of the Peshawar District*, 1898, 1910, 1933

—— *Selections from the Punjab Government Records*, Vols 7–8, 1912

—— *Papers connected with the Trial of Moulvie Ahmedoolah of Patna, and others, for Conspiracy and Treason 1864–65*, 1866, Punjab Index 538, undated

—— *Report on the Yoozoofzaee District by Lt H. B. Lumsden*, 1853, Punjab Index, 1954

Abdur Rahman [Abd al-Rahman Khan], *The Life of Abdur Rahman: Amir of Afghanistan*, 1900

Charles Raikes, *Notes on the Northwest Provinces of India*, 1852

—— *Notes on the Revolt in the Northwest Provinces of India*, 1857

T. E. Ravenshaw, *Patna Magistrate's Report*, 19 August 1852

—— *Historical Memorandum on the sect of the Wahabees, c. 1864*

Edward Rehatsek, 'The History of the Wahhabys in Arabia and in India', in *Journal of the Bombay Branch of the Royal Asiatic Society*, Vol. XIV, 1878–80

Frederick Roberts, *Forty-One Years in India; from Subaltern to Commander-in-Chief*, 1897

James Routledge, *English Rule and Native Opinion in India, from Notes taken in 1870–74*, 1874

Edward Alexander Samuells, *Remarks on Mr William Tayler's 'Brief Narrative of Events'*, 1858

Sayyid Mubarak Shah, 'Narrative of Sayyid Mubarak Shah', OIOC Mss. Eur. B138

Shah Ismail Shaheed, *Taqwiyat-ul-Iman*, 1827, translated as *Strengthening of the Faith* by Mir Shahamat Ali, with a preface by Ghulam Rasool Mehr, undated

William Tayler, *Our Crisis; Or Three Months at Patna during the Insurrection of 1857*, 1858

—— *Brief Narrative of Events Connected with the Removal of Mr Tayler from the Commissionership of Patna*, 1857

—— *Veritas Victrix; being Letters and Testimonials Relating to the Conduct of W. Tayler in the Indian Mutiny*, undated

—— *Thirty-Eight Years in India*, 1878

—— *Justice in the Nineteenth Century: an Appeal to British Honour*, 1885

Muhammad Jafar Thanesari, *Kala Pani: Tarikh e Ajeeb (The Black Water: a Strange Story)*,1884; translated and published as *In Exile (A Strange Story)*, 1964

Capt. L. J. Trotter, *William Tayler of Patna: a Brief Account of his Splendid Services, his Cruel Wrongs, and his Thirty Years' Struggle for Justice*, 1887

—— *Life of the Marquess of Dalhousie*, 1895

Sir Robert Warburton, *Eighteen Years in the Khyber, 1879–98*, 1898

James Wilson, *Why was Lord Mayo Assassinated?* 1872

H. C. Wylly, *From the Black Mountain to Waziristan*, 1912

G. J. Younghusband, *The Story of the Guides*, 1908

India, Pakistan, Afghanistan and Central Asia: secondary and modern sources (post-1947)

Anon., 'The Striving Sheik: Abdullah Azzam', in *Naidaul Islam Magazine*, July–September 1996

Aziz Ahmad, 'Political and Religious Ideas of Shah Wali-ullah of Delhi', in *Muslim World*, Vol. LII, 1, 1962

—— *Studies in Islamic Culture in the Indian Environment*, 1967

—— *Islamic Modernism in India and Pakistan, 1857–1964*, 1967

—— *An Intellectual History of Islam in India*, 1969

Khaled Ahmad, 'The Grand Deobandi Consensus', in *The Friday Times of Pakistan*, 4/2/2000

Qeyamuddin Ahmad, *The Wahabi Movement in India*, 1966; revised 1994

Akbar S. Ahmed, *Pukhtun Economy and Society*, 1980

—— *Millennium and Charisma among Pathans*, 1980

Hamza Alawi, *The Rise of Religious Fundamentalism in Pakistan*, undated

Charles Allen, *Soldier Sahibs: the Men who Made the North-West Frontier*, 2000

Fredrick Barth, *Political Leadership Among Swat Pathans*, 1959

A. K. Biswas, *Unsung Martyrs of 1857*, 2000

Jason Burke, *Al-Qaida: in the Shadow of Terror*, 2003

Sir Olaf Caroe, *The Pathans*, 1958

H. Chattopadhyaya, 'Mutiny in Bihar,'in *Bengal Past and Present*, Vol. LXXIV, Part II, 1955

—— *Insurgency of Titu Mir*, 2002

S. B. Chaudhuri, *Civil Disturbances during the British Rule in India*, 1955

John K. Cooley, *Unholy Wars: Afghanistan, America and International Terrorism*, 2000

Saul David, *The Indian Mutiny*, 2002

Mahasweta Devi, *Titu Mir*, 2000

Christine Dobbin, *Islamic Revivalism in a Changing Peasant Economy: Central Sumatra, 1784–1847*, 1983

Balkhi Fasihuddin, *Wahabi Movement*, 1983

Sir W. K. Fraser-Tytler, *Afghanistan*, 1950

Alexander Igantenko, 'Ordinary Wahhabism', in *Russian Journal*, International Eurasian Institute for Economic and Political Research, 27 December 2001

Lawrence James, *The Making and Unmaking of British India*, 1997

Ibrahim Kalin, 'Sayyid Jamal Al-Din Muhammad bin Safdar al-Afghani, 1838–1897',*www.cis-ca.org/voices*, 6 Jan. 2004

Narahari Kaviraj, *Wahabi and Farazi Rebels of Bengal*, 1982

N. R. Keddie, 'Sayyid Jamal al-Din al-Afghani', in Ali Rehnema, ed., *Pioneers of Islamic Revival*, 1994

Muhammad Asif Khan, *The Story of Swat: as told by the Founder, Miangul Abdul Wadud Badshah Sahib to Muhammad Asif Kahn*, undated (as quoted in Singer)

Muin-ud-Din Ahmad Khan, *Titu Mir and his Followers in British Indian Records*, 1977

Krishan Lal, 'The Sack of Delhi 1857–58 as witnessed by Ghalib', *Bengal Past and Present*, Vol. LXXIV, Part II, 1955

Christina Lamb, *Waiting for Allah: Pakistan's Struggle for Democracy*, 1991

Kamal Matinuddin, *The Taliban Phenomenon: Afghanistan 1994–1997*, 1999

Barbara D. Metcalf, *Islamic Revival in British India: Deoband 1860–1900*, 1989

—— '"Traditionalist" Islamic Activism: Deoband, Tablighis and Talibs', SSRC website, 2002

A. W. Miangul, *The Story of Swat*, 1962

Seyyed Vali Reza Nasr, 'Mawdudi and the Jama'at-i Islami: the Origins, Theory and Practice of Islamic Revivalism', in Ali Rehnema, ed., *Pioneers of Islamic Revival*, 1994

Taufiq Ahmad Nizami, *Muslim Political Thought and Activity in India during the First Half of the Nineteenth Century*, 1969

David Omissi, ed., *Indian Voices of the Great War: Soldiers' Letters 1914–18*, 1999

David Page, Editorial, *Kipling Journal*, September 2004

D. Pal, *The North-West Frontier 1843–1947*, 1949

M. Burhanuddin Qasmi, *Darul Uloom Deoband: a Heroic Struggle against the British Tyranny*, 2001

Tariq Rahman, 'The Madrassa and the State of Pakistan', in *Himal South Asian Magazine*, February 2004

—— 'Madrassas: Religion, Poverty and the Potential for Violence in Pakistan', in *IPRI Journal*, Vol. V, No. 1, Winter 2005

Ahmed Rashid, *Taliban: Militant Islam, Oil and Fundamentalism in Central Asia*, 2000, republished as *Taliban: the Story of the Afghan Warlords*, 2001

—— *Jihad: the Rise of Militant Islam in Central Asia*, 2002

Francis Robinson, *Islam and Muslim History in South Asia*, 2000

—— *The Ulama of Farangi Mahal and Islamic Culture in South Asia*, 2001

S. A. A. Rizvi, 'The Breakdown of Traditional Society,' in *Cambridge History of Islam*, Vol. II, 1970

Surendra Nath Sen, *Eighteen Fifty-Seven*, 1957

Yoginder Sikand, 'Madrassa Education in South Asia', in *Qualandar Magazine*, www.islaminterfaith.org

—— *Islamist Militancy in Kashmir: the Case of the Lashkar-i-Tayyeba*, 2003

André Singer, *Lords of the Khyber*, 1984

Eric Stokes, *The Peasant Armed: the Indian Revolt of 1857*, 1986

Percy M. Sykes, *A History of Afghanistan*, 1940

Murray Titmus, *Islam in India and Pakistan*, 1960

Various, 'Primer: A Guide to Religious and Extremist Groups in Pakistan', in *The Virtual Information Center*, 8 February 2002

Rahimullah Yusufzai, 'Wrath of God: Osama bin Laden lashes out against the West', in *Time Magazine*, 11 January 1999

Muhammad Qasim Zaman, 'Modernity and Religious Change in South Asian Islam', in *Journal of the Royal Asiatic Society*, Series 3, Vol. XIV, Part 3, 2004

General and reference: primary and secondary sources (post-1947)

Hamid Algar, *An Introduction to Islam*, 2000

Jason Burke, 'Making of the World's Most Wanted Man,' in *The Observer Focus Special*, 28 October 2001

—— *Al-Qaeda: Casting a Shadow of Terror*, 2003

Caleb Carr, *The Lessons of Terror: A History of Warfare against Civilians*, 2002

Peter Clarke, *The World's Religions: Islam*, 1998

John K. Cooley, *Unholy Wars: Afghanistan, America and International Terrorism*, 2nd ed, 2000

M. S. Doran, 'Gods and monsters', in *How Did this Happen? Terrorism and the New War*, 2001

John L. Esposito, *Islamic Revivalism*, 1985

—— *The Islamic Threat: Myth or Reality?*, 1999

—— *Unholy War: Terror in the name of Islam*, 2002

—— ed., *Oxford Encyclopaedia of the Modern Islamic World*, 1995

Reuven Firestone, *Jihad: the Origin of Holy War in Islam*, 1999

Terry Gambill, 'Abu Musab Al-Zarqawi: a Biographical Sketch,' in *The Jamestown Foundation Terrorism Monitor*, Vol. 2, Issue 24, 16 December 2004

H. A. R. Gibb & J. H. Kramers, *Shorter Encyclopaedia of Islam*, 1953

G. F. Haddad, 'Ahmad Ibn Taymiyya: A Brief Survey', in *Living Islam*, http://www.livingislam.org, 2002

Yvonne Haddad, 'Muhammad Abduh: Pioneer of Islamic Reform', in Ali Rehnema, ed., *Pioneers of Islamic Revival*, 1994

T. P. Hughes, *Dictionary of Islam*, 1895

Giles Kepel, *Jihad: The Trail of Political Islam*, 2002

Bernard Lewis, *What Went Wrong? The Clash between Islam and Modernity in the Middle East*, 2002

MEMRI, 'Al-Hayat Inquiry: the City of Al-Zarqaa in Jordan – Breeding Ground of Jordan's Salafi Jihad Movement', in *Special Despatch*, 17 January 2005

Rudolf Peters, *Jihad in Classical and Modern Islam*, 1996

Oliver Roy, *Global Islam: the Search for a New Ummah*, 2004

Raj Pruthi, *Encyclopedia of Jihad*, Vols II & IV, 2002

Samir Raafat, 'Ayman Al-Zawahri: the World's Second Most Wanted Man', in *Feature Article*, http://egy.com/people

Malise Ruthven, *Islam in the World*, 1998

—— *Fundamentalism: the Search for Meaning*, 2001

—— *A Fury for God: the Islamist Attack on America*, revised edition 2004

Edward Said, *Orientalism*, 1978

John O. Voll, 'Muhammad Hayat al-Sindi and Muhammad ibn Abd al-Wahhab: an Analysis of an Intellectual Group in Eighteenth Century Medina', in *Bulletin of the School of Oriental and African Studies*, Vol. 38, No. 1, 1975

—— 'Foundations for Renewal and Reform: Islamic Movements in the Eighteenth and Nineteenth Centuries', in *The Oxford History of Islam*, 1999

Benjamin Walker, *Foundations of Islam: the Making of A World Faith*, 1998

Index